LEO STRAUSS AND JUDAISM

LEO STRAUSS AND JUDAISM

Jerusalem and Athens Critically Revisited

Edited by
DAVID NOVAK

ROWMAN & LITTLEFIELD PUBLISHERS, INC.

ROWMAN & LITTLEFIELD PUBLISHERS, INC.

Published in the United States of America
by Rowman & Littlefield Publishers, Inc.
4720 Boston Way, Lanham, Maryland 20706

3 Henrietta Street
London WC2E 8LU, England

Copyright © 1996 by Rowman & Littlefield Publishers, Inc.

All rights reserved. No part of this publication may be reproduced,
stored in a retrieval system, or transmitted in any form or by any
means, electronic, mechanical, photocopying, recording, or otherwise,
without the prior permission of the publisher.

British Cataloging in Publication Information Available

Library of Congress Cataloging-in-Publication Data

Leo Strauss and Judaism: Jerusalem and Athens Critically Revisited / edited by
David Novak.
p.   cm.
Includes bibliographical references and index.
1. Strauss, Leo—Contributions in Jewish philosophy—Congresses.
2. Philosophy, Jewish—Congresses.   3. Strauss, Leo.   Jerusalem and
Athens.   I. Novak, David, 1941– .
BM755.S75J47   1996   181'.06—dc20   95-42221   CIP

ISBN 0-8476-8146-7 (cloth : alk. paper)
ISBN 0-8476-8147-5 (pbk. : alk. paper)

Printed in the United States of America

 TM The paper used in this publication meets the minimum requirements of
American National Standard for Information Sciences—Permanence of
Paper for Printed Library Materials, ANSI Z39.48—1984.

Library
University of Texas
at San Antonio

Contents

Introduction

Leo Strauss, although relatively obscure during his lifetime (1899–1973), is increasingly recognized as one of the great political theorists of the twentieth century. Strauss, a refugee from Nazism, was born into a pious Jewish family in Germany and was educated there, studying with, among others, Ernst Cassirer and Martin Heidegger. Although his earlier work was in the area of Jewish thought, his attention turned to general political theory, beginning with a pathfinding book on Hobbes in 1936. He emigrated to the United States in 1938, first teaching at the New School for Social Research in New York, and then as professor of political philosophy at the University of Chicago from 1949 until his retirement. Despite his role as a general political theorist, one who inspired significant disciples in that field, Strauss never lost his deep interest in the Jewish tradition and in the thought of Maimonides in particular. There is a growing recognition of the centrality of Judaism in Strauss's thought, a point too often overlooked by his admirers and detractors alike. This volume is an attempt to advance that recognition.

The essays in this volume are the result of an extraordinary conference, "Jerusalem and Athens Revisited: Leo Strauss and Judaism," which was held at the University of Virginia in Charlottesville on 10 and 11 October 1993. Original versions of all of the essays, except Chapter 2, were read as papers at the conference. Chapter 2 was drawn from a larger work and prepared especially for this book. The conference papers were subsequently rewritten to incorporate the intelligent and lively discussion that prevailed throughout the meeting. The discussion was of the quality that Strauss himself tried to stimulate as a teacher and a writer. As praise for the conference, someone who knew Strauss well stated that Leo Strauss himself would have very much enjoyed it.

The idea for a conference began in an informal conversation I had with Professor Jenny Strauss Clay, Leo Strauss's daughter and my colleague at the University of Virginia, in the spring of 1992. We recognized that the thought of Leo Strauss had become a topic of much discussion in certain learned circles. Two major debates prevailed. On one side sat the "Straussians," and on the other side sat, for want of a better term, the "anti-Straussians," a type of positivist who opposed both classical philosophy and revelation as having any normative force in our time. Their fierce opposition to Strauss and his agenda indicated that they had picked up the gauntlet Strauss threw down before them in his earlier critique of modernity. The second debate engaged the Straussians themselves, and involved those who were interested in Strauss's thoughts on natural right and those who were interested in Strauss's thoughts on esotericism.

However, it was on neither of these debates that Professor Clay and I felt a discussion of Strauss's thought should be focused. Instead, we wanted to create a forum for Strauss's Judaic interests, interests that usually get lost in the debates and are really crucial to understanding fully Strauss's teaching and writing. Furthermore, we believed these interests and Strauss's unique way of dealing with them should be entered into current discussions among Jewish thinkers and others who share their concerns. At this point in our conversation, the idea of a conference emerged.

The participants in the conference had to be carefully chosen with the goal of genuine intellectual interaction rather than memorials for a colleague we admired. Leo Strauss wanted others to be interested in his ideas, not in his personality. Therefore, we invited both Straussians and non-Straussians, and made their topic of discussion one of the cornerstones of Strauss's thought: the interrelation of Jerusalem and Athens, of revelation and reason. The non-Straussians are persons like myself who think that Leo Strauss raised the most important questions for humans to thoughtfully consider, even if we do not accept many of the answers he presented.

Reality exceeded our expectations. The dynamic of differing viewpoints promoted intelligent, interactive discourse. Our carefully chosen speakers, and attendees of the conference as well, joined thoughts and voices in a memorable intellectual medley. We believe it was worthy of Leo Strauss. We all hope this will spark greater interest in Strauss among Jewish thinkers and, indeed, in all those confronting the great questions of revelation and reason with which Judaism has wrestled for centuries.

Our subject is addressed in eight chapters. The introduction is by Hadley Arkes, who wrote his doctoral dissertation under Leo Strauss at the University of Chicago. In his chapter, "Athens and Jerusalem: The Legacy of Leo Strauss," Arkes states that "Strauss knew that the tradition of his fathers was—as he insisted at so many turns—a religion of reason" (p. 21). Ironically, Arkes connects Strauss with Hermann Cohen against whom Strauss argued both early and late in his career; indeed, Cohen's main work on Judaism is entitled *Religion of Reason Out of the Sources of Judaism*. However, what Arkes seems to be saying here is that despite their significant differences, both Cohen and Strauss could not or would not conceive of a Judaism that was not minimally hospitable to and maximally supportive of the philosophical enterprise. At this point in history especially, when relativism in its various guises is the enemy of both revelation and reason, Jews and others of like mind need to realize how necessary it is to retrieve the proper relation between revelation and reason that Strauss desired. Thus, Strauss's philosophical power cannot be appreciated and cannot be reinvoked without understanding his deep and abiding connection to the Jewish tradition, however untraditional that connection was. No matter how much one might differ from where Arkes himself (or Strauss) locates the relation between Jerusalem and Athens, his insistence upon the centrality of that relation for Strauss and those who want to learn from him and his insistence on its normative import here and now have set the necessary tone for the conference and for this volume.

Some might find it ironic that Susan Orr, author of Chapter 2, who now works in the public policy sphere in Washington, D.C., and who is one of the two non-Jewish contributors to the volume, actually presents the most Jewish version of Leo Strauss's thought. Orr's doctoral dissertation (a version of which was published in 1995 by Rowman and Littlefield under the title *Jerusalem and Athens: Reason and Revelation in the Work of Leo Strauss*), of which this chapter is a synopsis, was written at the Claremont Graduate School under Professor Harry V. Jaffa, who is Leo Strauss's first and oldest disciple. In "Strauss, Reason, and Revelation: Unraveling the Essential Question," Orr writes about Strauss that "both reason and revelation are presented as powers to be reckoned with. By making it possible to consider Jerusalem and Athens again, Strauss has begun the recovery of man, which is a noble task. And if he tips the scales at all, it is toward Jerusalem" (p. 50).

The main task of her essay is to counter the widely accepted view of Thomas Pangle and others that for Strauss the struggle between reason and revelation is basically reducible to the struggle Plato discussed between philosophers and poets. Just as it is clear that Plato regarded poetry to be no match for philosophy, so it is argued that Strauss regarded revelation to be no match for philosophy. If this view is true, then Judaism—the revealed religion in which Strauss was most interested—is nothing more than one more variety of clearly inferior poetry. But Orr's whole paper marshals considerable evidence for the distinctive role of Jerusalem and all it specifically stands for in Strauss's thought. How many readers will actually agree with Orr's bolder assertion, namely, that in truth Strauss saw the claims of Jerusalem being prior to those of Athens, is hard to tell. Nevertheless, many more readers should be persuaded by her more modest claim that Strauss did not subordinate Jerusalem to Athens in any way, and that anyone who wishes to follow in Strauss's path cannot ever forget Jerusalem.

When Jenny Strauss Clay and I designed the conference on Leo Strauss and Judaism as a discourse between Straussians and non-Straussians on the question of Jerusalem and Athens, we decided to divide that discourse into three areas: 1) Strauss and the medieval discussion of the question, 2) Strauss and the modern discussion of the question, and 3) *the* question itself and its significance for today and tomorrow. The medieval locus would have to be Strauss on Maimonides. For one could well see Strauss's own thought beginning not so much in his first book, *Spinoza's Critique of Religion* (1930), but, rather, in his second book, *Philosophy and Law: Contributions to the Understanding of Maimonides and His Predecessors* (1935). Strauss's never-ending fascination with Maimonides can be seen as the literary leitmotiv of his whole career as a teacher and a writer. No aspect of Strauss's literary interests has stirred more controversy than his treatment of Maimonides, particularly his treatment of Maimonides' most difficult work, *Guide of the Perplexed*.

An exposition and defense of Strauss on Maimonides is presented in Chapter 3 by Hillel Fradkin, who did his doctoral work at the

University of Chicago with two of Leo Strauss's closest disciples, Ralph Lerner and the late Allan Bloom. At the beginning of his paper, Dr. Fradkin writes that "we thus seem to be left with the troubling conclusion that Strauss did not offer any final and definitive account of the teaching of Maimonides, who according to him may be the most important thinker in human history and is certainly the most important in Jewish history" (p. 57). But if this is so, a number of scholars have argued that it seems Strauss has done us a disservice in any attempt to understand Maimonides. In other words, Maimonides himself is hard enough to understand, so what good has Strauss done for us by making him even harder to understand? Yet, as Fradkin notes about Strauss a little later on, "he follows very closely and strictly the manner in which Maimonides speaks" (p. 62). This seems to say that the very process of slowly and carefully uncovering deep secrets is where Judaism and philosophy come into authentic contact. In saying this, Fradkin shows how much Strauss objected to the modern notion that only what is immediately clear and evident can be taken to be true. Indeed, this notion goes back as much to Spinoza's rejection of a nonevident meaning of the Bible as it does to Descartes's rejection of anything esoteric in philosophy. For the modernity they established, it would seem that truth is something exoteric and, therefore, appropriable. But if both reason and revelation require of us lifelong dedication to the discovery of deeper and deeper truth, then that truth can never be appropriated; it must always be the worthy object of a quest coeval with one's very life. *Praxis* is always for the sake of *theoria*; their roles can never be reversed if we are to be left with either the life devoted to revelation or to reason. If that is the case, then Strauss has done us immeasurable good by introducing us to Maimonides' own way of thinking by example rather than by precept. Our task should not be to understand Maimonides but, rather, to think along *with* Maimonides.

A counterpart to these ideas is presented by Kenneth Seeskin, a Maimonidean scholar. In Chapter 4, Seeskin argues that Strauss misunderstood the role of esotericism in the *Guide of the Perplexed*. As he writes, "Strauss goes beyond the text in claiming that contradictions are the 'axis' of the *Guide* or that Maimonides makes contradictory statements on all important subjects. In fact, Maimonides limits the scope of this type of contradiction to *very obscure matters*. I take this to mean that he will use contradictions in those areas where there is no demonstration and little hope of finding one" (p. 90). Following this critique, Seeskin sees the contradictions of Maimonides to be *aporiai*, that is, those "knots" that no thinker can ever conclusively untie; a thinker can only suggest one "untying" as more plausible than another. Without any final resolution, the presentation of the knottiness of any *aporia* can only appear to be contradictory, that is, on the *prima facie* level. Seeskin traces this method of reasoning back to Aristotle. By doing this, however, Seeskin not only differs with Strauss in his interpretation of the method of the *Guide*, he also differs with Strauss in seeing Maimonides as both a theologian *and* a philosopher—indeed, as a theologian grounding his theology philosophically.

This approach is understandable if one is aware of the fact that Strauss's reading of Maimonides is one of several competing modern readings of this significant Jewish thinker, and that these readings say as much about the contemporary concerns of the respective readers as they do about Maimonides himself. Seeskin represents another way of reading Maimonides, one in the tradition of such Jewish scholars influenced by Kant as Hermann Cohen, Zvi Diesendruck, Julius Guttmann, and Steven S. Schwarzschild. In this view, Maimonides is a totally unified thinker, and that unity of thought can only be philosophical. In his critique of Strauss, then, Seeskin returns us to the exalted debate between Strauss and Cohen. Indeed, the very respectful way Seeskin differs with Strauss is reminiscent of the very respectful way Strauss differed with Cohen. The fact that Seeskin in no way dismisses Strauss and his concerns surely makes him anything but an "anti-Straussian."

Moving from the medieval into the modern, we take up the second area of discourse. Leo Strauss is perhaps best remembered as the modern thinker who raised again the "quarrel between the ancients and the moderns," siding with the former over the latter. Being situated within modernity, he could not very well return directly to what he believed to be better. Where he had to begin, then, was with a sustained critique of the pretensions of modernity. Whether he was successful or not in this effort, especially as pertains to the Athens/Jerusalem question, is addressed by Allan Arkush and Frederick G. Lawrence in Chapters 5 and 6.

On the more Straussian side of the discussion, one can locate Allan Arkush's chapter "Leo Strauss and Jewish Modernity." Here Professor Arkush concentrates on Leo Strauss's new preface (written in 1962) to the English translation of his first book, *Spinoza's Critique of Religion*, written over thirty years after its original publication in German. At the beginning of his essay, Arkush writes about Strauss's early awareness of "the untenability of all modern attempts to solve the Jewish problem. This road brought him to a juncture where he faced two positive alternatives: the unqualified reaffirmation of orthodoxy or the exploitation of the possibility of a return to premodern Jewish rationalism. We all know where he went from there" (p. 111). Arkush then shows how Strauss rejected the four basic modern solutions to the Jewish problem with modernity. These solutions are 1) liberalism, best argued by Hermann Cohen; 2) political Zionism, best argued by Theodor Herzl; 3) cultural Zionism, best argued by Ahad Ha'Am; and 4) the "new thinking" of Franz Rosenzweig. The fault of liberalism was its failure to understand the essential inability of the Jewish people to be assimilated. Political Zionism understood what the liberals did not, but failed to appreciate the spiritual necessity of Judaism for the Jewish people. Cultural Zionism understood the spiritual needs of the Jewish people, but failed to understand the religious basis of authentic Jewish culture. Rosenzweig's "new thinking," although certainly religious, was still too rooted in subjectivist notions of the primacy of human experience to adequately constitute the objective content of classical Judaism, namely, such doctrines as creation and miracle. Arkush concludes his perceptive analysis of Strauss's challenges to Jewish modernity by insisting that these challenges must set the agenda of both Orthodox and non-Orthodox attempts to develop a truly coherent contemporary Jewish thought. He cites the influential contemporary Jewish thinker, Emil Fackenheim, as one who has taken Strauss's challenge most seriously and responded to it most productively, even though Arkush himself has reservations about a number of points in Fackenheim's response.

In Chapter 6, "Leo Strauss and the Fourth Wave of Modernity," Frederick Lawrence asserts that Strauss did not overcome the limitations of modernity, and that Strauss suffers from those limitations himself. Professor Lawrence, a disciple of the late Bernard Lonergan, arguably the most profound Roman Catholic philosopher-theologian in this century, confronts Strauss's often-repeated claim that one cannot be both a philosopher and a theologian, but one can only be a theologian open to the challenge of philosophy or vice versa. For Lawrence this is not true, and with the precept and example of his teacher Lonergan close at hand, he argues with

Strauss. At the end of the chapter, Lawrence writes, "the dialectic between love of what is near and love of what is highest and best caused by the demand of the absolutely supernatural that humanism transcend itself . . . the explicit refusal to be open to the supernatural solution based on an exoteric pretended fidelity to the ancient's love of truth may be the foundation of a fourth wave of modernity in our time" (p. 148).

What Lawrence persistently and powerfully points out here is that the very desire to know the truth, which is the hallmark of classical philosophy, intends an unconditioned condition, one that is beyond nature, and one that religions have called "God." Because Strauss does not seem to have been able to follow the trajectory of his thought highly enough, he failed to realize that revelation completes what reason intends. In other words, one can move up from Athens to Jerusalem, without having to burn one's "Athenian" bridges behind in one's approach to God. In this overall assertion, Lawrence follows the fundamental assertion (albeit by Lonergan's "Transcendental Thomism," itself mediated by Kant's "return to the subject") that "grace does not annul nature but perfects it." Hence, the notion of an ultimately unbridgeable chasm between reason and revelation is itself one more example of the modern refusal to follow the full trajectory of the desire to know. In that sense, Lawrence sees Strauss as still being too modern by not being critical enough of what lies at the core of modernity's problem: its atheism.

The final section of this volume and third area of discourse concerns the "big" question, that of the normative significance of Strauss's views on reason and revelation. This question is discussed in Chapter 7 by Werner Dannhauser, Strauss's longtime disciple, and in Chapter 8 by myself, Strauss's sometime student.

In "Athens and Jerusalem or Jerusalem and Athens?" Werner Dannhauser, who wrote his doctoral dissertation at the University of Chicago under Leo Strauss, refers to himself as "a follower of the teaching of Leo Strauss" (p. 155). Moreover, Dannhauser identifies himself as "a Jew who has never been an atheist but who has had his share of trouble in choosing Jerusalem over Athens." In that way he seems to distance himself from his teacher, who, he believes, chose Athens over Jerusalem. Dannhauser believes that Strauss never explicitly stated his choice because of his love for the Jewish people and their way of life. So, he concludes by saying, "Love of the good, which is the same thing as love of the truth, is higher than love of one's own, but there is only one road to truth, and it leads through love of one's own" (p. 169). In other words, one cannot engage in the philosophical life if one is situated nowhere, that is, if one has no tradition as the matrix from which one comes and that one never finally overcomes. Clearly, such a loyalty is far more than the sentimental attachment to the Jewish people and their way of life that so characterizes the ethnocentric approach of many Jewish intellectuals today.

Finally, the last chapter in this volume is my own, "Philosophy and the Possibility of Revelation: A Theological Response to the Challenge of Leo Strauss." Close to the position of Frederick Lawrence, I am convinced that philosophy and theology are two separate disciplines, with distinct methodologies determined by two distinct objects—for philosophy, nature, and for theology, the word of God. Nevertheless, one does not have to choose between the two in orienting one's life. In the full and adequate search for the truth, philosophy intends theology and theology presupposes philosophy. The doctrine of natural law, which I delimit as "the province of philosophy and not theology precisely because it is not directly derived from the words of revelation but, rather, from reflection on the limits or ends of the human condition itself" (p. 184) is where the two come into the most intimate and fruitful contact. Philosophy, whose greatest achievement is its constitution of natural law, by providing a lower limit for the human condition, so to speak, prevents theology from the ready temptation to sink into fanaticism, superstition, and injustice. Philosophy saves theology from confusing the superrational with the subrational. The only quarrel theology has with philosophy is when philosophy attempts to declare revelation either impossible or irrelevant. But, we ask, in order for theologians to be able to do that effectively, or to be able to appropriate the proper reflections of philosophy, don't they have to first be philosophers? Thus, there is only an insuperable tension between philosophy and theology when either philosophers claim to have captured heaven or when theologians claim to have captured the earth. Perhaps Strauss did not see this point because he looked in the wrong place in the works of his favorite Jewish thinker, Maimonides, that is, in his metaphysical speculations rather than his reflections on the law as a jurist operating within the law. In other words, one can see Maimonides as most persuasive philosophically precisely where he is most authentically Jewish— not where he engages philosophy on it own ground, but where he brings coherent structure and intelligibility to the commandments (*ta'amei ha-mitsvot*) by theologically appropriating the methodology of philosophy. If this is where Judaism and philosophy come closest for Maimonides, then it certainly applies to any other Jew of lesser brilliance. That is my difference with Leo Strauss, but I could not sustain that difference without basically accepting the agenda of questions he presented to us all.

Our book closes with an afterword by Jenny Strauss Clay. These remarks, with which Professor Clay opened the conference in October 1993, offer a final Athenian weight to a discussion that seems to be weighted more toward Jerusalem.

The authors in this volume hope their ideas will continue to stimulate the type of intelligent discussion that accompanied their first presentation. We all are exceptionally grateful to the Lynde and Harry Bradley Foundation of Milwaukee, Wisconsin, for providing a generous grant that enabled us to conduct the conference and bring these works together as you see them here. And, finally, to Jayne Riew at the University of Virginia for all her efforts in the preparation of the manuscript.

1

Athens and Jerusalem: The Legacy of Leo Strauss

Hadley Arkes

Strauss Contra Spinoza

Leo Strauss once remarked archly on the presumption of Spinoza that the Bible could be read in the same way that one reads any other book: "there is no other standard for the intepretation of Scripture than the standard which is regularly applied to every other written work."[1] Along with that premise came the assumption, as Strauss said, that "the meaning of the Scriptures . . . is the literal meaning, [the] meaning which is accessible in equal measure to the devout reader and to the unbeliever."[2] That premise was the foundation of Spinoza's Bible science and his critique of religion. As Strauss contended, it was Spinoza's *petitio principii*, his begging of the question. It was a begging of the question because it took as its first principle the trust in the findings of one's own intellect.

Revelation, said Strauss, questions this trust in human reason, and so the philosophic inquiry into the Bible must begin by putting aside the claims of revelation. Such trust in the self-sufficiency of human reason is a begging of the question, because it does not advance to a disproof of revelation; it advances, or it begins its work, by presuming that revelation has no plausible bearing on the problem.

Spinoza began by detaching himself from revelation, and he detached himself quite as decisively from Judaism. As Strauss put it, he was "a Jew who had informally embraced a Christianity

1

without dogmas and sacraments." He would become the "father" or founder of a new kind of church, "which was to be universal in fact and not merely in claim, like other Churches, because its foundation," as Strauss said, "was no longer any positive revelation."[3] Spinoza would reject the resurrection of Christ, and he would reject the parts of the Old Testament that were redolent of a moral parochialism, not to say tribalism. God's promise to Solomon, he said, to make him the wisest of men, could not have implied a promise to preserve everyone else in ignorance.[4] In the same way, Spinoza wrote, the Jews "would have been no less blessed if God had called all men equally to salvation, nor would God have been less present to them for being equally present to others; their laws would have been no less just if they had been ordained for all, and they themselves would have been no less wise."[5] These readings were rendered plausible by the logic of morals, and the canons of morality were indeed supplying the thread of the new teaching. As Strauss complained, Spinoza put the Old and the New Testaments on the same plane; he treated them as documents, or teachings, of equal value. When the attempt was made in this way to find the thread that may link these two traditions, that common thread turned out to be, as Strauss said, "rational morality."[6]

It followed that the ground of the religious teaching would also supply the ground of the political. Spinoza had insisted that if the Hebrews had been a chosen or distinctive people, it was not because of the truth of their doctrines but the excellence of their political institutions. Yet, Spinoza sought to displace the notion of a distinctly Jewish State. The ground of the law would be found in the universal, rational morality. The Mosaic law might be followed among Jews, but it would no longer be what it was—and that was not merely a code for all of those who attached themselves to Judaism, but a political law, a doctrine that could be imposed, with the moral conviction and the authority of "law." As Strauss remarked, Spinoza was the first philosopher who was both a liberal and a democrat. He was the founder of liberal democracy.[7] By the logic of liberal democracy, the Mosaic law had to be displaced, decisively, as a governing doctrine. That is to say, it would have to be stripped of its claim to the standing of law. Something distinctive to Judaism would be lost, and Jews would have to give up the notion of a chosen people. What was held out to Jews now was the blessing of liberal society, a society in which "Jews and Christians can be equal members."[8]

Strauss would later concede that, while Spinoza detached himself from Judaism, he did not hate the Jews. Nevertheless, Strauss's critique of Spinoza began by gauging where, exactly, Spinoza stood, the place from which he took his bearings, and it made a difference for Strauss that Spinoza began by aligning himself against Judaism. Strauss, by indirection, would seem to have taken, decisively, the side of Judaism. Yet, with a close reading, these differences would become far more equivocal. Strauss must have appreciated in later years just where those points of equivocation could be found, and he must have recognized what was highly suggestive in that question he had raised earnestly in the critique of Spinoza: "whether the loyal and loving reshaping or reinterpretation of the inherited, or the pitiless burning of the hitherto worshiped is the best form of the annihilation of the antiquated, that is, of the untrue or bad."[9] It must have occurred to Strauss that the same question may plausibly be raised even about those people who sought to preserve the ancestral, especially if they thought to preserve the tradition by sifting out the strands that were no longer defensible, or no longer politic to preserve.

That is, it must have occurred to Strauss that his own efforts, inspired by devotion, could lead quite as well to the weakening of the tradition, no less than the efforts of Spinoza, animated by the most self-conscious purpose of displacing that tradition. For all of his reverent gestures toward revelation, Strauss approached his project with the canons of reason and with all of the formidable equipment that we associate with the most accomplished philosopher. The result might have been comparable to the effects produced by Spinoza: Strauss's own students, absorbing his temper and his style, might preserve their reverence for things ancestral, even as they detached themselves from Judaism. One of the most devoted students of Leo Strauss remarked to me once that he had raised his children on the *Nicomachean Ethics*. His grown children share his interest in political philosophy, but almost needless to say, they do not make a comparable part of their lives the putting on of *tefillin*.

Strauss the Philosopher

Strauss had not chosen to teach theology. He had deliberately taken as his vocation the study of political philosophy, and he wrote as a philosopher. His arguments in defense of revelation—his arguments about the limits of philosophy—were the arguments of a philosopher. He wrote books, which under the hazards of publication could be read by people who were not philosophers, but even more to the point, those books could be read by people who were both believers and nonbelievers. There was nothing on the surface to suggest that the writing contained in these books was not in fact accessible to beings of reason who have cultivated the arts of literacy, and the writing could be accessible, in that way, to Christians no less than Jews.

Surely, one of the most striking attributes, evident at once to the young student who entered a class of Strauss's for the first time, was the presence of a contingent of Catholic priests. They were not there as detached observers trying to scout the opposition. They were sitting at his feet, along with the rest of us, and there was, in the room, the most intense concentration, and the most pronounced reverence. Harry Jaffa has written that Strauss's distinct mission was to restore both reason and revelation against the tendency of modern science to deny them both. Both strands were unmistakably present in those classrooms: the interest in reason *and* revelation. It was evident that the thing that connected everyone in that room—from the Catholic priests to the young Jewish students—was the interest in standing against the world—*contra mundum*—standing against the current culture, with its variants of moral relativism. What connected everyone was the interest in what might be called "natural law": the conviction that there were indeed moral truths, grounded in human nature, and those truths would endure as long as that nature would endure. That is to say, what connected the Christians and Jews in that room was the religion of reason, or "rational morality." If there was something admirable and compelling about the common study of Christians and Jews in that classroom, one had to wonder why the same, shared understandings could not provide the ground of a common citizenship. Why could it not supply the foundation of a polity that would contain, as equal members, Christians and Jews? Professor Jaffa has been among the most dedicated and loyal students of Strauss, and in one of his most eloquent papers, Jaffa celebrated the American regime, as the best of modern regimes, for the character that was reflected in Washington's letter to the Hebrew congregation at Newport:

It is now no more that toleration is spoken of as if it were the indulgence of one class of people that another enjoyed the exercise of their inherent natural rights, for, happily, the Government of the United States, which gives to bigotry no sanction, to persecution no assistance, requires only that they who live under its protection should demean themselves as good citizens in giving it on all occasions their effectual support.[10]

Among the things that made the American republic new under the sun was that it took, as the ground of a common citizenship, the capacity to understand the same, moral principles, the principles that were summarized in the proposition "All men are created equal." That proposition, and the moral implications that flowed from that proposition, could be grasped by Jews as well as Christians. So, what was radically new in the American regime was that it was the first regime, in a civilized country, in which Jews and Christians could meet on the plane of a common citizenship. That, we know, was an achievement that Strauss thought eminently worthy of celebration, even more so in light of the barbarisms towards Jews of the twentieth century. Strauss thought the American regime worthy of celebration, for the same reasons explained by Harry Jaffa. But Strauss seemed to appreciate this achievement as a wonder of moderation, a wonder not to be disdained in a world that could cast up the passions of Nazism, and bring them forth in a country that had shown the deepest refinements of philosophy and culture. The notable, but problematic, achievement of America, that splendid modesty of a moderating Constitution, was part of what Strauss had in mind when he remarked that the American Founders had built on "low but solid ground."[11]

Christians and Jews could meet on the ground of a common citizenship only if there was nothing in the laws that favored Christianity over Judaism, or indeed nothing that made religiosity in any form a qualification for office or the rights of citizenship. The laws would have to be purged of any traces that might accord, to Christianity, or to religion, a preeminent respect. We know now that, as this logic has worked itself out in our own time, the separation of church and state has been taken to mean, in certain, influential quarters, that there is something divisive, and therefore something illegitimate, about religion in the life of a republic. Strauss was alert to these implications. A religion that was thrust into the private realm and treated merely as a species of personal passions or private interest, no better or worse than the interest in bowling or erotica, was a religion that was being diminished in its standing. Still, this arrangement, the arrangement of the regime of law, seemed to offer the best practicable arrangement for preserving religion in the modern regime. At the very least, it could mark off a domain of private belief with a claim to the respect and tolerance of nonbelievers. That modest regime, notably reduced in its aspirations, bore a decent chance of preserving the garden of religion from the corrupting intrusions of politicians.

That was an achievement of moderation and prudence and, as Strauss appreciated, it was a settlement that would ever be poised shakily on understandings that were problematic. A philosopher who saw the world rightly could never seriously hold that all people were born with an equal aptitude, say, for brain surgery, physics or philosophy. Nor could she say that everyone was born with an equal aptitude for rendering justice or reasoning about matters of right and wrong. There are many subtleties packed into that terse proposition, "All men are created equal." As Strauss seemed to understand, it was not prudent for the philosopher to inquire with a merciless honesty into the doubtful assumptions tucked away in that proposition, the proposition that Lincoln described as the father of all principles among us. As Strauss wrote, even the best of societies may be sustained with conventions that will not withstand a rigorous examination. The philosopher plays with a kind of political dynamite if he runs the risk of dislodging people from the wholesome conventions, or the useful prejudices, that support their own freedom. So, as Strauss recognized, even the philosopher writing in the most liberal regimes, without the danger of a censor, will still find it prudent to hold back part of the truth, and treat certain matters by writing between the lines.[12]

Strauss had been moved to defend Spinoza on this ground from the criticism leveled by Hermann Cohen. In the course of that defense, he pointed out that Cohen was writing with the freedom of the philosopher to express himself with a critical fulness; and he felt obliged to acknowledge out that this freedom on the part of philosophers had not been common in the past in other regimes. That freedom was a defining feature only of a liberal democracy, the regime shaped by the thought of Spinoza. Of course, Strauss made use of that same franchise, to write fully, and he too had come to be the practitioner of a vocation that could claim its fuller integrity in the regime that Spinoza had built. Strauss surely understood that he himself had to be the beneficiary of that regime created by Spinoza; the regime whose deepest foundations he was exposing now to his own, serious questioning.

By his own testimony, Strauss came to a more rounded view of Spinoza when he came to recognize, as he put it, the "harsh political verities"—the serious dangers—that were facing Spinoza in writing, and making it necessary for him to write between the lines. When Strauss began to look for that writing between the lines—when he suddenly saw the contradictions so plainly and deliberately placed—he began to trace the ellipses and lead himself back to the truer reading of Spinoza. He remarked, in his new preface to the book on Spinoza, in August 1962, that "I understood Spinoza too literally because I did not read him literally enough."[13]

If he now took Spinoza literally enough, if he now read him as closely as he deserved to be read, what exactly did he understand that had eluded him earlier? Strauss does not exactly say. Here, as in other places, he marks off an ellipsis and invites us to fill it in. I'm not confident that I have the wit to fill it in myself, but for the sake merely of discussion, I would ask a slightly different version of that question, namely, what was Strauss holding back, decorously, from the recognitions that came to him later in life? For the sake of discussion, I would offer this possibility: that Strauss had come to describe, in critical parts of his own life and teachings, the character he had attributed to Spinoza. His own classes offered a dramatic embodiment of a curriculum, a teaching, that brought together Christian priests and young Jewish students, with the sense of deeply shared moral commitments. The connecting thread was rational morality, or the religion of reason. The classes were in political philosophy rather than theology, and as Strauss had long taught, the central fact of political life, or indeed of social life, the fact than which only the natural phenomena were more fundamental, was the political regime. All of his teaching revolved about the question, running back to the ancients, of the best political regime, or, as he was quick to add, the best practicable regime. There was not much question that Strauss and his students took, as the best practicable regime, that regime built on low but solid ground.

Strauss's praise for that regime was shaded, and there were intimations, clearly signaled to his students, that Strauss was well aware of the fables and the conventional truths that sustained this, most eminently praiseworthy of modern regimes. *Natural Right and History* begins with the Declaration of Independence and with the celebration of the American regime as a regime founded on an understanding of natural right. This regime bore the main credit for defeating Nazism, but its intellectual class was in thrall now to doctrines of historicism and other variants of cultural relativism that were quite at odds with the understanding of the American founders. The educated classes in America were detaching themselves from the moral premises on which this good, practicable regime, perhaps the best practicable regime, had been founded. As Strauss remarked, with an edge of foreboding, "it would not be the first time that a nation, defeated on the battlefield . . . has deprived its conquerors of the most sublime fruit of victory by imposing on them the yoke of its own thought."[14] In the center of the book, Strauss intimates an understanding at odds with the storybook maxims, and the political fairy tales, that came along with the celebration of America. In a telling passage, at the center of *Natural Right and History*, Strauss was considering the exigencies of defending a decent regime against the wicked armed. Even a regime of high moral tone may find it necessary to use means that Immanuel Kant, or the World Council of Churches, would not endorse. Strauss wrote that

> a decent society will not go to war except for a just cause. But what it will do during a war will depend to a certain extent on what the enemy—possibly an absolutely unscrupulous and savage enemy— forces it to do. There are no limits which can be defined in advance, there are no assignable limits to what might become just reprisals. . . . The most just society cannot survive without "intelligence," i.e., espionage. Espionage is impossible without a suspension of certain rules of natural right. But societies are not only threatened from without. Considerations which apply to foreign enemies may well apply to subversive elements within society. [15]

With this passage, Strauss comes to the threshold of saying that we may have to suspend, even internally, the restraints of constitutionalism, or some of the implications that spring from the proposition, "all men are created equal." But then Strauss holds back, and in a telling, suggestive passage he says, "Let us leave these sad exigencies covered with the veil with which they are justly covered."[16] (That passage occurs on page 160, in a book of 323 pages—for those interested in certain arcane arts.) The challenge was to provide a worldly defense of the American regime that was not built on fairy tales. I think that something may be inferred from the fact that four of his most inspired and influential students, Harry Jaffa, Walter Berns, Martin Diamond, and Herbert Storing, made it their vocation, or their life's work, to provide a defense of the American regime that could be appreciated by the most worldly. My point is this: Strauss and his students were philosophers who depended, for the highest work of their lives, on the freedom that was afforded by a liberal democracy, or a regime of law. Even more than Hermann Cohen, Strauss had come to depend on that regime fashioned, to the most refined degree, from the thought of Spinoza.

Strauss and the Question of Natural Law

Along the way, Strauss might have judged that he was not as far from Spinoza's thoughts of thirty-five years earlier, and that Spinoza was not really as detached from Jewish thought as Strauss had contended.

It was hard not to find Spinoza appealing and disarming, for example, in that passage in which he anticipated Mel Brooks. Some people may recall Mel Brooks, in one of his movies, playing Moses coming down from Sinai with three tablets, each containing five commandments, and announcing that "the Lord God has given us these fifteen command— . . . " then suddenly dropping one tablet. Without missing a beat, he continues, "The Lord God has given us these ten commandments." Spinoza remarks, in the *Theologico-Political Treatise*, that the commandments would have been preserved for us, in our hearts, even if the original tablets had been lost. They would have been preserved for us in the understandings we could deduce from the notion of a just and merciful God. We would understand those commandments in the same way that we would understand that a just, merciful God would not withold grace or salvation from good people, with decent reflexes, who were too dim of wit to be philosophers. Or, we would know the commandments in the same way that we would know, in Spinoza's construction, that it would not be a denial of God's plan if the laws offered to the Hebrews for an upright life came to be adopted by all people, everywhere.[17]

Spinoza's understanding here found its ground in the canons of reason, or in the logical properties that attach to moral propositions—most notably, the property of universality. So, Spinoza's surety was grounded in a species of what might be called natural law.

Strauss insisted that there was no concept of natural law in the Old Testament, but on that point, he has been contested recently by his former student, David Novak. Novak has pointed to several commentators, over the generations, who have incorporated an understanding of natural law, or the logical equivalent of natural law, in Jewish teaching. Novak cites, in this vein, Saadiah, R. Judah Halevi, Nahmanides, and R. Joseph Albo.[18] As Gregory Dix once pointed out, it was precisely because of this universalism in Jewish thought that St. Paul saw, in the Jews, the natural constituency for a new church, built on the same premises of monotheism but incorporating a moral teaching that was even more explicitly universal.[19] Novak concedes that the Hebrew word for "nature," *teva*, is "not used in postbiblical or even in postrabbinic Hebrew," but he warns that the vocabulary should not be confused with the concepts or the understanding. People are aware of cause and effect even if they do not have the terms to express that relation. In regard to natural law, or moral judgment, I would be entirely in accord with Novak when he points out that we would be referring to a "transcendent criterion of judgment," in making distinctions between the things that are good or bad, just or unjust; a standard of judgment that cannot be reduced simply to the stipulations of the law or the conventions of the local tribe.

With that understanding, Rabbi Novak has pointed out the places in the Old Testament that clearly depend on the moral reasoning that is the hallmark of natural law. When Abraham argues with God over the punishment to be inflicted on Sodom and Gomorrah, he asks, "Shall the Judge of the whole earth not do justice?"—a question that bears no coherence if he simply took the command of God as the definitive measure of justice. He must have begun, as Novak says, with some "prior notion of justice," or a standard that could be used to measure, or judge, the instruction issued by God.[20] That itself creates no small problem for natural law in Judaism, if natural law implies a standard by which God may be judged—a standard, as it were, that God is powerless to alter. Nevertheless, when God held before the Jewish people the prospect of a covenant, it must be supposed, as Novak says, that the Jewish people had the competence to reckon the benefits and the risks, and to weigh their judgment. We must suppose, that is, that they had access to an understanding of the things that were good or bad, the things that served or disserved their own well-being, and the things that were just and unjust:

> In accepting God's offer of liberation, they judged freedom to be good and, therefore, rejected Pharaoh's enslavement of them as wrong. In other words, their response to God's presence presupposed that they had general criteria of good and evil, thus judging what acts are right and what acts are wrong. This is what made their response rational and not capricious.[21]

Even more deeply, as Novak suggested, a contract must presuppose that we are dealing with beings who have the competence of moral agents. Novak assumes, as I would, that we may not charge people with obligations that were imposed upon them under conditions of force or duress. We must assume that people were free to form their own commitments, that they had the competence to judge whether the covenant was decent or indecent, and whether it served their good. We do not, after all, make contracts with small children or with animals, with beings who do not possess the competence to weigh their interests and undertake an obligation. Novak quotes the halakic rule that "one is not liable for acts done under compulsion."[22]

This is a dictum I am especially pleased to recall, since it is close to one I have drawn myself, from the tradition of moral philosophy, where it often appears as the first law of moral reasoning—namely, that the language of morality comes into play only with those acts in the domain of freedom. It makes no sense to cast moral judgments on people, to condemn or commend, to blame or praise, for acts that people were entirely powerless to change.[23] If Smith is thrown out the window and on the way down lands on Jones, we do not hold Smith responsible for an assault. Nor do we hold a person responsible for honoring a contract to sell his or her house when he or she signs the document at the point of a gun. Whether East or West, in Jersey or Tahiti, we do not consider such a deed a valid contract enforceable as law. The point is that these recognitions are built into the notion of contracts, moral agents, and moral reasoning, and they must be folded into the logic of natural law, regardless of whether the rabbis happened to refer explicitly to a concept of natural law.

I would add one other illustration: that famous scene in II Samuel 12:1–7, where Nathan goes to David and tells him the parable of the householder who feeds a visitor by taking a lamb, not from his own, ample stock, but from the holding of a poor neighbor. The story is meant as a parable that will cover, or illuminate, David's own conduct in seeking to possess Bathsheba by putting out of the way Uriah, her husband. The force of the story comes through eliciting from David the avowal that the man who did such a thing deserves punishment. Nathan could instantly reply, "Thou art the man." The story would lose its meaning, and its moral force, unless the readers were expected to understand what some of us would call "the logic of morals": It had to be understood that the condemnation offered by David was a moral condemnation, and therefore it would have a universal and impersonal cast. It would encompass, in its judgment, anyone who described, in his or her own behavior, the features that defined the wrong acted out in the story. That is why Nathan offered the reproach to David in the form of a story, with its impersonal terms. The judgment elicited from David would encompass, then, even David the king if his conduct revealed the ingredients that gave rise here to the condemnation.

It should not require any refined arts of pleading to show that the Bible contains, in ample measure, an understanding of moral reasoning; but I would join David Novak in contending that this moral reasoning represents a critical, necessary ingredient in what we mean by natural law. On that point, we may be contested by other friends, and by Strauss himself; but packed away in this dispute would be a serious, vexing question of just how we find our way to the "nature" that forms the ground of natural right or natural law.[24] A whole day of papers could be offered for us on the question of whether we find the "natural" by induction, by drawing generalizations on the behavior of human beings over the millennia, or whether we would be obliged to bring to the problem a more demanding standard that involves propositions that are axiomatic, logically necessary, true a priori. If we draw generalizations from the checkered history of our species, we may be driven to conclude that incest and infanticide are consistent with natural law because they seem to be intractable parts of the human record. Some commentators, faced with continuities of that kind, have concluded that they must be in accord with natural law because they seem to spring from something rooted in human nature.[25] On the other hand, we may be driven to make distinctions, in the human record, among the things that are higher and lower for human beings. We may conclude, then, for example, that our capacity to give reasons over matters of right and wrong would be higher, better, more decisively human, than that capacity for brute, physical force that we share with other animals.

When we begin to measure nature in that way, when we seek a more demanding philosophic standard, I suspect that we will be appealing, again, to the logic of morals. That was the path of Spinoza's argument as he offered his own account of revelation. As Spinoza put it, "the power of reason does not extend so far as to determine for us that men may be blessed through simple obedience, without understanding."[26] Yet, what was the ground on which he claimed his own surety, or his own conviction, on this point? Was it not in fact the inference—drawn from the understanding of a just and merciful God—that God would not punish people for attributes that were morally irrelevant, attributes such as height and color of hair? Therefore, there was powerful reason to suspect that God would not hold back God's grace from dutiful, good people who simply could not understand syllogisms or show the brilliance of dialectics. It was almost needless to say, also, that these were inferences plausibly drawn from the attributes that Maimonides, no less than Spinoza, thought were necessary in God. Spinoza was led then to revelation through his reason. Revelation became plausible at the limits to the reach of reason, but the reach of reason was known to us through reason itself.

Reason and Revelation

Spinoza would claim no more than the separate domains marked off by Strauss and insist, as Strauss would later insist, that reason could not invade the province of revelation.[27] Reason could not judge, for their validity, the claims of belief; in the writing between the lines, it was plain that reason and therefore philosophy claimed an ascendance over revelation, for it was through reason itself that we understood these distinctions.

Strauss aligned himself against Spinoza, but in the end, his own account came back to the same thing. Like Spinoza, he sought to give an account of why it was reasonable to respect the claims of revelation. He sought to show that, while revelation could not refute the facts of nature or the laws of physics, science and philosophy could not refute revelation. By the common sense of reason, it was "only naturally or humanly impossible that the 'first' Isaiah should have known the name of the founder of the Persian empire." As Strauss quickly pointed out, "it was not impossible for the omnipotent God to reveal to him that name."[28] The parting of the Red Sea might be at odds with the laws of physics, unless of course those laws could be suspended by the God who was their creator. In all of these cases, a supernatural explanation remains a possibility, and the very possibility of that alternative explanation might be enough to give us pause before we settle in with a scientific explanation and rule out completely an account cast from revelation.

Now, leaving aside for a moment the way we judge this argument, it is nevertheless the case that Strauss does not ask us to accept this account as an understanding vouchsafed to us through revelation. He appeals to our reason, and he tries to weigh the question of how we can know whether the case for revelation is immanently plausible or implausible. As I remarked earlier, he does not approach this question from a posture of piety. He deliberately asks the question posed by a philosopher: How can we *know*? Or, how can we claim to have refuted the argument? Strauss seeks to make this problem comprehensible to us by drawing us to the logic of propositions. He tries to point up, in this respect, the intractable difference between an empirical proposition, a proposition that is confirmed or disproven through data drawn from the senses, and a logical proposition, which may be examined for its truth or falsity entirely on logical terms. Then, in a further step, he would try to bring out the difference that separates propositions of this character from propositions that can be judged for their validity *neither* by logic *nor* by empirical evidence.

This is the kind of exercise familiar to those people who make their livings as logicians or philosophers. It strikes me now as quite curious that Strauss should have put such a weight on this kind of argument. Consider, for a moment, how this brand of argument has become familiar to us in other settings. A person may claim, for example, that certain elves or leprechauns are responsible for the working of the watch on his wrist. We ask, How is that claim to be confirmed or refuted? Could we weigh the watch at different times? No, the answer runs, because the elves are imponderable, they are weightless. They are also invisible and inaudible; in short, they leave no traces that can form evidence for our senses. At the same time, the claim is not logically inescapable, for I can deny that there are elves in my watch without falling into contradiction. So, the conclusion may be a concession, offered with faint cheer, that indeed we cannot refute the claim that there are elves in the watch. Then the sobriety comes kicking in: neither can we claim, however, any ground for "knowing" that the elves are there; and for the same reason, we cannot supply the means by which other people may "know" of the elves and credit their existence.

It is at least puzzling, on the surface, that Strauss would raise the kind of question that signals the presence of a philosopher—the question of how we "know"—and then offer a proof in which the claim to know is surely most infirm. By this construction, revelation cannot be refuted, but neither can we claim to know that revelation is possible or that it deserves to be taken seriously. Again, this is a curious choice for Strauss, unless, of course, he chose deliberately the kind of proof that might reveal what is infirm in the things that philosophers claim to know. We may get a more precise sense of what we are risking, when we are lingering even playfully with arguments of this kind, if we consider how they have been used in a mischievous way in recent years. What I have in mind are those philosophers with an unaccountable drive to deny free will and preserve, as a live possibility, that our acts may not in fact be authentically our own. They would urge us to consider that we are controlled, that our behavior is "determined," by agents or forces we may not even comprehend. As Daniel Robinson points out, we are compelled to ask these writers whether this argument is indeed theirs; whether they offer it earnestly as their own, or whether it might be put through their lips by agents and powers outside themselves.[29]

I will not rehearse the ways, quite fascinating and mirthful, in which this kind of argument collapses on itself. There is nothing mirthful, however, about the implications that may be drawn from this argument if it is taken seriously and left unrefuted. We may consider, at length, on another day, just what effect may be generated for our laws or our daily lives if we begin crediting certain unexaminable, unverifiable claims of this type: "You saw me act as the agent in killing Jones, but I was not responsible; someone else at that moment was in control of my mind and my body." We have, curiously enough, commentators who wish to make us suggestible to propositions of this character, which would dissolve any sense of personal responsibility. In the sweep of their advocacy, these writers seem willing at the same time to strike at the premises of free will and moral agency that lie behind the proposition that "all men are created equal." I think it is plain that we would never credit for a moment these claims of determinism as a way of dissolving the responsibility that real persons may have for assaulting victims; we are not inclined to displace a regime of consent, or free elections, on the ground that the elections are bogus, because no one, after all, is acting "freely."

My argument is this: these variants on the untestable, metaphysical argument would never be taken seriously for a moment on any practical matter, or any matter of moral consequence. A similar argument put forth about revelation or God would be condemned, again, to be a metaphysic without moral consequence. In that event, we must ask why Strauss would have given such weight to a form of argument that is so wanting in moral significance, so incapable of supporting a judgment on any moral or political matter that he regarded as important.

I revert to the possibility I held out earlier: that Strauss chose an example that would deliberately undercut the claim of philosophers to know. At one moment, in his preface on Spinoza, Strauss had sought to establish a symmetry of incapacity by showing the way in which revelation and philosophy could generate their own refutations. He showed a remarkable prescience in marking off the way in which philosophers and jurists would persuade themselves that reason finally cannot establish its own truths: they would persuade themselves on that point mainly by noting that even the most accomplished philosophers fall into disagreement over moral truths. With this kind of argument, men as varied as John Rawls, Laurence Tribe, Robert Bork, and Harry Blackmun have sought to "prove" that there are no moral truths, or at least no propositions that could be installed as "truths," in our law. However, this argument resolves into this proposition: that the presence of disagreement on any matter of moral consequence is sufficient to establish the absence of truth. Now, I would be obliged to register my own disagreement with this proposition, and by its own terms, that should be quite sufficient to establish its falsity. There are no tricks; it is simply an example of the kinds of propositions that have been quite familiar to philosophers as "self-refuting" propositions. Strauss himself, in other writings, showed his own awareness of the falsity of this proposition (that the want of consensus marked the absence of truth), which is to say, he showed his awareness that this proposition could be known, unmistakably, as wrong because it ran afoul of the law of contradiction. But in that event, there could be no such symmetry of the kind Strauss had suggested, with revelation and reason casting up the arguments that would stymie themselves. The argument that supposedly shows the limits of philosophy, or reason, was a transparently false argument, and it could be known as false through the canons of reason that were known to philosophy. Of course, a fiction could be preserved that reason had reached its limits, a certain modesty could be preserved for the claims of philosophy, by a philosopher who was willing to mask, in a benign haze, the things that he or she really knew. In that style, Strauss could scale down the claims of philosophy by gently concealing what he knew; anyone tutored in philosophy would readily notice what he was doing. It was a gesture of self-effacement, carried out by a philosopher, but evident to other philosophers. And yet, what was concealed so elaborately in this maneuver but the superiority of philosophy in judging the claims about the things we can know?

Strauss and the Return to Judaism

Not long after Leo Strauss's death in 1973, Milton Himmelfarb was doing a commemorative piece on Strauss, and as he tried to estimate Strauss's relation to Judaism he remarked that Strauss had not been seen often in the synagogue. I remember calling Milton at the time and recounting to him a story I had been told about Strauss's appearance for a lecture at Amherst—a few years before I had arrived at Amherst. After his lecture, he was approached by a professor of English, a man of Jewish ancestry who made it a deliberate project to remove from his life any attachment to things Jewish. He ran up to Strauss and said, "But if I follow what you've said, you would have to believe in revelation." To which Strauss replied, "But I'm a Jew." The professor of English said, "But what does that mean—these days?" To which Strauss said, "That's not my problem."

Milton Himmelfarb listened to this story and said, "Well, it was Athens and Jerusalem, wasn't it? His heart was in Jerusalem, his head was in Athens, and the head is the organ of the philosopher." After all the shadings and turns in the argument, after all of the ellipses and writing between the lines, that may be, in the end, the truth of the matter. But it cannot be such an unequivocal truth,

since Strauss evidently strained to render the matter more complicated.

Several years ago I was teaching *Natural Right and History*, and
returning to that book after many years. I still had the copy I had
bought and marked up thirty years earlier, when I was preparing to
encounter Strauss in the classroom for the first time. I asked my
students to keep the book closed and tell me how it began: What
was on page 1 and what were the opening sentences? The book
began, in the first sentence, with the mention of what Strauss calls
"a passage" in the Declaration of Independence. He then remarks
that this passage has been quoted often, but by its very weight and
elevation it may be rendered immune to that familiarity that breeds
contempt and misuse. He then quotes the passage: "We hold these
truths to be self-evident, that all men are created equal, that they
are endowed by their creator with certain unalienable rights . . ."
In that passage, he has the core of a teaching about natural rights.
He has moral truths, and the Creator of the universe that contains
moral truths. This is the first principle of that decent, moderate
regime, the regime in which Christians and Jews can meet on a
common plane of citizenship. They can meet there because that
first principle of the regime is accessible to all creatures of reason.
Natural Right and History begins with that document written by
statesmen-philosophers, with "the proposition," as Lincoln called
it, that could be understood, through reason, by all people, everywhere.

Then I was pleasantly surprised when one of my students remarked, "No, that's not how the book begins." This student had
been with me in other courses, and he had apparently absorbed
Strauss, or he had anticipated what I would do in other parts of the
book. He held the book up. Page 1 does begin as I had described
it, in the opening sentences, but as the book is opened to that first
page, page 1 is on the right. To the left of page 1 are two short
paragraphs set in italics—the epigraph for the book. They are not
drawn from the work of philosophers, and they do not form an
appeal to sovereign reason. They come from the Old Testament.
One was the story I alluded to earlier told by Nathan to David.
Strauss truncates the story by letting the fragment end in this way:
"And there came a traveller unto the rich man, and he spared to
take of his own flock and of his own herd, to dress for the wayfaring
man that was come unto him; but took the poor man's lamb, and
dressed it up for the man that was come to him." Strauss draws

on Nathan's account of the injustice, but he ends before the confrontation, when Nathan brings home to David the point of the story, and says, "Thou art the man." That is, Strauss ends before the problem is cast in the impersonal terms of the "logic of morals."

The second fragment is more revealing. That passage is from I Kings 21 and reads in this way:

Naboth the Jezreelite had a vineyard which was in Jezreel, hard by the palace of Ahab king of Samaria. And Ahab spake unto Naboth, saying, Give me thy vineyard, that I may have it for a garden of herbs, because it is near unto my house: and I will give thee for it a better vineyard than it; or, if it seem good to thee, I will give thee the worth of it in money. And Naboth said to Ahab, The Lord forbid it to me, that I should give the inheritance of my fathers unto thee.

In the second passage, unlike the first, there is no description, or offer, of injustice. The only semblance of an impropriety that could stir the indignation of Naboth is the suggestion that he should think of trading away his patrimony, the property that was given to him by his fathers. The appeal in this passage is to the things that are ancestral—the respect due to fathers, but due to them mainly on the strength of the Lawgiver. The offer might hold great utility: it is certainly not foreclosed by anything stemming from the law of contradiction. But, he says, "The Lord forbid it to me," perhaps because it is inconsistent with the honor due to "thy father and mother."

Once again, though, there is a truncating, and a deeper injustice masked from view in this fragment. Ahab's wife, Jezebel, manages to have Naboth accused falsely and stoned to death. Both stories are about the abuse of kingly power, of men in lawful authority acting wrongly. David uses his power as king to dispose of Bathsheba's husband and possess Bathsheba; and Ahab secures, through the wickedness of his wife, the land that Naboth would not willingly sell. It is made clear, in the text, that the kings committed deep wrongs, even abominations. It is not exactly clear that the kings acted "lawlessly." The stories clearly imply that the readers have access to standards of judgment, in judging the deep wrongs done by kings. When we press on to the ground of those judgments, we find that it does not depend finally on the ancestral. It depends on understandings of right and wrong that should be evident even to people who are not Jewish. What looks on the surface like an appeal to the biblical tradition, turns into something else. The hidden lesson of the story takes us beyond the ancestral, and beyond revelation; it takes us back, after all, to rational morality.

Strauss professed to understand Spinoza better than he had at the age of twenty-five, and he must have understood that the differences he drew so sharply, between himself and Spinoza, might not have been entirely warranted. Yet, he did not alter, in 1962, the sense of the alignments that put him on the side of Judaism and Spinoza on the side of philosophy detached from the Jews. In my own sense of the matter, the explanation might be found in that remark of Strauss's in the new preface on Spinoza: The world had seen now something novel, "the only German regime—the only regime ever anywhere—which had no other clear principle than murderous hatred of the Jews." After the Holocaust it was even more important not to equivocate and to stand decisively with the Jews. As Emil Fackenheim reminded us, the Holocaust brought home to us that certain Jews at the turn of the century virtually condemned their children to death by the decision to raise them as Jews. That danger could be averted only by a decision not to raise them as Jews. But a decision of that kind, taken now, has even more significance than the same decision made before the Holocaust, because it would mark a willingness to give Hitler his posthumous victory. It would make Jews accomplices in the project of removing Jews from the world.

Strauss might have borne the reservations of a philosopher, but he was not going to build those reservations toward a decision to overthrow, on his own, the religion that had been handed down to him by his father, and by his father before him. He would earnestly preserve his reverence, and that reverence might have been shown in his willingness, precisely, to mute or submerge his philosophic doubts.

Then, too, we must remind ourselves that the embrace of the ancestral could not have been, for Strauss, a simple proposition. He knew that the praise of the old could be done with an utter suspension of moral judgment, as it is done by certain conservatives, who are even willing to say a redeeming word about slavery if it can be said that slavery was part, after all, of the American "tradition." For Strauss, the honoring of tradition meant the honoring of a legacy of serious reflection about the laws, about the things that were right and wrong. Some of our friends may be inclined to dispute us over the question of whether the principles of moral judgment can indeed be known to us, even across those tribes and traditions that have formed our languages and character. Putting that aside, Strauss knew that the tradition of his fathers was—as he insisted at so many turns—a religion of reason. If there was anything that stood out in the work of Leo Strauss—anything that was evident in his classroom—it was the concern to set himself against the current of his time, in resisting relativism. It was plain even to the dimmest onlooker that Strauss stood against that tendency, diffusing itself through the academy, to reduce morality to conventions, or to the habits of the local tribe. Strauss attached himself to a tradition of prophets and scholars, and even when those teachers were searching and confessedly puzzled, they spoke on certain matters with moral conviction. They did not speak with the accents of relativism. At the limit of their own wit, they could still summon the conviction that there was something to be known; that there were moral laws that had their source finally in the Lawgiver. Strauss was quite far, then, from those primates we find now on campuses, the colleagues who tell us earnestly that we must engage in moral reasoning even though there are no moral truths to supply the substance of that reasoning. They tell us, with a sweep of sentiment, that we must ever strive to "know," even though we must always fall short, for there is nothing, finally, that we can reliably know. A notable philosopher once explained that there could be knowledge without a knower—that the Pythagorean theorem was true even before Pythagoras came to know it. But our recent, affable colleagues tell us that we must all seek to be knowers, although there is nothing to be known. For all of the mysteries that Strauss was willing to encourage about his own teaching, no one would suggest that a skepticism, or a bewilderment, of that kind, could be hidden anywhere in his subtleties.

Of course, we know that it was part of Strauss's design to preserve a bit of puzzle for us, and to hold certain things discreetly back. In the chapters ahead we will explore that puzzle a bit further, with readers who have been closely attentive to the writings that Strauss left us. I have sketched in here the tentative lines of my own judgment, but I hesitate to claim the position of the authoritative commentator or claim to understand Strauss better than he understood himself. I am sure, though—now, more than ever—that I understood him too literally, in the past, because I did not understand him literally enough.

Notes

1. Leo Strauss, *Spinoza's Critique of Religion* (New York: Schocken Books, 1965), 263.

2. Ibid., 123.

3. Ibid., 17.

4. Spinoza, *A Theologico-Political Treatise*, trans. R.H.M. Elwes (New York: Dover, 1951) 44. (Cited hereafter as *Theologico-Political Treatise*.)

5. Ibid., 43.

6. Strauss, *Spinoza's Critique of Religion*, 117.

7. Ibid., 16.

8. Ibid., 20.

9. Ibid., 25.

10. J. C. Fitzpatrick, ed., *The Writings of George Washington* (Washington, D.C.: U.S. Government Printing Office, 1939), 185–186.

11. Cf., in this vein, Strauss's commentary on that tendency sprung from the Enlightenment to put education and secular morality in the place of religion:

Karl Marx, the father of communism, and Friedrich Nietzsche, the stepgrandfather of fascism, were liberally educated on a level to which we cannot even hope to aspire. But perhaps one can say that their grandiose failures make it easier for us who have experienced those failures to understand again the old saying that wisdom cannot be separated from moderation and hence to understand that wisdom requires unhesitating loyalty to a decent constititution and even to the cause of constititutionalism. ("Liberal Education and Responsibility," in Strauss, *Liberalism Ancient and Modern* [New York: Basic Books, 1968], 24).

12. See Strauss, *Persecution and the Art of Writing* (Glencoe, Ill.: Free Press, 1952), 34–35.

13. Strauss, *Spinoza's Critique of Religion*, 31.

14. Strauss, *Natural Right and History* (Chicago: University of Chicago Press, 1953), 2.

15. Ibid., 160.

16. Ibid. Strauss completes the thought, however, by noting that "it suffices to repeat that in extreme situations the normally valid rules of natural right are justly changed, or changed in accordance with natural right; the exceptions are as just as the rules."

17. See Spinoza, *Theologico-Political Treatise*, 44.

18. See David Novak, *Jewish Social Ethics* (New York: Oxford University Press, 1992), 25.

19. See Gregory Dix, *Jew and Greek; A Study in the Primitive Church* (Westminster, Md., 1955).

20. Novak, *Jewish Social Ethics*, 30–31.

21. Ibid., 29.

22. Ibid., 28.

23. See Arkes, *First Things* (Princeton: Princeton University Press, 1986), 53–54, 88–89, 96–98, 167–68.

24. See Ernest L. Fortin, "The New Rights Theory and the Natural Law," *Review of Politics* 44 (1982): 590–612.

25. In this manner, Judge Richard Posner has been willing to treat Social Darwinism as a theory of nature that may plausibly qualify as a species of "natural law." See Posner, *The Problems of Jurisprudence* (Cambridge, Mass: Harvard University Press, 1990), 235–36.

26. Spinoza, *Theologico-Political Treatise*, 194–195.

27. Ibid., 190, 194–95, 198.

28. Strauss, *Spinoza's Critique of Religion*, 28.

29. See Daniel N. Robinson, "Determinism, 'Hard' and 'Soft,' " *Philosophy of Psychology* (New York: Columbia University Press, 1985), chap. 2.

2

Strauss, Reason, and Revelation: Unraveling the Essential Question

Susan Orr

What has political science to do with God?[1] Leo Strauss showed that the two are inextricably linked. Strauss perceived that what is highest in a person leads him or her to either philosophy or theology. Today we understand political philosophy more deeply in light of what he posed as the permanent problem of the conflict between philosophy and theology, or as he would have it, reason and revelation.

In *Natural Right and History*, he puts it succinctly: "The fundamental question, therefore, is whether men can acquire knowledge of the good without which they cannot guide their lives individually or collectively by the unaided effort of their natural powers, or whether they are dependent for that knowledge on Divine Revelation. No alternative is more fundamental than this: human guidance or divine guidance."[2]

That his work should be taken seriously is something that few would now deny.[3] From those skeptical of the Straussian enterprise to those who applaud it, all are forced to come to terms with this twentieth-century master. Whether or not we appreciate his ideas, we must confront them, refute them, or agree with them. It appears that Allan Bloom is correct when he says "Echoing the *Apology* with what will seem a threat to some, a blessing to others, I believe our generation may well be judged by the next generation according to how we judged Leo Strauss."[4]

Yet, it is not an easy task to find out what Leo Strauss thought.

The problem is twofold: The first obstacle is the structure of the writing itself. It is usually in the form of commentary upon a given text written to bring the ideas within that text to life. It is often difficult to distinguish between Strauss's elucidation of a text and his own thought: it is difficult to separate the philosopher being analyzed from the analyzing philosopher. The second problem is the one for which Strauss and his school have been most excoriated: his teaching on esotericism, or reading between the lines.

Fundamental to Strauss's teaching is that it is not always prudent to make one's views apparent. Wishing to avoid a tyrant's ire is only one obvious example of why it is necessary to write with caution, especially when writing on political philosophy. As he states in *Thoughts on Machiavelli*, "to speak the truth is sensible only when one speaks to wise men."[5] By its very nature, of course, the written word cannot control who reads it, thus making esoteric writing necessary. Upon reflection, it is fairly easy to grasp that there are different types of speech, that is, that people speak differently to different people. Hence, one would speak more openly to a friend than to a stranger. When considering his work, therefore, it is best to proceed with caution and to assume that there are different levels of meaning to be found: some that are meant for friends, others for strangers.

Two Schools of Straussians: East and West

The difficulty of discerning what Strauss thinks is compounded by dissension among his students, each claiming to be carrying on the tradition begun by Professor Strauss and each carrying out a decidedly different project. The dispute over the legacy of Leo Strauss dissolves into two camps: East and West. The East Coast Straussians are those who collapse the distinction between ancient and modern philosophy and claim that the real dispute is between philosophy and poetry or philosophy and revelation. As Thomas Pangle writes, "What is most essential in the quarrel between Plato and the Bible is already present in the quarrel between Plato and the poets . . ."[6] According to the East Coast version of Strauss, any talk of god or gods is political, only a noble lie and an attempt to disguise his nihilism. Thus, any distinction between Zeus and the Judeo-Christian God is only one of degree in the end, a matter of taste. Against this claim, Harry V. Jaffa, the preeminent exemplar of the West Coast school, explicitly denies that Strauss was an Epicurean in disguise. Jaffa understands Strauss's contribution to political philosophy thus: "Strauss's distinctiveness—indeed, his uniqueness, I had thought—lay above all else in the fact that he was the first great critic of modernity whose diagnosis of the ills of modernity did not end by seeking a solution of those ills through a radicalization of the principles of modernity."[7] Using Strauss's esotericism as a shield, the East Coast Straussians insist that Jaffa has missed the point, that he only succeeds in getting the political or exoteric teaching of Strauss, but misses the inner core that reveals the hidden emptiness of the political realm, namely, that morality has no real grounding.[8] One wonders which of these accounts of Strauss is the correct one? Whatever the answer may be, we can assert at least in the beginning that Strauss seems to have imitated Plato successfully by writing ironically.[9]

There is no dispute, however, about what Strauss thought of modern political science. He held that political scientists were busily translating the ideas found in Darwin and Einstein to political science without accounting for any difference between atoms and human beings. Departments of political science, enthralled by the fact-value distinction that eliminated any notion of a transcendent good, had become frivolous. As Strauss noted trenchantly:

> Only a great fool would call the new political science diabolic: it has no attributes peculiar to fallen angels. It is not even Machiavellian, for Machiavelli's teaching was graceful, subtle, and colorful. Nor is it Neronian. Nevertheless one may say of it that it fiddles while Rome burns. It is excused by two facts: It does not know that it fiddles, and it does not know that Rome burns.[10]

Embracing this relativistic science and translating it to politics, the new political science rejected any hierarchical understanding of people. In refusing to recognize any limits inherent in men, women, or anywhere else, political scientists blindly placed their faith in progress. It was left to Strauss to show his colleagues that, while they mistakenly thought themselves free, they had indeed bound themselves more completely than the medievals they despised to chains of superstition: for they had replaced the belief in God with the belief in the inevitable march of history toward progress.

Strauss's interest in the serious consideration of the claims of revelation was one that, with few exceptions, modern political scientists and philosophers alike scorned. Indeed, as Strauss noted, "The new science uses sociological or psychological theories regarding religion which exclude, without considering it, the possibility that religion rests ultimately on God's revealing Himself to man."[11] The Enlightenment had tossed aside religion as monkish superstition, the only purpose of which was to enslave others; religion had retained that tarnish within academia. But Strauss would not let revelation go at that. He understood only too well what we had lost by giving up the notion of the divine, or even of considering its possibility. He understood that the highest questions that political philosophy asks—for example, what is justice?—point to questions about God. As he states in the final sentence of *The City and Man*, "Only by beginning at this point will we be open to the full impact of the all important question which is coeval with philosophy although the philosophers do not frequently pronounce it—the question *quis sit deus* [who is God?]."[12]

The Theological Question in Strauss

Understanding that the theological question is important to the political realm does not necessarily imply that God is only a political concept for Strauss. Thus, the key question for the serious student of Strauss to answer is whether or not he held the door open to revelation. In a new introduction, written in 1962 for the English translation of his first book, *Spinoza's Critique of Religion*, Strauss states:

> The genuine refutation of orthodoxy would require the proof that the world and human life are perfectly intelligible without the assumption of a mysterious God; it would require at least the success of the philosophic system: man has to show himself theoretically and practically as the master of his human life; the merely given world must be replaced by the world created by man theoretically and practically.[13]

To suggest that Strauss remained skeptical regarding people's ability to accomplish this task would not be putting it too strongly. The question remains, however, whether this is simply his exoteric teaching.

His most thorough articulation of the problem of reason and

revelation can be found in his lecture "Jerusalem and Athens: Some Preliminary Reflections."[14] It is an essay that is so carefully crafted that every examination of it leads to a further understanding of Strauss and the competing claims of reason and revelation.

Strauss gave this lecture at the City College in New York in 1967, and it was published in an abbreviated version in *Commentary* later that same year.[15] That Strauss published it in a journal of opinion like *Commentary* indicates that he considered what he had to say on the topic to be important for more than just the academic world. It is also interesting to note that the book that Strauss was working on at the time of his death was to have the essay on Jerusalem and Athens as its central chapter. That is another indication of the importance he placed on this work in particular and the subject as a whole.[16]

That this essay is pivotal to answering the question of what Strauss thought of the relationship between reason and faith is beyond doubt. It is his fullest reconsideration of whether the moderns were correct in their denigration of the sacred. He captures the entire history of the battle for the human soul: first, by showing us that modern men and women are lost, then by showing us the path to recovery. Similar to the task Maimonides set for himself in an earlier age, Strauss has undertaken a recovery or a revitalization of the West by testing the limits of reason. The essay is a debate or dialogue between the two rival claimants, revelation and reason, in their own words, that is, in the words of the author of Genesis and the prophets and the words of the Greek poets and philosophers, in particular Hesiod and Socrates. Here are reason and revelation at their peak: the account of the creation according to the Bible compared with the account found in Greek poetry and philosophy in the first part of the essay; the prophets' mission versus Socrates' in the second.

It is not possible, in this chapter, to undertake a thorough analysis of Strauss's lecture. Instead, by concentrating on some of the salient features of "Jerusalem and Athens," I hope to be able to suggest which account of Leo Strauss is more accurate: the cautious nihilist or the reluctant believer? In "Jerusalem and Athens," he tackles this important philosophic question most directly: is it to reason or revelation that one should look for answers about the highest things?

What does it mean to choose between Jerusalem and Athens and why does Strauss insist that there must be a choice? Is it simply that faith is irrational, that is, a choice against reason, or is it deeper than that? The question of Jerusalem and Athens is the question of how people guide their lives, how they choose what is best for them: does philosophy or revelation give them the answer? In other words, the question of Jerusalem or Athens is whether one can know the good on one's own, or if one has to be told. Strauss first lets us look at the biblical answer, then he shows us the alternatives from poetry and philosophy.

Even before we turn to the essay, we already have some inkling of the importance of the two great cities of Jerusalem and Athens. Jerusalem, fountain of Judaism and Christianity, stands for the claims of faith or revelation. Athens represents what people can accomplish through unaided reason. Both cities have something to say about the contemplative life, that is, the highest activity that people can accomplish, and about political life, or how people should live their daily lives—since even the best person can neither philosophize nor pray all of the time. It is also important to note that these two cities are ancient cities. Thus from the outset, we are asked to look back, to turn away from modernity to a more ancient understanding of things.

In another work, Strauss argues that Jerusalem, not Athens, takes the theme of political philosophy most seriously, takes the desire for justice most seriously; Jerusalem longs for justice.[17] Her longing for justice reflects an incompleteness: a desire for justice because we do not possess it, just as philosophy is a longing for a wisdom that we do not possess. The faithful city is incomplete because while she strives for justice, she must ultimately wait for God to bring it. Athens is incomplete as well, but in a different way. For Strauss, wisdom begins in doubt of the divine law, and finds its home in Athens, an admittedly imperfect regime. To attain wisdom, however, one needs not only Athens, but a little help from "the sun," or from nature, as well.[18]

"Jerusalem and Athens": An Analysis

A few preliminary remarks are in order regarding the structure of "Jerusalem and Athens." The first thing that should be noted about it may at first appear obvious; but as we have seen, Strauss always cautioned his students that one learns many things by the words that wise people choose. Surface and structure are important.[19]

Thus, it is not unimportant that the essay is entitled "Jerusalem *and* Athens" and not "Jerusalem *or* Athens." In an essay about what Strauss considered the most fundamental choice, he does not force us to begin by choosing one over the other. In keeping with this method, the essay takes both claims seriously. Also interesting is the fact that Jerusalem has the pride of place not only in the title but in the argument itself.

One omission in "Jerusalem and Athens" is as intriguing as it is surprising. In an essay dealing with reason and revelation, one would expect to find some reference to Maimonides. It is strange not to find even one reference to *The Guide of the Perplexed*, especially since Strauss claims:

> The *Guide* is then devoted above all to biblical exegesis, although to biblical exegesis of a particular kind . . . The *Guide* is then devoted to "the difficulties of the Law" or to "the secrets of the Law." The most important of these secrets are the Account of the Beginning (the beginning of the Bible) and the Account of the Chariot (Ezekiel 1 and 10). The *Guide* is then devoted primarily and chiefly to the explanation of the Account of the Beginning and the Account of the Chariot.[20]

Strauss does not, at least not openly, take his understanding of the beginning from Maimonides. Instead, Strauss replaces Maimonides, becoming the new guide for perplexed moderns.

Strauss divides the lecture into two parts: "The Beginning of the Bible and Its Greek Counterparts" and "On Socrates and the Prophets." "Jerusalem and Athens," of course, can be subdivided even further, and although the division is not arbitrary, Strauss does not tell us how to break it down.[21] The entire essay is forty-one paragraphs long. The first part, "The Beginning of the Bible and Its Greek Counterparts," is composed of thirty paragraphs and can be divided into five sections: an introduction of one paragraph; a critique of culture that takes up four paragraphs; a section on biblical criticism, four paragraphs; the biblical account, fifteen paragraphs; and finally its Greek counterparts, six paragraphs. Thus, Strauss devotes the major portion of the first part and indeed the entire essay to the biblical account. In contrast, only six paragraphs are dedicated to the Greek understanding of the beginning of things.

The second part, "On Socrates and the Prophets," is much shorter, only eleven paragraphs. This part of the essay is dedicated

to a comparison of the different missions of the prophets and
Socrates. The difference in length between the two parts could be
a reflection of the fact that the account of the beginnings of
things, either in Genesis or Greek poetry and philosophy, is more
important. The account of the beginning lays the groundwork
upon which morality, which is of tantamount importance to both
Socrates and the prophets, rests. Perhaps Strauss is simply imitat-
ing the difference in status between the Torah and the prophets
within Judaism, that is, the difference in status between Moses and
those prophets who come later: only Moses spoke with God face
to face. Both Socrates and the prophets are concerned with morality: the prophets, with getting the Israelites to remain true to their
covenant with the God of Abraham, Isaac, and Jacob; Socrates
with teaching his fellow citizens to remain true to knowledge, and
thereby, attain virtue. The prophets, however, are much more
successful in their endeavors, as Strauss points out at the close of
his lecture.

Strauss begins "Jerusalem and Athens" with a critique of modern
social science that is devastating despite its brevity. We know
from the beginning that we cannot count on a modern answer to
"illuminate our trackless way."[22] Through Nietzsche, Strauss
shows us the emptiness of the cultural relativism hailed by social
science. Strauss begins with Nietzsche because Nietzsche did not
mock Athens and Jerusalem, but rather had a "deeper reverence"
than any other modern for these two ancient cities and what they
stand for; yet, he was unable to return to either one.[23] Elsewhere,
Strauss informs us that Nietzsche cannot simply return to classical
paganism: "He is an heir to that deepening of the soul which has
been effected by the Biblical belief in a God that is holy. The
philosopher of the future, as distinct from the classical philosopher,
will be concerned with the holy."[24] This deepening of the soul that
Strauss notes is an indication of the inherent superiority of Jerusalem to classical mythology. There is a distinction to be made
between the Judeo-Christian God and Zeus. Whatever we will learn
from Hesiod or the other Greek counterparts, we will not learn that
Zeus is holy.

After he has shown that social science is filled with self-contra-
dictions, Strauss looks to what theology and philosophy think
about the beginnings of things, or the first things. But before he can
begin, he must demonstrate that Spinoza was wrong, that the Bible

is not full of "self-contradictory assertions, of remnants of ancient prejudices or superstitions, and of the outpourings of an uncontrolled imagination."[25] How does Strauss do this? Surprisingly, by admitting preemptive defeat.

Strauss turns to the two accounts of wisdom. Jerusalem and Athens each say wisdom is something different. The distinction between the two is immediate. The Torah, a work (for we still have not been told whether or not it is a book) and not a person, asserts it is God's "wisdom in the eyes of the nations."[26] The Greeks make no such claim. Strauss lets our first encounter with the Bible leave the impression that it is knowable to everyone who approaches it with care. The Bible says that fear of the Lord is the beginning of wisdom. Strauss contrasts this account of wisdom with the Greek understanding that wisdom begins with wonder. On their face, these two notions of how to attain wisdom appear decidedly different and Strauss insists that they are mutually incompatible; because we are not wise, we must listen to each claim. His next statement that he has already decided in favor of Athens by even considering the question comes as something of a surprise. In asserting this, Strauss must insist that this openness or willingness to consider either claim is somehow contrary to Jerusalem. It is easy to see that philosophy, if it is understood as a search for wisdom, must remain open; but apparently, faith cannot remain open.

This decision in advance for philosophy is contrary to what we had thought from simply looking at the inclusive nature of the title "Jerusalem *and* Athens" of the lecture. It would seem, therefore, that we need proceed no further, that philosophy has won. If even considering the two claims violates the principles of Jerusalem, then thoughtful human beings must side with Athens; if, in order to be faithful to Jerusalem, we must somehow deny our ability to reason, then it seems almost inhuman to side with Jerusalem. But Strauss does not stop here. Indeed, he proceeds at great length. Is this not a contradiction? Could it be that he does not think it is as simple as he presents it here?

No matter what fear of the Lord is, the first thing that should be said about it is that it must be learned; the prerequisite for this Judeo-Christian virtue is faith. Although faith may be understood as a gift, we are not born with it, nor is it something simply intuited. Similar to philosophy, we must learn about it. Unlike philosophy, it is not something that we can learn through studying nature. Revelation is necessary precisely because human beings by their very nature are limited in what they can know about God on their own. God must reveal God's self: One thus has to hear about revelation whether, as in the case of Judaism, it be from the prophet directly, the writings he leaves behind, or from tradition. In other words, we have "to hear first" and then decide. It therefore seems that we are confronted with an assertion that is not meant to be taken seriously, although many take this as Strauss's final word on the subject.[27] Indeed, as we will soon find out the Bible itself has a reasonable beginning; and at the close of the section on biblical criticism, he rescinds his determination to make an advance decision in favor of Athens. Jerusalem, therefore, cannot be completely irrational. Strauss constantly tells his readers that first-rate minds do not make obvious mistakes. This seems to be one, and therefore it must be intentional. If it is, what does it mean to cloak the compelling rationality of Jerusalem? Could it be that he is lulling the atheists to sleep? As we shall see, this is exactly what he does.

With the next paragraph, he grants further ground to the opposition saying that it seems necessary "for all of us who cannot be orthodox" to "accept the principle of the historical-critical study of the Bible."[28] Despite this accession, he vigorously assaults biblical criticism's understanding of the Bible. He insists that the first shortcoming of biblical criticism is that it fails to understand the Bible as it was understood by the immediate addressees of the Bible. A not so subtle distinction is made between how Strauss says the Bible ought to be read versus how he has said other great books must be read. Strauss contends that the proper way to read a great book is to read it as it was understood by the author of the book. In contrast, Strauss focuses our attention here on the addressees of the Bible. It would, of course, be impious to suggest the possibility of understanding the author of the Bible if that author is God.[29]

Despite its being taken as a collection of memories, Strauss presents Genesis as a coherent whole—an idea shored up by Strauss's reliance on the Jewish biblical scholar Umberto Cassuto. Strauss does not turn to tradition for guidance in interpreting any given passage of the Bible. His critique of the biblical critics allows him an advantage that is not insignificant. Strauss can quite rightly assume his audience's ignorance of anything more than the most basic outline of Genesis. By sticking to the text of the Bible, Strauss is able to retell those events and make them new for us. Curiously, Strauss does not explore the question of inspiration. By leaving the question of God's inspiration aside, he allows the reader to acquire an admiration for the coherence of the text itself: to see that it is not an irrational account, that to consider revelation seriously does not require choosing between following reason or an irrational call to blind obedience. Thus, his exegesis of the Bible does not allow us to bring with us any assumptions or prejudices, good or bad.

Strauss's recounting of Genesis begins with creation and ends with Abraham's sacrifice of Isaac. He closes with a consideration of who the God of Abraham, Isaac, and Jacob is through an examination of God's revelation of God's name to Moses. In imitation of Genesis, people become the focus of Strauss's analysis of the Bible. Hence, Strauss lets us learn about the biblical God through God's interaction with people. The first principle that we learn is that, in beginning at the beginning, "the Bible begins reasonably."[30]

Strauss too begins reasonably, with an exegesis of the account of creation. Through his analysis, he demonstrates to the careful reader that Genesis presents a complete and coherent account of the whole, an account that is in fact a rebuke to philosophy. The lesson of the creation is that people are higher than the heavens in importance. It is worthwhile to quote Strauss at length here: "What the heavenly lights lose, man gains; man is the peak of creation. The creatures of the first three days cannot change their places; the heavenly bodies change their places but not their courses; the living beings change their courses but not their 'ways'; men alone can change their 'ways.' Man is the only being created in God's image."[31]

Note what Strauss says that people share with God. He does not speak of people's endowment with reason, but rather their ability to change their ways. Thus, the creator God first comes to sight as one who can change God's ways. For Strauss, the God of the Bible is first and foremost an incomprehensible God who can and does change God's ways. Therefore, God cannot be known or understood because God's ways are unpredictable. Strauss's interpretation of the events within Genesis serves also to confirm this understanding. Philosophy cannot touch the biblical God. As Strauss will tell us at the close of "The Biblical Account of the Beginning," the passage from the Bible that speaks most tellingly of the God of Abraham, Isaac, and Jacob is "I shall be gracious to whom I shall be gracious and I shall show mercy to whom I shall show mercy."[32] God is unpredictable, even if in marvelous ways.

What is the central teaching of the Bible? For Strauss, it is an implicit rejection of philosophy: the central teaching of the Bible is that people are meant to live in simplicity. In fact, the central paragraph of the entire essay (paragraph twenty-one), which falls within the first section on the beginnings, encapsulates this message. This paragraph deals with Noah's curse of his grandson Canaan, the excellence of Nimrod, and the destruction of the tower of Babel, events occurring between the two covenants of Noah and Abraham. This paragraph echoes the lesson from Cain and Abel: the foundations of civilization are laid in blood. Each episode in the central paragraph demonstrates people's attempts to circumvent the moral law and how God, sometimes with people's assistance, confounds that attempt: Canaan is cursed by Noah because he is the result of incest; Nimrod, his descendant, is a mighty hunter and warrior who builds an empire, which the Bible teaches is an evil thing; finally, God brings about a "milder alternative to the Flood" to prevent Nimrod's success.[33] God divides people into nations and therefore prevents Nimrod's empire from encompassing all of humankind. This paragraph is a further commentary on politics and civilization or people's constant attempt to overcome their own limitations. From what we have learned from Strauss's biblical exegesis thus far, the lesson is that God sometimes intervenes on behalf of God's creatures to prevent them from greater harm: people cannot be left alone to obey the law themselves.

The Greek accounts, in contrast to the coherent whole of the biblical account, are varied and numerous; each Greek presents a different understanding of the beginning of things. Indeed, some are poets and some are philosophers; poetry and philosophy, moreover, do not agree. Yet neither poetry nor philosophy agrees with the account presented by the author of Genesis. This entire section is an ascent: the section moves from poetry to philosophy, from the mythology of Hesiod to the philosopher whom Strauss believes comes closest to agreeing with the biblical account, Plato.

Strauss spends a lengthy paragraph discussing the poetry of Hesiod. *Theogony* and *Works and Days* give us Hesiod's account of the beginning of the gods and of humankind. For Hesiod, there are no transcendent beings. There is nothing eternally preexistent in Hesiod's cosmos. This is because according to Hesiod "everything that is has come to be."[34] There is no notion present in

Hesiod's poetry, or in any Greek thought for that matter, that the universe and all it contains did not need to exist, that it is a gift of creation. Instead, Hesiod presents the Greeks with gods that are far from perfect. These gods can and indeed often do commit evil deeds. Thus, speaking of Zeus, Strauss wryly notes, "Given his ancestors it is not surprising that while being the father of men and belonging to the gods who are the givers of good things, he is far from being kind to men."[35] Zeus is far from the eternal and perfect being who is outside of time, who intervenes in time when he wills, who covenants with his creation.

This teaching is confirmed by Hesiod's account of people. Although Zeus may destroy a town for one unjust person, his interest in people is unpredictable at best. The biblical God required "well-nigh universal wickedness" before God repented of God's creation.[36] After the destruction of the Flood, God makes a covenant with Noah promising never to undertake such destruction again, even if people are universally wicked. Later, God confounds man's speech so that there cannot be such widespread corruption. Lastly, God covenants with God's chosen people. In other words, God provides for creation, even when God's creatures are disobedient. In contrast, Zeus is unconcerned with sparing the righteous from destruction, much less with confounding the wicked. Furthermore, the notion that Zeus or any god would covenant with a mortal, or consider making a person his moral partner as God did with Abraham, is completely unthinkable to the Greeks.

Philosophers and Prophets

Part 2 of "Jerusalem and Athens" is rather short. It is also difficult to break down into subsections. Strauss begins the second part with an analysis of Hermann Cohen and his understanding of Plato and the prophets which takes up four paragraphs; the next section on the prophets is covered in a mere two paragraphs. The subsequent two paragraphs are spent considering Socrates' mission according to Plato. The final three paragraphs compare Socrates and the prophets.

Strauss begins with a critique of Hermann Cohen's "The Social Ideal in Plato and the Prophets." Cohen's interest is focused on the prophets, not the Torah, and this is not accidental. His intent was to distill a religion from Judaism based on the principles of reason. As Strauss notes, "The religion of reason leaves no place for absolute obedience or for what traditional Judaism considered the core of faith."[37] Thus, for example, Abraham's willingness to obey God's command to sacrifice Isaac becomes incomprehensible under the religion of reason. Here, Strauss presents a figure who stands for both Jerusalem and Athens, "a passionate philosopher and a Jew passionately devoted to Judaism."[38] Yet because Cohen presents a modern solution to the problem, we cannot turn to him as our guide. Again, Strauss emerges as the only one who can possibly lead us out of our present trouble.

While the first part of "Jerusalem and Athens" has no middle paragraph, there is one in "On Socrates and the Prophets" (paragraph thirty-six); it addresses the problem of distinguishing between true and false prophets. Here Strauss admits that not only true prophets have claimed to be sent by God. Most people, therefore, are left in a quandary over whom to believe. Even those who have heard both are unsure as to whom they should turn. The Bible's answer to the problem is simple: false prophets lie; they tell the people what they most want to hear. False prophets promise peace. Strauss sums up the difference beautifully:

> The false prophets trust in flesh, even if that flesh is the temple in Jerusalem, the promised land, nay, the chosen people itself, nay, God's promise to the chosen people if that promise is taken to be an unconditional promise and not as part of a Covenant. The true prophets, regardless of whether they predict doom or salvation, predict the unexpected, the humanly unforeseeable—what would not occur to men, left to themselves, to fear or to hope.[39]

We are reminded of Strauss's change of God's name to "I shall be What I shall be," which keeps the God of Israel radically free.[40] He even uses the Hebrew word for God's name in the next sentence to ensure that we see the connection. It is interesting that Strauss fails to make the traditional arguments for distinguishing false from true prophets: first, that false prophets are those who contradict Mosaic law; and second, that true prophets demonstrate the veracity of their calling through miracles.[41] Again Strauss reminds us of the difficulty that revelation presents to us: does it really come from God and how do we know this? This time, however, we understand at least one fundamental test. A true prophet will not let us settle for anything less than God.

Although there are many more lessons to be drawn from "Jerusalem and Athens," after this cursory glance, it is possible to draw various strands of his argument together to weave at least some preliminary conclusions regarding what Strauss wants to teach us about reason and revelation. "Jerusalem and Athens" is a most exacting essay filled with many allusions and many difficulties. There is little about it that is simple. Strauss makes us work to understand the problems behind reason and revelation. Everything important is understated and the conclusions are often left unsaid. To say the least, "Jerusalem and Athens" is not without ambiguity. Yet, it is possible to come to some determination of Strauss's purpose.

It is helpful first to remind ourselves of the obvious. "Jerusalem and Athens" is a relatively short piece, forty-one paragraphs all told. Even so, it is an amazingly compact account that presents a coherent case for a return either to classical philosophy in the form of Socrates or to biblical revelation. Remember what Strauss had originally presented as the problem in his introduction: "In order to understand ourselves and to illuminate our trackless way into the future, we must understand Jerusalem and Athens."[42] Having listened to Strauss, we can say that he has accomplished his task. With Strauss as our guide, we can at least say that we are no longer lost on a trackless way; we have two clear choices set before us. We even understand at least on some level what those choices are. The question is, what does the future hold now that we understand our past? The quarrel involves which way he suggests we should go—to Jerusalem or Athens?

Return: To Athens or to Jerusalem?

The question that must then be asked is, after understanding these two cities, does Strauss suggest a progress or a return? It is safe to say that he calls for an unqualified return. At the same time, it appears that he leaves it open as to which city to look to for guidance, in other words, to which city we should return. His allegiance remains intentionally unclear throughout the essay. This unwillingness to speak clearly about this most important subject is a lesson as well, but one that is difficult to arrive at. His failure to come down clearly on one side or the other may at times be frustrating, but the result is not: by refusing to stand with either

Athens or Jerusalem, he saves both possibilities. His concluding remarks in "Progress or Return? The Contemporary Crisis in Western Civilization" bear witness to this: "No one can be both a philosopher and a theologian nor, for that matter, some possibility which transcends the conflict between philosophy and theology, or pretends to be a synthesis of both. But every one of us can be and ought to be one or the other, the philosopher open to the challenge of theology or the theologian open to the challenge of philosophy."[43] Strauss may resemble Nietzsche in this essay, that is, he may appear as simply a beholder of Jerusalem and Athens. If this is so, he is one with an essential difference: he shows the impossibility of uniting Jerusalem and Athens, even at their highest level. He does not foretell the solution of a superman.

Strauss always cautions us to approach any thoughtful writing with care. Therefore, we can make this general remark about this particular essay: the manner in which he writes also indicates his purpose. Alan Udoff notes that, as a general rule, in Strauss's writing "the texts are cited without identifying their sources; that is to say, the authoritativeness of the texts is to rest on their instruction, not their authorship. For Strauss, anonymity is a sign and preserve of philosophy."[44] This observation about Strauss's style is particularly true of "Jerusalem and Athens." Strauss often fails to cite where he has drawn a particular text from. This is most noticeable in his discussions on the Bible and Plato. In "Jerusalem and Athens," the authoritativeness of the texts he uses is not only based upon their instruction, but upon his interpretation of them. Strauss thus makes himself the guide for perplexed moderns who are wandering their trackless way toward the future; he establishes himself as the new guide for those who wish to understand biblical teaching, as well as for those who wish to pursue the philosophic life. In keeping with this strategy, many times Strauss chooses to assert things in "Jerusalem and Athens" that he finds necessary to demonstrate more forcefully elsewhere. In "Jerusalem and Athens," Strauss is the authority; he believes his word alone is sufficient for the truth of any given statement. Thus it is quite probable that this essay presents his authoritative view on the subject. That stated, what exactly has Strauss taught us in "Jerusalem and Athens"?

The first lesson is the most profound. Its profundity is not lessened by the fact that it is obvious. It is perhaps the only unqualified lesson in "Jerusalem and Athens." Above all, Strauss wants us to abandon any notion that a modern synthesis of reason and revelation is possible. Thus, he begins both parts of "Jerusalem and Athens" with devastating critiques of the modern solutions, first with a denunciation of social science that claims neither Jerusalem nor Athens to be important, second with an indictment of the possibility of a synthesis of the two through his analysis of Hermann Cohen.

The second lesson is not as obvious as the first but is, nonetheless, profound: Strauss has begun the recovery of Jerusalem, a task much more difficult than the recovery of Athens. It is more difficult because, in some sense, Athens presents the possibility of a continued search, a constant questioning; it appeals to our modern souls more immediately than the life demanded by the Bible. A life of free and independent inquiry is certainly not as constraining as a life of obedience, even if that life of questioning may eventually lead to virtue.[45] It looks as if Strauss intentionally cloaks the compelling nature of Jerusalem by making the case against revelation appear stronger than it actually is. Indeed, there are several instances in which Strauss appears more impious on the surface than he is upon deeper examination. Two examples are: 1) his insistence that asking the very question of Jerusalem or Athens means an advance decision in favor of Jerusalem, and 2) his assertion that the Bible is the work of compilers, containing relics that were not intended.[46] Both imply that Jerusalem is on very shaky ground. Yet his exegesis of Genesis belies this first impression and shows the inherent coherence of the text. The question thus becomes, why does Strauss appear to make the weaker speech the stronger?

The case can be made that he proceeds in this fashion in order to convince "those of us who cannot be orthodox" to listen to him.[47] As argued earlier, atheism has certainly become the reigning academic fashion. The problem then becomes how to get bright young students to consider the possibility of revelation, that is, to consider the possibility that revelation might be true. To do so, one must proceed cautiously. James Steintrager has suggested that Strauss veils the case for Jerusalem in order to make conventional students feel safe.[48] Thus, Strauss begins by granting the opposition's position: the Bible is a collection of "memories of memories"; it does not claim that the collection itself is miraculous; it may even contain unintended relics. By beginning with an advanced decision in favor of Athens, he allows us to consider what the Bible has to say openly, without feeling threatened by the idea of God, especially that God whom we thought we had outgrown and left behind in childhood.[49] As James Schall writes in a penetrating analysis of Strauss:

> Strauss constantly, and rightly, worried that the fact of revelation might lead to the corruption or elimination of philosophy. The oft-quoted theological phrase—*credo quia absurdum*—would seem to lend strength to Strauss' worries. But likewise, Strauss also wondered that if revelation was indeed a fact, philosophers might well violate their vocation by refusing to consider even its possibility. Strauss' *secret* writing was thus sometimes necessary to protect philosophers, even philosophers from themselves.[50]

Strauss's method is ingenious for he draws the reader into discovering the Bible only after he has sufficiently disarmed her by allowing her to hold on to her prejudices, at least temporarily. Then, through his exacting exegesis of the Bible, he brings the text to life, and the text itself demands that we respect it.

The Secrets of the Torah

In order to succeed with this project, Strauss had to confront and answer the charges of Spinoza. We are now in a position to see that he has succeeded in destroying Spinoza's argument. Strauss's use of Cassuto and his own analysis show that it is more than possible for an intelligent man to understand the Bible and learn from it, although it must be studied with care in order to see that it is God's wisdom before the nations. His greatest feat has been to demonstrate that, far from being a miscellany of superstitious tribal relics, Genesis provides a comprehensive account of the whole, and can even be understood as a rebuke to philosophy. The Bible is not the work of fevered imagination, but one of reason informed by faith.

Did Strauss leave any problems unresolved? Of course. It may be helpful to consider again what Strauss fails to cover in this essay. For instance, he never discusses anthropomorphisms in the Bible. He avoids discussing such things as God walking in the Garden of Eden or God descending to earth to see what God's creatures are doing in the kingdom of Babel. However, Strauss does point to them. One wonders, why is he silent? Is it because these things are inherently superstitious? That might seem to be the answer at first glance. However, there are explanations that make more sense. The first one is that the problem of corporealism is no longer a serious threat; no one today is making the argument that the Bible teaches that God has a body. To that extent, Maimonides' project had succeeded. Second and more important, because God is fundamentally mysterious, it is impossible to speak about God without the use of metaphors and anthropomorphisms. Here, Strauss's argument regarding the mysteries of the Bible, the *sithre Torah*, should be mentioned. It is the cautionary reminder that we may not be able to speak about God and God's interaction with people without contradicting ourselves. One of the things this means is that since we are finite beings, we cannot speak coherently of the infinite and omnipotent God except through analogy. The use of analogy may be the only way to demonstrate God's concern for God's creation.

A related problem is the one of providence. Strauss points to it in his discussion of Aristotle to suggest that it cannot be understood philosophically. But Strauss knows that it is not sufficient to say that because Aristotle's god is incapable of providence, providence itself is impossible. As Strauss notes in "The Mutual Influence of Theology and Philosophy," philosophy "suffers a defeat as soon as it starts an offensive of its own, as soon as it tries to refute, not the necessarily inadequate proofs of revelation, but revelation itself."[51] In order to come to grips with this problem, it may be best to turn away at least momentarily from Strauss so that we can see the problem from a different angle.

Ronald Knox illustrates that the problem of providence is not one for philosophy alone. Even if we believe that God is watching over us, it is still sometimes hard to trust and obey, as difficult as it must have been for Abraham. Even Sarah laughed. Knox shows us the difficulty by reminding us of the account of the storm on the Lake of Galilee in which the apostles themselves, desperately afraid for their lives, had to wake up Christ so that He would calm the storm. As Knox points out, there is a tremendous lesson to be found both in the apostles' panic and in Christ's seeming disregard of their peril. It is a hard lesson for people. As Knox remarks:

> In his later parables, our Lord seems to change both the symbolism and the emphasis. Almighty God is represented not as a man who goes to sleep, but as a man who goes off on a journey to some far-off

country, leaving his servants behind him on their good behaviour. The change of symbolism does not matter much; evidently the man who goes off on a journey, like the man who falls asleep, is in no position, here and now, to interfere; *It is God's apparent neglect of his creation that is thrown into relief* [emphasis mine]. But the change of emphasis is more important; our Lord is no longer concerned to arm us against despair, he is warning us against negligence. Because God seems to take no notice, man is tempted to take no notice either.[52]

The lesson is that God's providence is not always as obvious as we would like it to be; it may even appear as neglect. Again, it is a mystery, one of the *sithre Torah*, one of which faith is well aware. As Strauss says in "Jerusalem and Athens":

> The apparent contradiction between the command to sacrifice Isaac and the divine promise to the descendants of Isaac is disposed of by the consideration that nothing is too wondrous for the Lord. Abraham's supreme trust in God, his simple, single-minded, child-like faith was rewarded, although or because it presupposed his entire unconcern with any reward, for Abraham was willing to forgo, to destroy, to kill the only reward with which he was concerned; God prevented the sacrifice of Isaac.[53]

The mystery of God's providence is somehow connected with the preservation of people's freedom to choose whether or not to serve God. Remember that Strauss speaks of people's resemblance to their creator by stressing that people, alone among creation, can change their ways; this is also connected with their elevation above the heavens.

God and Personal Experience

Another theme that Strauss avoids in "Jerusalem and Athens" is the possibility of a personal experience of God. He alludes to it only in a footnote in his discussion of Halevi by referring to *Persecution and the Art of Writing*, the only time he cites another of his own works. That in itself is important. When we look at the lengthy passage to which he refers, we find Strauss mentions personal experience of the divine twice. First, he speaks in terms of the philosophic stance of invincible ignorance because "a philosopher is untouched by, or has never tasted, that 'Divine thing' or 'Divine command'(*amr ilahi*) which is known from actual experience to the actual believer, the Jewish scholar, and the potential believer, the king."[54] His next reference to personal experience comes when he speaks of the natural limits of Halevi's arguments, which are "convincing to such naturally pious people only as have some foretaste of Divine revelation by having experienced a revelation by an angel or at least a rudimentary revelation of one kind or another."[55] Thus, we are left with the impression that invincible ignorance of God is possible. But, when we turn to his new "Introductory Essay" in the old book on Spinoza, Strauss makes the following argument:

> God's revealing Himself to man, His addressing man, is not merely known through traditions going back to the remote past and therefore now "merely believed," but is genuinely known through present experience which every human being can have if he does not refuse himself to it. This experience is not a kind of self-experience, of the actualization of a human potentiality, of the human mind coming into its own, into what it desires or is naturally inclined to, but of something undesired, coming from the outside, going against man's grain. It is the only awareness of something absolute which cannot be relativized in any way as everything else, rational or non-rational can; it is the experience of God as the Thou, the father and king of all men; it is the experience of an unequivocal command addressed to me here and now as distinguished from general laws or ideas which are always disputable and permitting of exceptions. Only by surrendering to God's experienced call which calls for one's loving Him with all one's heart, with all one's soul and with all one's might can one come to see the other human being as one's brother and love him as oneself.[56]

This personal experience, Strauss is quick to admit, will not, in and of itself, lead to the biblical God who is essentially mysterious. Strauss's assertion that this experience is available to every person, not simply to the naturally pious, is a startling admission. Of course, we are also free to refuse this call. It is important not to underestimate this admission.

This call coincides with what Strauss says is the central teaching of the Bible: "God rightfully demands that He alone be loved unqualifiedly: God does not command that we love His chosen people with all our heart, with all our souls and with all our might."[57] Although Strauss's emphasis in "Jerusalem and Athens" is always upon the obedience that this love requires, it is an obedience that also liberates. James Schall summarizes the teaching of the Old Testament thus:

> The Old Testament, in a sense, is an effort to prevent men and nations from settling for anything less than Yahweh. From this point of view, it is a much more graphic endeavor than that found in *The Ethics* of Aristotle with its relation to *The Metaphysics* or even in first questions of the Prima Secundae of Aquinas' *Summa Theologica* about the location of human beatitude. The net effect, consequently, is to prevent the nation from being an idol, an absolute, even though it is a good. Already in the Old Testament, we are aware that the most dangerous threat to human worth and dignity will probably be from a political system claiming the prerogatives of Yahweh. This is the power to set up a nation's own definition of right and wrong, its own idols, of which itself, the nation, the political power, is the most perilous and the most tempting.[58]

That Strauss would agree with this assessment is, I think, beyond question. As he has shown, the biblical god is certainly more than a tribal god, for this is certainly one of the lessons of the kingdom of Babel. Indeed, Strauss reminds us of this fact at the end of the essay by pointing to Nathan's rebuke of David; the lesson is that even the king is not above God's law.

Yet this very liberation is not without its problems. As Strauss informs us in *Natural Right and History*: "The recognition of universal principles thus tends to prevent men from wholeheartedly identifying themselves with, or accepting, the social order that fate has allotted to them. It tends to alienate them from their place on earth. It tends to make them strangers, and even strangers on the earth."[59] Strauss's discussion of the prophets concentrates on the Messianic promise in which people will beat their swords into plowshares. His critique of Hermann Cohen centers on Cohen's desire to achieve the Messianic promises through people's scientific achievement. A concern with a world outside of our own making, a city of God, is not unique to Christianity. This is possibly why Strauss chose to argue in terms that include both Christian and Jew.

However, this lack of rootedness, when properly channeled, is not a bad thing. Because modernity attempted to attain the city of God on earth, it is easy to overlook the fact that the ability to see universal principles can also have a good effect upon the body politic; for example, it allows people to see that they need not blindly serve tyranny. As Schall puts it, "Finally, since evil can occasion good—the patience of the sufferer, the humility of the proud—no social order or situation is hopeless. Nor is any well-governed society completely secure. . . . From the worst social orders can come the best men and women."[60] Thus, the ability to transcend our present situation is liberating; we can use it for good or ill. Just what an important insight this is seems to have escaped some of Strauss's East Coast students, although it did not escape him.

According to Thomas Pangle's analysis of Strauss, the Bible is simply a subset of poetry. All of the essential elements of the quarrel between philosophy and revelation are already present in the quarrel between Plato and the poets.[61] For Pangle, Strauss's teaching is that philosophy, as represented by Socrates, is the only true guide for people. As he states most clearly and forcefully in his debate with Jaffa,

> If Jaffa believes that the "most essential" issue regarding prophecy or the Divine Law emerged only after the time of Plato, or in texts unknown to Plato; if he supposes that the most essential issue was not and could not have been addressed by Plato's philosophic spokesman in his dialogue with the poets and the statesmen and gentlemen who are the poets' followers—then it seems to me Jaffa has either broken with Strauss's teaching or failed to comprehend it.[62]

Pangle's collapse of the distinction between Yahweh and Zeus, and his attribution of this teaching to Strauss does not seem to be warranted. Even though Strauss points to the similarities between Plato and the Bible, he still recognizes the profound differences, the unbridgeable gaps. As Strauss has shown throughout "Jerusalem and Athens," the understanding or possibility of a God who is holy changes forever how people view the world; it deepens their view. God's holiness, moreover, is not the same as God's goodness, a tenet that Plato and the Bible hold in common. The god of the *Timaeus* and the God of Genesis, although both are creators, are not alike. Pangle is wrong about Plato and Strauss's understanding in this respect. Plato did not envision the possibility of a God who is holy. That does not make him any less of a philosopher. It just means he is not a theologian: the God of the Bible has to be revealed to be known. Strauss, I think, understood that difference. Strauss never allows Athens to triumph over Jerusalem.

The Socratic Enterprise

That being said, the recovery of Jerusalem does not lessen the importance of the Socratic enterprise for Strauss. With the destruction of the understanding of the natural order wrought by modern science, the whole once again appears incomprehensible, and philosophy, impossible. Yet Strauss points to a way out. Again, Strauss's insight from *What Is Political Philosophy?* bears repeating:

> Socrates was so far from being committed to a specific cosmology that his knowledge was knowledge of ignorance. Knowledge of ignorance is not ignorance. It is knowledge of the elusive character of the truth, of the whole. Socrates, then, viewed man in the light of the mysterious character of the whole. He held therefore that we are more familiar with the situation of man as man than with the ultimate causes of that situation. We may also say he viewed man in light of unchangeable ideas, i.e., of the fundamental and permanent problems.[63]

Strauss's insistence on the Socratic alternative to Jerusalem also has another interesting effect: it allows Strauss to maintain his piety. The Socratic enterprise is preeminently concerned with "human things." As he explains in *The City and Man*, "A pious man will not investigate the divine things but only the human things, the things left to man's investigation. It is the greatest proof of Socrates' piety that he limited himself to the study of human things. His wisdom is knowledge of ignorance because it is pious and it is pious because it is knowledge of ignorance."[64]

Harry Jaffa, too, sheds illumination on why Strauss focused his attention on the Socratic enterprise:

> Socratic progress in wisdom—such progress as may be said to result from every Socratic conversation—always is accompanied by an increased awareness of what we do not know. How can a Socratic know that his "progress" is in "wisdom" if the goal of philosophy recedes with every supposed advance? Does not philosophy—

confidence in the ultimate significance of reason—depend upon an act of faith as much as a belief in the God of the Bible?[65]

In the end, there is a certain degree of mystery to both Jerusalem and Athens.

Thus, we begin to understand why Strauss has such a peculiar and untraditional definition of philosophy: "Philosophy is essentially not possession of the truth, but quest for the truth. The distinctive trait of the philosopher is that 'he knows that he knows nothing' and that his insight into our ignorance concerning the most important things induces him to strive with all his power for knowledge."[66] Strauss realized that modernity in attempting to answer all questions, destroyed itself. He therefore keeps the philosopher as one who is searching in order to preserve the possibility of faith.

Strauss's tactic is reminiscent of Plato. In his "Second Letter," Plato gives us a hint as to why he wrote in the manner that he did. Plato's dialogues present philosophy, through Socrates, as something new and beautiful; Socrates on his own is not either of these things, but through the Platonic art, he becomes compelling; the dialogues make Socrates and, through him, philosophy attractive.[67] It would not be going too far to say that Strauss imitates Plato by rarely writing in his own voice. Instead of writing in the form of a dialogue, however, he chose to write exegetical accounts of other texts. Strauss, too, was capable of making the search for wisdom beautiful as is demonstrated most aptly by the opening paragraph of "Jerusalem and Athens." This essay itself is a rare combination of personal reflection and dialogue: for in this essay Strauss is more revealing of himself than usual and also allows reason and revelation to carry on a conversation that is not unlike a dialogue. As we have seen, Strauss employs his art to make both alternatives attractive. His unwillingness to come down on either side may also be a result of the caution he expresses in the following passage from his essay, "What Is Liberal Education?"

Philosophy, we have learned, must be on its guard against the wish to be edifying—philosophy can only be intrinsically edifying. We cannot exert our understanding without from time to time understanding something important; and this understanding may be accompanied by the awareness of our understanding, by the understanding of understanding, by *noesis noeseus*, and this is so high, so pure, so noble an experience that Aristotle could ascribe it to his God. This experience is entirely independent of whether what we understand is primarily pleasing or displeasing, fair or ugly. It leads us to realize that all evils are in a sense necessary if there is to be understanding. It enables us to accept all evils which befall us and which may well break our hearts in the spirit of good citizens of the City of God. By becoming aware of the dignity of the mind, we realize the true ground of the dignity of man and therewith the goodness of the world, whether we understand it as created or as uncreated, which is the home of man because it is the home of the human mind.[68]

If, as Strauss has suggested elsewhere, the surface of things is the heart of things, then it behooves us well to look at the surface of "Jerusalem and Athens." What we find there is that both reason and revelation are presented as powers to be reckoned with. By making it possible to consider Jerusalem and Athens again, Strauss has begun the recovery of people, which is a noble task. If he tips the scales at all, it is toward Jerusalem. Just as Socrates' attempt to show that Apollo made a mistake in attributing wisdom to him ends with a vindication of the god, so, too, Strauss's exegetical defense comes to the aid of the God of Abraham, Isaac, and Jacob. Such an endeavor may be considered a bit impious; but it is nonetheless undertaken with pious intentions and pious results.

Notes

1. This chapter is adapted from my book, *"Jerusalem and Athens": A Study of Leo Strauss* (Lanham, Md: Rowman & Littlefield, 1995).

2. Leo Strauss, *Natural Right and History* (Chicago: University of Chicago Press, 1953), 74; hereafter cited as *Natural Right*.

3. See books recently published on Strauss such as Shadia Drury, *The Political Ideas of Leo Strauss* (New York: St. Martin's Press, 1988); Alan Udoff, ed., *Leo Strauss' Thought: Towards a Critical Engagement* (Boulder, Colo.: Rienner Publishers, 1991); Peter Emberley and Barry Cooper, eds., *Faith and Political Philosophy: The Correspondence between Leo Strauss and Eric Voegelin, 1934–1964* (University Park, Penn.: Penn State Press, 1993); Kenneth Hart Green, *Jew and Philosopher: The Return to Maimonides in the Jewish Thought of Leo Strauss* (Albany, N.Y.: SUNY Press, 1993); and Kenneth L. Deutsch and Walter Nicgorski, eds., *Leo Strauss: Political Philosopher and Jewish Thinker* (Lanham, Md.: Rowman & Littlefield, 1994).

4. Allan Bloom, *Giants and Dwarfs: Essays 1960–1990* (New York: Simon and Schuster, 1990), 255.

5. Leo Strauss, *Thoughts on Machiavelli* (Chicago: Free Press, 1958), 34; hereafter cited as *Thoughts*.

6. Introduction to Leo Strauss, *Studies in Platonic Political Philosophy*, ed. Thomas Pangle (Chicago: University of Chicago Press, 1983), 20.

7. Harry Jaffa, "The Legacy of Leo Strauss Defended," *Claremont Review of Books* 4 (1985): 20.

8. Thomas Pangle, "The Platonism of Leo Strauss: A Reply to Harry Jaffa," *Claremont Review of Books* 4 (1985): 18–20.

9. See *Thoughts*, 40.

10. *Liberalism: Ancient and Modern* (New York: Basic Books, 1968), 223; hereafter cited as *Liberalism*.

11. Ibid., 218.

12. *The City and Man* (Chicago: Rand McNally, 1964), 241; hereafter cited as *City*.

13. *Spinoza's Critique of Religion*, trans. E.M. Sinclair (New York: Schocken Books, 1982), introductory essay, 29; hereafter cited as "Introductory Essay." The original book is titled *Die Religionskritik Spinozas als Grundlage seiner Bibelwissenschaft* (Berlin: Academie-Verlag, 1930).

14. All citations from this essay will be taken from *Studies in Platonic Political Philosophy* (Chicago: University of Chicago Press, 1983), 147–173; hereafter cited as "Jerusalem."

15. *Commentary* 43 (1967): 45–57.

16. See Harry V. Jaffa, "The Legacy of Leo Strauss," *Claremont Review of Books* 3 (1984): 17. Another sign that Strauss wanted this essay to be understood as his final view on the subject is the fact that he says that Hermann Cohen's essay entitled "The Social Ideal in Plato and the Prophets" was Cohen's "final view on Jerusalem and Athens and therewith on *the* truth" by arguing that Cohen repeated this lecture shortly before his death ("Jerusalem and Athens," 167). So, Strauss followed Cohen's example in his "Jerusalem and Athens." Cohen's 1916 essay, "Das soziale Ideal bei Platon und den Propheten" was published in *Jüdische Schriften* I, ed. B. Strauss (Berlin, 1924), 306–30. There is an abridged version in English translation by Eva Jospe, "The Social Ideal as Seen by Plato and the Prophets," in *Reason and Hope: Selections from the Jewish Writings of Hermann Cohen*, ed. E. Jospe (New York: Norton, 1971), 66–77.

17. In his essay "What is Political Philosophy?" which he first gave as a lecture in Jerusalem, Strauss speaks of the sacred city in this manner: "In this city and in this land, the theme of political philosophy—'the city of righteousness, the faithful city'—has been taken more seriously than anywhere else on earth. Nowhere else has the longing for justice and the just city filled the purest hearts and the loftiest souls with such zeal as

on this sacred soil" (*What Is Political Philosophy?* [Westport, Conn.: Greenwood Press, 1959], 9; hereafter cited as *What?*).

18. *City*, 231.

19. As Strauss tells us in *Thoughts*, "There is no surer protection against the understanding of anything than taking for granted or otherwise despising the obvious and the surface. The problem inherent in the surface of things, and only in the surface of things, is the heart of things" (p. 13).

20. *Liberalism*, 142–43.

21. One is reminded of Strauss's exegesis of Maimonides' *Guide* in which he provides the structure that is also not obvious at first glance.

22. "Jerusalem," 147.

23. Ibid., 148.

24. *The Rebirth of Classical Political Rationalism: An Introduction to the Thought of Leo Strauss*, ed. Thomas Pangle (Chicago: University of Chicago Press, 1989), 41.

25. "Jerusalem," 150.

26. Ibid., 149.

27. In taking this as his final word, one is not following Strauss's own instructions for reading texts with care. For two recent examples of this opinion, see John G. Gunnell, "Strauss before Straussianism: Reason, Revelation, and Nature," in *Leo Strauss: Political Philosopher and Jewish Thinker*, 107–28, and James L. Wiser, "Reason and Revelation as Search and Response: A Comparison of Eric Voegelin and Leo Strauss," in *Faith and Political Philosophy*, 237–48.

28. "Jerusalem," 150.

29. This change also means that later interpretations cannot be considered.

30. "Jerusalem," 152.

31. Ibid., 153.

32. Ibid., 162.

33. Ibid., 160.

34. Ibid., 164.

35. Ibid., 164.

36. Ibid., 158.

37. *Studies in Platonic Political Philosophy*, 237.

38. Leo Strauss and Jacob Klein, "A Giving of Accounts," *St. John's Review* 22 (1970): 2.

39. "Jerusalem," 170.

40. Ibid., 162.

41. Earlier in "Jerusalem and Athens," Strauss tells us that miracles only persuade those who believe in the possibility of a god: "The biblical signs and wonders convince men who have little faith or who believe in other gods; they are not addressed to "the fools who say in their hearts 'there is no God' " (p. 151).

42. Ibid., 147.
43. "Progress or Return? The Contemporary Crisis in Western Civilization," *Modern Judaism* 1 (1981): 44–45.
44. Introduction to *Leo Strauss' Thought*, 6.
45. Glaucon, for example, is someone who was tamed by philosophy. See Plato, *Republic*, Bk. II/357Aff.
46. "Jerusalem," 150, 163.
47. Ibid., 150.
48. "Political Philosophy, Political Theology, and Morality," *The Thomist* 32 (1968): 307–22.
49. This modern desire to transcend religion is perhaps best summed up by G.K. Chesterton's opening statement in *Orthodoxy*: "It recounts my elephantine adventures in pursuit of the obvious. No one can think my case more ludicrous than I think it myself; no reader can accuse me of trying to make a fool of him. I am the fool of this story, and no rebel shall hurl me from my throne. . . . I did, like all other solemn little boys, try to be in advance of the age. Like them I tried to be some ten minutes in advance of the truth. And I found that I was eighteen hundred years behind it" (*Collected Works*, I [San Francisco: Ignatius Press, 1986], 214).
50. "Revelation, Reason, and Politics I: Catholic Reflections on Strauss," *Gregorianum* 2–3 (1981): 354.
51. "The Mutual Influence of Theology and Philosophy," *Independent Journal of Philosophy* 3 (1979): 116.
52. *A Retreat for Lay People* (Harrison, N.Y.: Sheed and Ward, 1955), 45.
53. "Jerusalem," 163.
54. *Persecution and the Art of Writing* (Westport, Conn.: Greenwood Press, 1952), 105.
55. Ibid., 106.
56. *Spinoza's Critique of Religion*, 8–9.
57. "Jerusalem," 161.
58. *The Politics of Heaven and Hell* (Boston: University Press of America, 1984), 7.
59. *Natural Right*, 13–14.
60. *The Politics of Heaven and Hell*, 123.
61. Introduction to *Studies*, 20.
62. "The Platonism of Leo Strauss: A Reply to Harry Jaffa," *Claremont Review of Books* 4 (1985): 19.
63. *What?*, 38–39.
64. *City*, 20.
65. "Leo Strauss, the Bible, and Political Philosophy," in *Leo Strauss: Political Philosopher and Jewish Thinker*, 199–200.
66. *What?*, 11.
67. See "Second Letter" 314C-D.
68. *Liberalism*, 8.

3

A Word Fitly Spoken: The Interpretation of Maimonides and the Legacy of Leo Strauss

Hillel Fradkin

Considering the legacy of Leo Strauss, one natural focus is his interpretation of Moses Maimonides, the twelfth-century Spanish Jewish thinker. Strauss authored a number of writings devoted in whole or in part to Maimonides' thought.[1]

The large number of Strauss's works devoted to Maimonides expresses implicitly the judgment he stated explicitly. According to him, Maimonides is "the central figure of Jewish medieval philosophy."[2] But even such statements do not adequately convey the quality and measure of Strauss's enthusiasm for Maimonides. He says in the opening sentences of his only book devoted to Maimonides, *Philosophy and Law: Essays toward the Understanding of Maimonides and His Predecessors*:

> According to Hermann Cohen, Maimonides is the "classic of rationalism" in Judaism. This seems to us to be correct in a more exact sense than Cohen probably meant it. Maimonides' rationalism is the truly natural model, the standard that must be carefully guarded against every counterfeit. . . . The purpose of the present work is to arouse a prejudice in favor of this conception of Maimonides or rather, to excite a suspicion against the powerful prejudice to the contrary.[3]

It is easy to say that this is strong stuff. It is perhaps more appropriate to say that this is an amazing or fantastic claim. Taken literally and in its most unrestricted sense, Strauss's declaration appears to claim that Maimonides is not only the central figure in Jewish thought, but the central figure of all human thought.

To repeat, is not such a view simply fantastic? What could have led Strauss to make such a claim? How can he defend it?[4]

It is tempting to understand this claim as a bit of youthful enthusiasm and hyperbole. (After all, Strauss was only thirty-six when he made it.) Besides, Strauss apparently revises and tempers this claim in the same paragraph by speaking of his goal as the arousal of a "prejudice" or the exciting of "a suspicion against a . . . prejudice." Above all, it is tempting to set aside this early claim in favor of another, later, and thus apparently more mature claim for which Strauss is well known. Everyone knows or thinks they know that Strauss claimed that the truly natural model of rationalism and therewith the deepest and most important form of human thought is to be found among certain Greek authors, especially the heirs of Socrates: Plato and Aristotle, of course, but also Xenophon. Strauss apparently devoted the greater part of his mature years to the study of these authors and the theme they permit one to explore: the problem of Socrates.[5]

It is true that this later claim may also be regarded as fantastic. Indeed, it often is, as is the fact that Strauss drew heavily on Xenophon and Aristophanes for his understanding of Socrates and classical thought. Still, it is likely to be considered more plausible than the one he raised on behalf of Maimonides by the vast majority of our contemporaries, that is, all or most non-Jews. We may say, then, that according to a certain common view, Strauss was a scholar or thinker who made amazing or fantastic claims. In his youth, he made wild claims on behalf of Maimonides. In later years, he made somewhat more sober claims regarding Plato and Xenophon, with the emphasis on the "somewhat."

Although it seemed necessary to present the questions that attend the place of Maimonides in the heart and mind of Strauss, it goes without saying that this is not the place to address them at length.[6] It is certainly not my task. Above all it is obviously, not possible to determine how important Strauss thought Maimonides' teaching is, before considering what Strauss thought that teaching to be.

Strauss's Last Statement on Maimonides

What then, is Strauss's interpretation of Maimonides' teaching? This is a simple enough question that unfortunately lacks a simple answer. More precisely, it lacks a definite—that is, comprehensive and final—answer. Strauss tells us this in his last extended discussion of Maimonides' *Guide of the Perplexed*, an essay entitled "How to Begin to Study *The Guide of the Perplexed*." At the conclusion of this essay, the mature fruit, Strauss tells us, of twenty-five years of study, Strauss writes, "We have been compelled to put a greater emphasis on Maimonides' perplexities than on his certainties, and in particular on his vigorous and skillful defense of the Law, because the latter are more easily accessible than the former."[7]

This statement seems to confirm and explain the import of the title of the essay from which it is drawn. Strauss's readers are at the beginning of their study of the *Guide of the Perplexed*, the most important and also most difficult expression of Maimonides' thought. With Strauss's guidance, they may advance beyond this beginning, but how much further is unclear.[8] Nevertheless it is Strauss's last extended treatment of the *Guide*. It is true that readers inspired and instructed by this essay may go on to learn more about and from Maimonides. It is also true that this essay may be supplemented by three later ones that treat Maimonides' thought.[9] However, two of those three are extremely short and in none is the *Guide* the primary subject. They are devoted to other Maimonidean works. But the *Guide* is the most perfect expression of his most important views and it is with this work that Strauss and we must chiefly be concerned.[10]

To sum up, we seem to be left with the troubling conclusion that Strauss did not offer any final and definitive account of the teaching of Maimonides, who according to him may be the most important thinker in human history and is certainly the most important in Jewish history. I leave aside or defer consideration of what one is to make of this—why Strauss leaves his readers in this state—to concern myself with what one is supposed to do with it . . . How is one to proceed?

The only immediately practicable solution seems to be to try to identify and follow the main lines of Strauss's account of Maimonides. In light of Strauss's remarks quoted above, these can only be regarded as provisional. That is, I may be obliged to stress Strauss's perplexities more than his certainties, since the former may be "more easily accessible" than the latter. Nevertheless, I trust that my remarks will not have a misleading effect or that they will be taken with the large grain of salt they deserve. As the essay "How to Begin to Study *The Guide of the Perplexed*" is Strauss's last major statement on the *Guide*, my remarks will tend to focus on this essay.

The Literary Problem of Maimonides

It seems natural to begin with that aspect of Strauss's interpretation that is the proximate source of his difficulties and my own: the literary problem of Maimonides. One of the most salient, well-known, and distinctive characteristics of Strauss's treatment of Maimonides is the fact that he is concerned not only with the substance of Maimonides' teaching but the literary form or forms in which it expressed itself. What he has to say about literary questions is at least as extensive as what he conveys concerning substantive ones. In fact, beside *Philosophy and Law*, his two other most extensive treatments of Maimonides begin from and focus on literary questions: the essay just cited and another earlier one suitably entitled the "Literary Character of the *Guide of the Perplexed*." This focus derives from the fact that Strauss regards Maimonides' works as presenting especially grave and daunting literary problems and questions, so grave that their treatment is the necessary and very extended preliminary to understanding the substance of Maimonides' thought. To put it most simply, according to Strauss, Maimonides wrote esoteric books, which concealed many if not all parts of his teaching.

The discovery or rather rediscovery of the practice of a form of writing known as esoteric, is a teaching for which Strauss is famous, or infamous. In the view of Strauss, several important thinkers of the past practiced this form of writing.[11]

It would seem that Strauss's judgment concerning Maimonides on this point admits of no question. Maimonides was remarkably open and emphatic about his esotericism, at least in the *Guide*, especially when compared to other esoteric authors such as Plato, Xenophon, Machiavelli, Hobbes, and Locke.[12]

Indeed, many critics of Strauss are ready to grant him his assertion concerning Maimonides. However, this is only to say that they regard his study of Maimonides as having distorted his view of other authors by leading him to apply inappropriately the lesson of Maimonides to them. In short, they think Maimonides is a special and perhaps unique case.

As regards the uniqueness of Maimonides, Strauss might be said to agree with such critics, but to think them "correct in a more exact sense" than they mean. What I mean by this is as follows: Almost all the other works that Strauss regarded as esoteric and interpreted as such were written by men who were philosophers and are philosophic books. They are regarded so generally and also by Strauss. However, according to Strauss, Maimonides and the *Guide* are different and almost unique. The *Guide* is not a philosophic book and cannot be understood if it is taken to be one.[13]

This assertion is shocking. Is not Maimonides *the* medieval Jewish philosopher? If he is not a philosopher, what medieval Jew is? Is there, then, such a thing as a medieval Jewish philosopher? Above all, what kind of book is the *Guide*? The answers to the first three questions are (1) yes and no, (2) nobody, and (3) maybe not.

The answer to the fourth question is that the *Guide* is a Jewish book. This is less shocking, but what does it mean? Strauss made a general comment about Jewish books and philosophers. A Jewish book is:

a book written by a Jew for Jews. Its first premise is the old Jewish premise that being a Jew and being a philosopher are two incompatible things. Philosophers are men who try to give an account of the whole by starting from what is always accessible to man as man; Maimonides starts from the acceptance of the Torah. A Jew may make use of philosophy and Maimonides makes the most ample use of it; but as a Jew he gives his assent, where as a philosopher he would suspend his assent.[14]

What does this mean more concretely? To begin with and in accord with the character of the Torah and Jewish works generally, the *Guide* is a work devoted to law. Maimonides wrote two other large works, the *Commentary on the Mishnah* and the *Mishnah Torah*, both of which are manifestly legal works. Hence, Strauss's judgment concerning the *Guide* means that all of Maimonides' major works are legal in character. So, too, are most of his minor ones.[15] But as just noted, there are two other large works, more commonly and more readily regarded as legal works. In what way is the *Guide* different? Strauss answers as follows: there are according to Maimonides different sciences of the law, or more precisely two: the legalistic science of the law or jurisprudence and the true science of the law. The *Guide* is devoted to the latter.

What is the true science of law? Strauss says,

Its first purpose is to explain biblical terms and its second purpose is
to explain biblical similes. The *Guide* is, then, devoted above all to
biblical exegesis, although to biblical exegesis of a particular kind.
That kind of exegesis is required because many biblical terms and all
biblical similes have an apparent or outer and a hidden or inner
meaning; the gravest errors as well as the most tormenting perplexities arise from men's understanding the Bible always according to its
apparent or literal meaning. The *Guide* is then devoted to "the
difficulties of the Law" or to "the secrets of the Law." The most
important of these secrets are the Account of the Beginning (the
beginning of the Bible) and the Account of the Chariot (Ezekiel 1 and
10). The *Guide* is then devoted primarily and chiefly to the explanation of the Account of the Beginning and the Account of the Chariot.[16]

More strictly speaking then, the *Guide* is a work of biblical
exegesis. In particular, it is preponderately concerned with the
opinions expressed in or taught by the Torah rather than the actions
commanded by it. More particularly still, it is devoted to bringing
to light the secret opinions of the Bible or the esoteric teaching of
the Bible. The most exalted though not the only components of the
secret teaching are the Account of the Beginning and the Account
of the Chariot, that is, the biblical account of creation and the
account of God and the Divine World presented through Ezekiel's
vision. The concern with opinion and the difficulties of biblical
expression appear to be the ground of Maimonides' use of philosophy and, as Strauss states, Maimonides makes ample use of philosophy. Indeed, in clarifying the meaning of biblical terms and
similes, Maimonides seems to discover there the teachings of
philosophy or philosophers. But is this not what is meant by calling
Maimonides a Jewish philosopher and does this not make the *Guide*
a philosophic book?

No, Strauss insists. The clarification of biblical language and
opinion by means of philosophy may be helpful and even necessary.
It does not mean that the procedure or even the opinions in question
are philosophic, even when the Bible and philosophy agree.[17]
Moreover, there are cases where they disagree, even if only
slightly. For example, Maimonides sometimes presents the teaching
of the Bible as being in substantial agreement with philosophic
teaching, but substantial is not identical. In such cases Biblical
teaching corrects philosophic teaching. (An example is Maimonides' discussion of prophecy.)[18] In such cases, Maimonides is called
upon not only to clarify Biblical teaching but to defend it. All the

more so in cases where philosophy and the Bible manifestly or directly contradict one another. (The most important example is the question of whether the world is created or eternal.[19]) Hence, the *Guide* is not only a work of exegesis but of apologetics, including antiphilosophical apologetics. It is similar in intention though not in method to that form of theological apologetics known as Kalam, or dialectical theology, that was cultivated by Muslims and adopted to some degree by Jews. It is devoted to demonstrating the roots or fundamental opinions of the law.[20] In pursuing this intention, one may say that Maimonides fulfills an important duty of the law. Accordingly, the *Guide* is a legal work from several points of view.

Notwithstanding the fact that Strauss has recourse to express statements of Maimonides, in particular the latter's declaration that the subject matter of the *Guide* is the true science of the law, one might still want to raise some questions about his conclusion. Does Maimonides really mean this? Does Strauss really understand him to mean this?[21]

We may put these questions in a different and more concrete way: Why, if the *Guide* is not a philosophic book, is it an esoteric book? Why would it need to be? In other treatments of the sort of esoteric literature with which he is concerned, Strauss makes it clear that such works have their origin in a certain problem: "The problem of the relation between philosophy and politics."[22] He indicates that he became "familiar with the problem mentioned while studying the Jewish and the Islamic philosophy of the Middle Ages."[23] As a matter of fact, he makes this declaration in the preface to a book entitled *Persecution and the Art of Writing*, which collects several essays that all deal with this problem.[24] Included among those essays is one entitled the "Literary Character of the *Guide of the Perplexed*."

On the basis of these general circumstances it seems reasonable to repeat our question. If the *Guide* is an esoteric book, does not that mean it is philosophic? If it is not, why is it esoteric? Once again Strauss replies: the law. As we have already indicated, the law, or Bible, has itself an esoteric teaching: the Account of the Beginning and the Account of the Chariot. Moreover, the law expressly forbids public instruction in this teaching. As he observes, this means that it forbids the presentation of these subjects in a book. Maimonides is then in violation of the law. However, Maimonides was compelled to break the law. He sought to reduce his transgression by writing in a manner that preserves and serves the intention of that law. He adopted a particular form of esoteric writing. In other words, in conformity with the law he presents an esoteric interpretation of the esoteric teaching of the law.[25]

Law then is Strauss's first word and his last word. The *Guide* and Maimonides' presentation of his thought must be understood within a legal rather than philosophic framework, however unusual that framework may be or however much, from time to time, it or its contents may appear to resemble philosophy.[26]

Strauss does not mean to deny that Maimonides is a great student and admirer of philosophy. He means, that Maimonides' treatment of philosophy is presented not only in formal subordination to the law, but within a framework genuinely defined by the characteristics of the law as law. Strauss's conception of the legal framework of Maimonides' thought has additional aspects that we may consider later.

For the moment, it is sufficient to note that here, as elsewhere, it is the case that he follows very closely and strictly the manner in which Maimonides speaks. Still, however solid the premises and orderly the reasoning therefrom, Strauss's conclusions regarding the literary and substantive character of the *Guide* are unnerving.

They would perhaps be less so if Strauss had provided a clear account of Maimonides' secret teaching on the two most important subjects of the *Guide*—the Account of the Beginning and the Account of the Chariot. It would seem that such an account would provide us with an opportunity to grasp both the concrete character of Maimonides' teaching and the difference between it and philosophy. In addition to general considerations that render this likely, there is the fact observed and even stressed by Strauss that Maimonides indicates that there is an important and direct relationship between the esoteric teaching of the Bible and philosophy. Maimonides asserts in several places that the Account of the Beginning and the Account of the Chariot are identical to natural science and divine science or physics and metaphysics, respectively.[27] This statement has inclined any number of Maimonidean scholars to regard the *Guide* and Maimonidean teaching as essentially philosophic and his esotericism or pronouncements thereof as a relatively minor figleaf rather easily removed by the contemporary scholar.[28] The latter is a view Strauss apparently rejects, but to repeat: his rejection would be more easily understood if he presented his own account of Maimonides' esoteric teaching.

Strauss appears to have denied that he provided such an account by declaring that he has focused on Maimonides' perplexities. Whether he cannot or will not must for the present remain an open question. More specifically, he denies that Maimonides' apparent identification of the esoteric teaching of the Bible with physics and metaphysics offers an easy and clear insight into the esoteric teaching of the *Guide*. He declares that what Maimonides means by this is profoundly unclear and is perhaps the secret *par excellence* of the *Guide*.[29]

The basis of this assertion is the fact that Maimonides contradicts himself regarding this identification. Indeed, Maimonides contradicts himself a great deal and this obviously makes it difficult to identify Maimonides' substantive teaching, secret or otherwise.[30]

Moreover, this, as Strauss brings out, is not accidental or unconscious on Maimonides' part. Maimonides declared openly that he adopted the practice of contradicting himself. He did so in response to the character of his subject matter and the strictures of the law concerning it. Furthermore, he has made matters more difficult by several other means of concealment, including the practice of concealing many of his contradictions.[31]

In accord with these remarks, Strauss apparently defers an account of Maimonides' substantive teaching. He devotes himself to the immediate task of describing Maimonides' mode of writing and developing means by which it may be interpreted. This is meant to prepare a way for an understanding of Maimonides' teaching. In light of the fact that Maimonides not only employs contradictions to conceal his teaching but hides them as well, Strauss must first labor to bring such contradictions and other difficulties to light. He must first bewilder the reader (and himself) before enlightening her. Indeed, he suggests that bewilderment is the first form of enlightenment. The reader may be pardoned if she sometimes thinks that the two are simply identical.[32]

To put it another way, as the title of Strauss's essay declares, he offers his readers guides on how to study Maimonides or how to begin to study Maimonides. Strauss's essays combine the features of two related kinds of books so common in contemporary bookstores—the do-it-yourself book and the self-improvement book. They may also be regarded as analogous to another contemporary form of writing, the instructions that come in the package of products marked, "Some assembly required." Strauss's essays may easily inspire the same dread as these three terrifying words. Nevertheless, if we want to consider Strauss's interpretation of Maimonides, we have no choice but to focus on and try to follow his discussion of the literary character of the *Guide*. Moreover, this may occasionally bring us into contact with the substance of Maimonides' teaching. Indeed, for reasons to be indicated later, it cannot help but do so. Thus we may find that Strauss does after all have something to say about the substantive teaching of the *Guide*, or provides hints about this teaching.[33] Nevertheless, always and from the beginning he forces the reader to begin from the literary question or problem.

Philosophy and Law

Before starting, however, there is another matter it would be useful to consider: This is the conception of the theme of medieval Jewish rationalism or enlightenment as the relationship of philosophy and law, a conception developed in Strauss's earliest work and maintained with modifications later on. At the outset it distinguished Strauss's interpretation from others and bore implications for the character of his inquiries, on which it is useful to elaborate.[34]

Like others, Strauss understood this tradition to be concerned with the relationship between classical philosophy and the Bible, especially their conflicts. But where others chose to refer to this relationship in the terms of reason and revelation, Strauss referred to it as the relationship of philosophy and law. This, according to Strauss, is more precise and, hence, preferable. The preference for the term "law" in place of "revelation" is explained by the fact that revelation is too general a term for a phenomenon that is emphatically particular in its alleged occurrences. It is therefore imprecise. Jewish revelation takes the form of law. Other revelations do not. The difference is crucial. Maimonides' usage, that is, his practice of referring to biblical teaching as the teaching of the "opinions of the law," reflects and confirms this.

This also has an impact upon the manner in which reason is seen and understood. As law is primarily concerned with action, the law, which is the Bible, tends to see the cultivation of reason less as a body of doctrine than as an activity. Philosophy, or the pursuit of wisdom rather than its possession, conveys more precisely the sense of reason as an activity. Moreover, since the authority of the law is primary, it is this conception of reason that is definitive for the manner in which reason ought to be conceived, at least initially. This is so much so the case that the first question to be addressed concerns not what philosophy teaches, but whether it is lawful as an activity. Is it forbidden or permitted or even obligatory?

This is true whether or not the opinions of the philosophers happen to conflict with those featured in the law, although such conflicts are the most likely circumstance to raise the question of the legal standing of philosophy.

According to this analysis, the fact and priority of law not only raises the question of whether philosophy may be pursued, but also affects how it will be pursued. Indeed, the two are connected, since the justification of philosophy within a legal framework will inevitably solicit an interpretation of that framework. Indeed, the legal defense of philosophy would seem to require such an interpretation as evidence of the contribution philosophy may make to the law. The need for such an interpretation will have different consequences than those that might arise if revelation were viewed in terms other than law. The most immediate consequence is the unusual importance of a particular branch of philosophy, political philosophy. Political philosophy is that part of philosophy that treats law as a theme.[35]

The focus on political philosophy is a feature of Strauss's interpretation that is immensely important for his understanding of Maimonides. This is reflected in the fact that Strauss devoted a number of essays to the subject of Maimonides' political science. In fact, it is only some exaggeration to say that these essays are the only ones expressly devoted to some portion of the substance of Maimonides' teaching.[36]

The primary purpose of these essays is, of course, to clarify Maimonides' political science. However, in order to do that, Strauss found himself obliged to turn to the works of other authors, in particular, the thought of Al-Farabi, the great Muslim philosopher. Strauss observed that due to the priority of law as well as other reasons in his own works, including the *Guide*, Maimonides presupposes a certain understanding of philosophy and philosophic teachings. In order, then, to grasp his view of philosophy it is at least helpful, if not necessary, to turn to his philosophic authorities. Of course, Aristotle plays a large role in such efforts. In a decisive respect, Farabi plays a role equally important.[37]

In the earliest of these essays, Strauss proved that Maimonides' political science was derived and adapted from the teaching of Farabi. In these and other essays devoted to Farabi, Strauss further proved that Farabi's political philosophy, and in a certain way his philosophy as a whole, is adapted from Plato. He also showed that Maimonides follows Farabi in this respect. This is true notwithstanding the fact that Farabi was the first Muslim philosopher to promote the study of Aristotle and thus initiate the medieval tradition of Muslim and Jewish Aristotelianism, of which Maimonides is the greatest Jewish exemplar.[38]

Put most simply, according to Strauss both Farabi and Maimonides are Platonists, at least in certain fundamental and decisive respects. This is another of Strauss's claims that seems remarkable. However, in later essays, Strauss continued his study and elaboration of the political science of Farabi and Maimonides. Although in the case of Maimonides, this partially entailed the study of works other than the *Guide*, it has a fundamental bearing on his interpretation of the *Guide*, literary and otherwise. This in turn depends decisively on his understanding of Farabi, for which reason it is useful to consider his interpretation of the latter.

Since space does not permit a full treatment of this subject, I will summarize some essential points. The character of Farabi's political philosophy is expressed in two ways. One is the kind of works Farabi wrote. As the admirer and student of Aristotle, Farabi composed a number of commentaries on Aristotle's logic. Maimonides praised these works highly in a well-known letter to Ibn Tibbon and recommended to him that he study nothing but these in his efforts to learn logic. Farabi also provided a number of general presentations of his thought and of philosophy that he identified with the teaching of Plato and Aristotle. All these works have the remarkable feature of being presented within a political framework. Among these works is one entitled the *Political Regime*. This work is singled out for praise by Maimonides in the same letter mentioned above under the title *The Principles of the Beings*.[39]

What is characteristic of this and the other works of this kind is that the whole of philosophy, or its themes, is presented within a framework of the virtuous or perfect city. The *Political Regime,* for example, consists of two main parts, an account of metaphysics or cosmology and an account of political science. The guiding theme of the latter is the perfect city and the cosmology that precedes it is meant to be appropriate to the understanding of that city or the citizens of that city. The presentation of the whole of philosophy from the perspective of the best regime resembles Plato's approach in works like *The Republic* and *The Laws*. This resemblance is one powerful expression of Farabi's Platonism.[40]

The second way in which Farabi's political science expresses itself is through his political teaching. More specifically, Farabi makes the prophet or prophecy a theme of his political philosophy. This is grounded in understanding the distinctive purpose of prophecy as legislation, and the purpose of such legislation as the founding of the perfect city. In order for prophetic legislation to have this goal and effect, the prophet must be wise. The prophet must have the qualities that Plato's philosopher-kings have and produce the kind of legislation presented by the Athenian Stranger in *The Laws*. As Farabi puts it, "the idea of the Philosopher, Supreme Ruler, Prince, Legislator and Imam is but a single idea."[41] Farabi's prophet is Plato's philosopher-king and fulfills the conditions Plato proposed for such a person.[42] These conditions being reasonable, philosophy permits one to understand and make intelligible revelation.

Strauss drew attention to the great debt Maimonides owed to Farabi's views. He stressed the fact that Maimonides' own prophetology is based upon Farabi's and that in other respects Farabi's political science was taken over by Maimonides. Moses is the philosopher-king or the most perfect fulfillment of the need uncovered and elaborated by Plato through the proposal for philosopher-kings.[43]

Strauss observes and admits that political science occupies a relatively small portion of the *Guide of the Perplexed* (perhaps comprising at most part 2, chapters 32–48, and part 3, chapters 8–54). Moreover, the most important subjects of the *Guide* are not political—the Account of the Beginning and the Account of the Chariot. However, as Strauss also observes, since the subject of the *Guide* as a whole is the true science of the law, Maimonides' political thought informs throughout the character of the *Guide*. Indeed, the conjoining of the highest theoretical themes and political science in the same book resembles Farabi's procedure in works like the *Political Regime*.[44]

Considerations like the ones just mentioned may be thought to show that the *Guide* is, after all, a philosophic book. However, in Strauss's account they provide additional evidence, perhaps the most solid evidence, of the opposite: the nonphilosophic character of this book. The elaboration of Farabi's thought in general and his political science in particular permitted Strauss to establish the philosophic teaching in the strict sense. It is true that this is important for understanding Maimonides' views, since the latter derives from it but does not always make that debt clear. However, the comparison of Maimonides' account with the philosophic teaching serves to bring out the differences, including and especially in the area of political science.[45] This is most obviously true of Maimonides' prophetology, which expressly modifies the philosophic teaching. It is also true in other respects as well.[46] In keeping with Strauss's stress on the importance of literary features, his observation that the *Guide* bears a formal resemblance to the plan of such works as the *Political Regime* and the view that underlies it would seem to be a very important indication of Maimonides' debt to Farabi and the philosophic teaching. And it is! But in addition to the similarities, there are differences—differences in the order of themes and their treatment. Strauss attributes these differences to the impact of the law. Accordingly, the plan of the *Guide* would seem to be the result of two principles of understanding and organization, one stemming from philosophy and the other from the law.[47]

While these principles are not and cannot be simply heterogeneous, they are sufficiently different for the question of their relationship to arise: Which is the primary and ultimately dominant principle? The answer is the law. This would imply that the very plan or structure of the *Guide* reflects and is the embodiment of Maimonides' understanding of the relationship of philosophy and law or the fundamental question. This is an additional reason why Strauss places such emphasis on the literary character of the *Guide*.[48] It is also why, in following Strauss's literary analysis of the *Guide*, we can hope to learn something about the substance of the *Guide*'s teaching. This brings us back to the point from which we digressed: the intention to try to understand how Strauss means for us to begin our study of the *Guide* and what we may learn from it.

A Table of Contents for the Guide

What then does Strauss regard as the most important literary problem of the *Guide*? Strauss answers this question by beginning his essay abruptly and surprisingly with the following remark: "I believe that it will not be amiss if I simply present the plan of the *Guide* as it has become clear to me in the course of about twenty-five years of frequently interrupted but never abandoned study."[49] One sentence later he fulfills this intention by providing a two-page account of the plan of the *Guide*. He supplies us with the table of contents the *Guide* lacks.

Strauss draws our attention to the plan or order of the *Guide*. His reasons are twofold. First, Maimonides places great stress on this issue by declaring that every word in the *Guide* was chosen and arranged with exceeding care and precision. The *Guide* is an extremely well-articulated whole. Second, the orderliness of the *Guide* is far from obvious. Indeed, it may appear very disorderly. Though it has a careful plan, this plan is very obscure, but intentionally so. A certain disorder is part of Maimonides' plan.[50]

One of the causes of this obscurity is the fact that the *Guide* deals with the esoteric teaching of the Bible, particularly the Account of the Beginning and the Account of the Chariot. According to the law, anyone in possession of this teaching may communicate only the chapter headings. Maimonides adheres to this restriction by scattering the "chapter headings" of this teaching. The question of order then, is a most important key to understanding the *Guide* and its secret teaching.[51]

While Strauss's offer of the plan of the *Guide* is meant to be helpful and may be so in the long run, it leads immediately to the following conclusion: "The simple statement of the plan of the *Guide* suffices to show that the book is sealed with many seals."[52] The burden of the rest of Strauss's essay is to consider how these seals may be opened. As Strauss observes, the plan of the *Guide* is not entirely obscure. The demarcation, character, and development of several large sections of the work are tolerably clear. The plan is most obscure at the first part of the *Guide* and especially in its first seventy chapters. Accordingly, the greater part of Strauss's essay is devoted to dealing with the problems of this section, which is the first and perhaps most important key to understanding the teaching of the *Guide*.[53]

The obscurity of this section manifests itself in several ways. It is devoted by and large to the exegesis of various biblical terms that have a bearing upon the Bible's true teaching regarding God. In particular, they are concerned with two themes—God's incorporeality and God's unity. As such, they might be thought to belong to divine science or to the Account of the Chariot.

While divine science is obviously important to the ultimate purpose of the *Guide*, a number of questions arise: Is it in fact divine science? Why should Maimonides begin with divine science? Why should he begin by pursuing it in this fashion? Moreover, Maimonides takes up the doctrine of God's character in an order that is not obvious, beginning with the question of God's incorporeality, rather than God's existence or God's unity. Finally and most concretely, the character and development of Maimonides' exegesis is peculiar in a number of specific ways. Strauss observes that in keeping with the exegetical character of this section, a very large number of its chapters are of a type that Strauss calls "lexicographic." These are chapters that begin with some Biblical term or terms that are to be explained. While this kind of chapter is natural to the character of this section, Strauss shows that there is a considerable and even bewildering variety of such chapters. He also brings out that Maimonides' selection of terms to be explained is often perplexing, including the omission of obvious candidates for explication and that the order of their treatment is often unclear. Finally he observes that despite the exegetical character of the section, there are relatively large numbers of nonlexicographic chapters whose presence requires explanation, especially as they often interrupt Maimonides' exegesis in unexpected ways. As one might expect, Strauss stresses such details and this has mixed consequences. As Strauss notes cheerily in a related matter, it is one thing to observe such features and quite another to understand them.[54]

Strauss does not limit himself to cataloging these difficulties but presents an account of his approach to them. If this does not, as Strauss admits, resolve every question, it is nonetheless very helpful. Above all it provides a foundation for the study of the *Guide*. Strauss first offers an explanation of the selection of incorporeality as the initial theme and then shows how and why the discussion of this question may be divided into subsections. This paves the way for a similar account of its sequel, the discussion of God's unity. While this comprises the bulk of Strauss's treatment, building upon this discussion, he also considers certain aspects of other and later parts of the *Guide*.[55]

Space does not permit a full account of Strauss's discussion. Indeed, we must confine ourselves to the first part of the *Guide* and further limit our focus to the discussion of God's incorporeality, that is, to the beginning of the beginning of the *Guide*. Finally, even here only a compressed summary is possible. Still it is implied in Strauss's title that a good beginning is very important.

Before turning directly to the discussion of incorporeality, one general observation is useful since it applies to the whole of Strauss's treatment. Strauss stresses the fact that Maimonides presents a twofold teaching from the beginning and throughout the *Guide*. One part of Maimonides' teaching is public. The other is private. In other words, his teaching has both an outer and an inner or hidden meaning. In this respect Maimonides' teaching corresponds formally to its purpose, the interpretation of the Bible; according to Maimonides, the Bible, too, has an outer and inner meaning. This similarity—the fact that the *Guide* is the esoteric interpretation of an esoteric teaching—means that the *Guide* not only presents literary problems but also makes them one of its themes. In this sense it might be suggested that the question of literary interpretation forms part of the substance of the *Guide's* teaching.[56]

One may further suggest that Strauss adopts this view and that it is perhaps the most fundamental reason he stresses the question of literary interpretation. This means that the account of the literary problems permits and even solicits some important substantive observations, even if these are not regarded by Strauss as conclusive.

The first application of this is Maimonides' discussion of God's incorporeality. But, initially, Strauss must explain why this is Maimonides' initial theme. According to Maimonides, the doctrine of God's incorporeality is one of three fundamental verities concerning God, along with God's existence and God's unity. It is not necessarily the *most* fundamental. Its priority in the *Guide* derives from several factors, but among them is the fact that although the Bible's teaching regarding God's existence and unity is relatively clear and well accepted, its teaching on God's incorporeality is not. The Bible often speaks in terms that suggest God has a body. Clarity on this subject is therefore most urgent.[57]

Moreover, since the philosophic sciences teach that God is incorporeal, the Bible's corporealism leads to the kind of difficulty that is the immediate occasion for the *Guide*. The typical reader of the *Guide* is a person who knows the Bible and other Jewish texts and is at least somewhat familiar with philosophic teachings. This reader will thus be aware of the conflict between the literal meaning of the Bible and the teaching of philosophy. This conflict will give rise to perplexity.[58]

As one might suppose, Maimonides' general approach to this kind of difficulty is based on the notion that the Bible and biblical terms have more than one meaning. It may be that the literal or common meaning of biblical terms conflict with philosophy and science. There is, however, another more uncommon or hidden meaning that does not conflict and that is the true meaning.

For various reasons, this distinction is especially applicable to the Bible's description of God and important for its understanding. This is especially true of the Bible's teaching on God's incorporeality. The Bible abounds in passages that suggest God has a body. Nonetheless, these represent the outer meaning of the Bible. The true meaning teaches that God is incorporeal.

This is all very well and good but the question arises: How does Maimonides know of this distinction and how it is to be applied? This question applies with particular force to the area in which it is most needed—the question of God's incorporeality. As was just noted, the Bible and the Torah abound in corporealisms. Moreover, the force of this question is increased by the fact that Maimonides draws attention to passages in the Bible that describe the divine world in corporeal terms, and that do not admit of a nonliteral interpretation.[59]

Maimonides is thus obliged to give a fuller and more complicated account of this distinction and to provide a justification of it. Maimonides could have and to some degree does appeal to the tradition of post-Biblical Jewish interpretation, which had shown a marked tendency toward interpretating the Bible in incorporeal ways. However, Maimonides denies that in the most fundamental sense, the exegesis he offers in the *Guide* rests on an available tradition. Moreover, as Strauss notes, due to the rise of Karaism, the Jewish movement that rejected rabbinic or post-biblical tradition and appealed to strict adherence to biblical teaching, such a solution would not have been altogether satisfactory. It would not have satisfied Maimonides.[60]

From this it appears that Maimonides is obliged to show that the Bible solicits, in a manner of speaking, the kind of interpretation he offers. This, according to Strauss, is what Maimonides in fact does. His account of the grounds of his interpretation of the Bible is partly open and partly hidden. Some of its most hidden aspects

are not surprisingly interwoven with the discussion of God's incorporeality. This means that the grounds of the interpretation of the
hidden teaching of the Bible are themselves hidden or form part of
the hidden teaching. Accordingly, Strauss's treatment of the literary problem of the *Guide* may be said to be not only a preliminary
to the treatment of its esoteric teaching but part of that treatment.

Strauss approaches those questions by way of the more open
grounds of Maimonides' interpretation. We may do likewise. The
key to this appears to be the question of idolatry.

It is the prohibition of idolatry that first solicits and justifies
Maimonidean interpretation. Strauss summarizes his line of reasoning as follows:

> It was of course universally known that idolatry is a very grave sin,
> nay that the Law serves, so to speak, no other purpose than to
> destroy idolatry (I35, III29 end). But this evil can be completely
> eradicated only if everyone is brought to know that God has no
> visible shape whatever or that He is incorporeal. Only if God is
> incorporeal is it absurd to make images of God and to worship such
> images. Only under this condition can it become manifest to everyone
> that the only image of God is man, living and thinking man, and that
> man acts as the image of God only through worshipping the invisible
> or hidden God alone. Not idolatry, but the belief in God's corporeal-
> ity is a fundamental sin.[61]

It is clear to any thoughtful student of the Bible that this argument
carries great weight. Nevertheless, it leaves unexplained why the
Bible describes God in corporeal terms. As Strauss indicates,
Maimonides does indeed offer an explanation that is part and parcel
of his framework for interpreting the Bible. The main features are
as follows: The Bible must be interpreted in light of the character
of the people to whom it was revealed. These like all the rest of
their contemporaries were idolaters. While it was desirable and
possible to prohibit idolatry in the strictest sense, given the general
character of people, it was not possible to eradicate all aspects of
idolatry immediately. The people, who were thoroughly imbued
with the teachings or beliefs of idolatry, which Maimonides refers
to as Sabianism, could not abandon them quickly or even over a
period of time. This is due to both the force of habit and the fact
that it is extremely difficult for people to understand a being that is
not a body or in a body.[62]

The revelation of the Torah, or law, is designed to initiate a process of education though which people will progress to a complete understanding of the eternal truths that are the basis of that law. This process may take a long time and in fact has. Even in Maimonides' time, it was not fully complete. Maimonides' interpretation of the Bible carries it forward.

This view of Maimonides' interpretative procedure and argument is relatively clear from certain later passages in the *Guide* where he provides a thematic account.[63] Strauss brings out its application to and effect upon the earliest parts of the *Guide*. Moreover and more significantly, he shows that it is incomplete. Maimonides has, according to Strauss, additional grounds for arguing that the Bible means to initiate a progressive education. These emerge through Strauss's consideration of the difficulties of Maimonides' plan. To begin with, Strauss shows that these difficulties become more intelligible once one realizes that certain particular biblical passages underlie this discussion. These passages present difficulties not only when compared with philosophic teaching but with one another. In the case of two such passages and the subsection that is defined by them, a comparison raises the possibility of an intrabiblical progress in the Bible's public teaching concerning God and especially incorporeality.

This progress takes place between Moses' account of God and that of Isaiah and Ezekiel. For obvious reasons, the possibility of such progress and still more the fact that it actually occurred enormously strengthens Maimonides' undertaking and position. Seen in this light, Maimonides' treatment of the Bible is not only an interpretation but also an imitation of it or an imitation on several levels. His imitation of the Bible is the grounds of his interpretation.[64]

Strauss's account of Maimonides' discussion of this possibility is very helpful for understanding the difficulties of this section of the *Guide*, including the reason for these difficulties in the first place, that is, why Maimonides conceals this discussion. The possibility of intrabiblical progress that Maimonides raises may solve some problems. It also raises others that are extremely grave due to the unique authority that Moses and his prophecy possess, a uniqueness Maimonides is otherwise at great pains to define and defend. It is this uniqueness that is the ground of the absolute and unalterable authority of the law. As Strauss observes, Maimonides' suggestion of a progress beyond Mosaic prophecy may be limited to a progress in the public teaching of the fundamental truth of that prophecy and, hence, does not alter in any fundamental sense the superiority of Mosaic prophecy and the authority of the law. All the same, it alters the understanding of that superiority or authority in a way shocking to common understanding. Strauss gives expression to this shocking character by describing the relationship between the *Guide* and the Bible as the relationship of the Torah for the perplexed and the Torah for the unperplexed.[65]

When one turns from intrabiblical progress to that Maimonides seeks through his own efforts, Strauss himself offers some shocks and surprises. The immediate source of this is Strauss's description of the role of Aristotle.

As Strauss indicates, for Maimonides, the work of Aristotle is one of two conditions for an advance beyond the Bible's mode of expression. (The other is the eradication of paganism through the rise of Christianity and Islam and their universal propagation of forms of monotheism.) Aristotle's discovery of the art of demonstration, or teaching, of it makes possible the demonstration of certain roots of biblical teaching, such as God's incorporeality.

Here there is a complication. While Aristotle may be thought to teach that God is incorporeal, Strauss notes that he was nonetheless an idolater. This suggests that idolatry is not contrary to reason. Although it is somewhat unclear what Strauss means by this, it at least means that Aristotle was a member of a pagan and idolatrous society and did not see an absolute reason for opposing idolatrous practice. Moreover, it is not clear that according to Aristotle, God or the gods are completely and utterly incorporeal. He regards the heavens as divine and at all events more appropriate images of God than human beings.[66]

Strauss's discussion leads to the strange implication that despite the abundance of corporealistic language in the Bible, it may be the case that it is the Bible and only the Bible that teaches the incorporeality of God in the strictest sense. Strauss's account of Maimonides' subsequent discussion of God's unity leads to an analogous conclusion that he does state and that is worth quoting in this context:

> Thus we understand why the doctrine in question, in spite of its philosophic origin, can be regarded as the, indeed unbiblical but nevertheless appropriate expression of the biblical principle, namely, of the biblical teaching regarding the hidden God who created the world out of nothing, not to increase the good—for since He is the complete good, the good cannot be increased by His actions—but

without any ground, in absolute freedom, and whose essence is
therefore indicated by "will" rather than by "wisdom." (III 13)[67]

If this be the case, it is clear that the *Guide* is not only formally but
also fundamentally a Jewish and not a philosophic book.

Returning, however, to the discussion of incorporeality, it is
necessary and even crucial to stress that the clearest difference
between the Bible and philosophy to emerge from this discussion
concerns the status of idolatry and, hence, is practical or political
in character. As Strauss observes, to Maimonides, Aristotle is an
idolater. That is, he does not reject idolatrous worship as communal
or politically unreasonable; but the Bible of course does. Even if it
were or should prove to be the case that Aristotle's view of God's
incorporeality were identical to the Bible's, this practical difference
would remain and its consequences would be significant. As Strauss
notes, the Bible's insistence on the eradication of idolatry serves
to justify violence and even war to that end. It is true that partially
upon the basis of Aristotle, Maimonides seeks a progress beyond
such practices. The success of Maimonides' quasi-philosophical
theology would eradicate idolatry peaceably. However, in this
event, it emerges that only the means are philosophic; the end is
defined and even made possible by biblical grounds, among them
the notion that general or universal progress in human understanding is possible. This would seem to have been denied by Aristotle.[68]

Strauss's stress on progress, on the progressive character of
Maimonides' undertaking and its roots in what may be called the
Bible's progressive mission arises through his attempt to resolve
the literary problem of the *Guide*. At the same time it brings to
light the fundamental differences between the Bible and philosophy
or at least classical philosophy and their impact on Maimonides'
teaching. In particular, it makes clear why Maimonides' interpretation of the Bible may be truly regarded as the explication of a law,
as Maimonides' formulas claim. This is true despite, or rather
because, of the fact that law has the most unusual purpose of
teaching the absolute and unfathomable unity and incorporeality of
God. Further reflection would tend to indicate that it is this teaching
that authorizes biblical law and its purposes and that it is such a
law that can provide such a teaching and its corollaries. The subject
of the *Guide* is thus aptly termed the true science of the law.[69]

Needless to say, the full meaning of this conclusion is not
immediately clear. The inquiry that leads to this conclusion leads

also to the conclusion that the problems of the *Guide* have their origin in the internal problems of the Bible, at least as much as the problems of the Bible's relationship to philosophy. It thus brings one into ever greater contact with the deepest problems of biblical teaching. To solve both these problems and the related problems of the *Guide* would require a further and much deeper understanding of the true science of the law. To acquire this science, it is now tolerably clear that we are obliged to take more seriously than is our custom the phenomenon of law. We now appreciate more deeply how seriously Maimonides takes this as his beginning point.[70]

It is also true that we must try to understand better the other term in Maimonides' formula: "science" or "true science" and its relationship to philosophy. We must try then to address more deeply the question of philosophy and law. But is this truly necessary and even possible if the most fundamental problems of the *Guide* are essentially biblical in origin or if the *Guide* is a Jewish and not a philosophic book?

The proper answer to this question no doubt entails a variety of considerations. Here I must limit myself to suggesting that Strauss's response to this question is partially expressed in his observation concerning the first seven chapters of the *Guide*, which constitute the first subsection of the treatment of incorporeality.

Beginning with the literary problem of this section, Strauss shows that the key to its plan is supplied by the fact that it is based on two biblical passages. These passages suggest more than any other that God has a body. However, as Strauss's discussion also reveals, somewhat less explicitly, those passages raise an additional problem: the question of the Bible's understanding of the relationship of human reason and human morality or, as we might also say, the relationship of reason and law. It thus appears that the Bible or the law itself presents this theme and presents it problematically.[71]

Strauss's direct discussion of these seven chapters does not fully resolve the literary problem it presents. Still less does it resolve the substantive problem that it raises. His subsequent discussion is addressed most directly to the development of the treatment of God's incorporeality. At the same time it is addressed to the question of reason or philosophy and law. At this point this must remain an open question.

Still, from these considerations, we are now in a better position to understand two things: (1) how important it is to make a good beginning in the study of the *Guide of the Perplexed*, and (2) how much and how regrettably, we are still beginners.

Notes

1. See "Maimunis Lehre von der Prophetie und ihre Quellen," *Le Monde Oriental* (Uppsala) 28 (1934): 99–139, 1936 (reprinted in *Philosophie und Gesetz*, see next entry); *Philosophie und Gesetz: Beiträge zum Verständnis Maimunis und Seiner Vorlaüfer* (Philadelphia: Jewish Publication Society, 1935); English translation by F. Bauman, *Philosophy and Law* Philadelphia, 1987). Citations are to the English translation; "Quelques rémarques sur la science politique de Maimonide et de Farabi," *Revue des Etudes Juives* 100 (1936): 1–37 (reprinted in *Maimonide*, ed. R. Brague [Paris: 1988]). Citations are to this edition as "Quelques remarques"; "Der Ort der Vorsehungslehre nach der Ansicht Maimunis," *Monatschrift für Geschichte und Wissenschaft des Judentums* 81 (1937): 83–105 (translated and reprinted as "Le Lieu de la doctrine de la providence d'apres les vues de Maimonide," in *Maimonide*, ed. R. Brague. Hereafter cited as "Le Lieu"; page references are to Brague; Review of Moses Hyamson's edition of Maimonides, *The Mishneh Torah*, Book 1, *Review of Religion* 3 (1939): 448–456; "The Literary Character of *The Guide of the Perplexed*," in *Essays on Maimonides*, ed. S. W. Baron (New York: AMS Press, 1941), 37–91. Reprinted in *Persecution and the Art of Writing* (Glencoe, Ill: Free Press, 1952). Hereafter cited as "Literary Character" with page references to *Persecution and the Art of Writing*; "Maimonides' Statement on Political Science," *Proceedings of the American Academy for Jewish Research* 22 (1953), 115–30. Reprinted in *What Is Political Philosophy?* (Glencoe, Ill.: Free Press, 1959). Citations are to *What Is Political Philosophy?*; "How to Begin to Study *The Guide of the Perplexed*," in *Maimonides' Guide of the Perplexed*, trans. Shlomo Pines (Chicago: University of Chicago Press, 1963), xi–lvi. Reprinted in *Liberalism Ancient and Modern* (New York: Basic Books, 1968). Hereafter cited as "How to Begin" with page references to *Liberalism Ancient and Modern;* "On the Plan of *The Guide of the Perplexed*," in *Harry Austryn Wolfson Jubilee Volume* (Jerusalem: Academy for Jewish Research, 1965), 771–91. (Shorter version of the preceding entry); "Notes on Maimonides' Book of Knowledge," in *Studies in Mysticism and Religion Presented to Gershom G. Scholem* (Jerusalem: Magnes Press, 1967), 269–83. Reprinted in *Studies in Platonic Political Philosophy* (Chicago: University of Chicago Press, 1983). Citations are to *Studies in Platonic Political Philosophy;* "Note on Maimonides' *Letter on Astrology*," in *Studies in Platonic Political Philosophy;* "Note on Maimonides' *Treatise on the Art of Logic*," in *Studies in Platonic Political Philosophy*.

See also, "On Abravanel's Philosophical Teaching and Political Teaching," in *Isaac Abravanel*, ed. J. B. Trend and H. Loewe (Cambridge: Cambridge University Press, 1937), 93–129. In order to clarify the specific character of Abravanel's teaching, Strauss develops at some length the character of Maimonides' teaching. This is partially because Abravanel identifies himself as an heir to Maimonides. For the same reason, Strauss's characterization of Abravanel serves to clarify Maimonides' teaching.

2. "On Abravanel's Philosophical Tendency and Political Teaching," 95.

3. *Philosophy and Law*, 3.

4. Even if we attempt to understand these remarks in a more restricted sense in light of the context, that is, a book largely devoted to medieval thought, Strauss's claim still seems to be extraordinary. In that event, Strauss seems to claim that Maimonides is the most important figure in medieval thought. Hence, it is important to stress that Strauss is well aware of rival claimants. Strauss had studied thoroughly the whole tradition of medieval Jewish rationalism, both Maimonides' predecessors and his successors, including his critics. His footnotes abound with citations of all major figures from Saadiah to Abravanel and many less-famous authors as well.

Equally if not more important is his awareness of a powerful objection to the seriousness with which he took medieval Jewish rationalism generally: the excavation and recovery of that form of Jewish thought known as Kabbalah effected by the research of Gershom Scholem. Strauss was a contemporary and a friend of Scholem. He was aware of his work from its early stages, followed it closely thereafter, and admired it greatly. Moreover, here and there Strauss indicates that he had reflected on the relevance of Scholem's work and the mystical tradition to his own endeavors. (See "How to Begin to Study Medieval Philosophy," in *The Rebirth of Classical Rationalism*, ed. T. Pangle [Chicago: University of Chicago Press, 1989], 212–5.)

The case is somewhat similar if we turn from medieval Jewish thought to medieval thought. Strauss was a student of Christian and Islamic thought as well, and contributed heavily to the revival of their study. Here, too, one sees the shadow of Maimonides inasmuch as the study of Christian and Muslim authors is often pursued with a view to the contribution they might make to the clarification and understanding of Maimonides. One example, though a most important one, may suffice.

Among the things Strauss undertook to do was to revive the study and understanding of Al-Farabi, the great Muslim philosopher who lived in the ninth and tenth centuries. While Strauss was not without predecessors and colleagues in these efforts, no one equalled him in taking Farabi seriously and in dedication to solving the considerable difficulties of his thought. Farabi is intelligible today, if still relatively ignored, due to Strauss's own efforts and those he inspired among a handful of students, especially Muhsin Mahdi. Still we first encounter Farabi in Strauss as the teacher of Maimonides and thus as a man who may therefore illumine the obscurities of Maimonides' thought.

As Strauss observes, Maimonides presents his own thought, especially in the *Guide of the Perplexed* as a correction of "the philosophic view." Farabi derives his importance from the fact that he is for Maimonides the most important philosophic authority after Aristotle. More precisely, he is the most important philosophic authority after the rise of revealed religion. He is then the most important philosophic authority simply for understanding Maimonides. See "Quelques remarques," 143, 147, 148, and "Le Lieu," 191, 192, and above all, "Farabi's Plato," 357.

5. Despite this general inclination, there are some readers of Strauss who believe that Maimonides remained the most important figure for him throughout his career. See Remi Brague, "Leo Strauss and Maimonides," in *Leo Strauss' Thought: Towards A Critical Engagement*, ed. A. Udoff (Boulder, Colo.: Rienner Publishers, 1991), 93–114. One may also observe that the last book that Strauss prepared for publication before his death in 1973, *Studies in Platonic Political Philosophy*, contains three essays on Maimonides.

6. These questions are addressed by Nathan Tarcov and Thomas Pangle in "Epilogue: Leo Strauss and the History of Political Philosophy," in *History of Political Philosophy*, ed. Leo Strauss and Joseph Cropsey, 3d ed. (Chicago: Rand McNally, 1987); N. Tarcov, "On a Certain Critique of 'Straussianism,' " *Review of Politics* 53 (1991), 3–18; and T. Pangle, "Editors Introduction," *The Rebirth of Political Rationalism*. See also, H. Fradkin, "Philosophy and Law: Leo Strauss as a Student of Medieval Jewish Thought," *Review of Politics* 53 (1991): 40–52; H. Fradkin, "Leo Strauss," *Interpreters of Judaism in the Late Twentieth Century*, ed. Steven Katz (Washington: B'nai Brith, 1993), 343–67.

7. "How to Begin," 183–4.

8. Strauss's locution here is strange. It seems to say that it is precisely Maimonides' perplexities that are least accessible. However that may be, it is clear that Strauss regards his presentation of these perplexities as his most immediate contribution to progress in understanding Maimonides. For obvious reasons, in this event, progress has a somewhat ambiguous meaning.

9. "Notes on Maimonides' Book of Knowledge"; "Note on Maimonides' *Letter on Astrology*"; "Note on Maimonides' *Treatise on the Art of Logic*."

10. In an earlier essay, Strauss considered at length the view that the *Mishneh Torah* should be regarded as superior in importance to the *Guide*. He rejects this view. (See "The Literary Character," 77–94.)

11. See "On a Forgotten Kind of Writing," in *What Is Political Philosophy*, 221–32.

12. See *Guide of the Perplexed*, Introduction.

13. "How to Begin," 142; "Literary Character," 42.

14. "How to Begin," 142.

15. There are some nonlegal works, but almost all of these are medical and as such not strictly speaking philosophic. There is only one work that might deserve to be called philosophic—an early work entitled the *Treatise on Logic*. (See also "The Literary Character," 38.)

16. "How to Begin," 142–3; "The Literary Character," 41–42.

17. "Literary Character," 40–43.

18. See *Guide*, 2.32; "Farabi's Plato," 357.

19. *Guide*, 2.13.

20. "How to Begin," 144, 151, 179–81; "Literary Character," 40–41; "Le Lieu," 187–9.

21. The last question is connected with the possibility that Strauss's own presentation is esoteric. Strauss discusses this possibility in "The Literary Character of the *Guide of the Perplexed*," and there notes that there were such interpretations of Maimonides in the Middle Ages. In that event, one would have an esoteric interpretation of an esoteric interpretation of an esoteric teaching. Strauss denies that such relationships make it necessarily more difficult to understand the original teaching. Parody, if one may use this term, can be helpful as an explicative tool. Nonetheless, Strauss appears to deny that his presentation is esoteric ("Literary Character," 56, 60–61).

22. *Persecution and the Art of Writing*, Preface, 5.

23. Ibid.

24. Ibid. The problem in question stems from several factors. To begin with, the desire of certain thoughtful people who love wisdom or the truth to communicate that truth as they understand it to other thoughtful lovers of the truth. This kind of person is extremely rare, so that there is a fundamental distinction between the lovers of truth or wisdom and the vast multitude of people. The latter cannot understand and bear the truth. To take it seriously would require a radical change in their attachments and their whole way of life. As a result they may well be hostile to the truth and the people who offer it. This supplies one of the motives of the art of esoteric writing: to protect the lovers of truth from the hostility of others. There are, however, other more generous motives. The resistance of the multitude to the truth is not willful but a function of its nature, its natural incapacity. The people deserve then to be protected from that portion of the truth that is harmful to them. While this distinction among people makes it necessary to conceal the truth, it also makes it possible. Since the majority of people are not thoughtful and do not have a burning desire to know the truth, it is possible to devise literary forms of expres-

sion that can both conceal the truth from most people and reveal it to others who are willing to make proper application of thought and effort.

This intention is assisted by the fact that the true audience of such books is not the actually thoughtful lovers of the truth but the potentially thoughtful. They are people who initially share the opinions of their contemporaries but who may be led to see their problematic character through thinking them through seriously. Accordingly, such books must be formulated in the idiom of conventional or orthodox opinion.

There may be certain general techniques that permit this kind of communication. Still it is important to stress that according to Strauss, the literary forms that serve these purposes may and have varied enormously. This is due to the fact that the fundamental condition that requires this mode of expression is the inclination of most people to adhere to the common, conventional, or orthodox opinions of their times and places. But these vary enormously from time to time and place to place. Included among these variations are the literary forms that are considered customary and even permissible, such as dialogues, treatises, histories, and commentaries.

In short, this kind of literary expression will always be in an important way relative to and determined by the prevailing circumstances. This is all the more the case due to the additional factor that the thoughtful few are at the outset only the potentially thoughtful, or are under the sway of and share prevailing opinion. Their pursuit of the truth must begin from such opinions and indeed may rest on taking such opinions sufficiently seriously to become aware of their problematic character.

To repeat then, the literary forms to which this general practice gives rise will vary and even be highly individual and particular. This means that Strauss denies that there is any general method of interpreting these works, not to mention others. Every such author, and in fact every writing of every such author, may be a special case requiring very detailed and complicated literary considerations. Indeed at the outset, the most tangible or only reliable indication of their intentions and thoughts is the literary form they have adopted. As a consequence, the results of these literary investigations will be decisive for the hope of interpreting them.

25. "How to Begin," 143–4; "The Literary Character," 55, 60–61.

26. What remains puzzling is Strauss's reference to Jewish philosophy in the preface to *Persecution and the Art of Writing*. In light of such reference, it seems natural to take him to understand Maimonides as a representative of such philosophy. However, in the body of the work, Strauss consistently rejects this identification. This includes the "Introduction," where Strauss indicates that he hopes to gain a better understanding of medieval philosophy from Maimonides and Halevi, not because they are philosophers but despite the fact that they are not and are even opponents of philosophy (*Persecution and the Art of Writing*, 11; "Literary Character," 42–46, 71; "Le Lieu," 195).

27. See *Commentary on the Mishnah*: Hagigah 2.1; *Mishneh Torah*: Yesodei ha-Torah, 4.13 and Talmud Torah, 1.12; *Guide*, Introduction.

28. Among the factors that suggest to contemporary scholars it has become easier for us to see behind this figleaf is the fact that we no longer live under the sway of either biblical religion or classical philosophy. This is to say that as we no longer believe in the force of either of these teachings and, hence, no longer care about their conflicts, we see more easily through Maimonides' biblical rhetoric to his Aristotelian or philosophic teaching. According to Strauss, however, if we approach Maimonides in this spirit, we lack the interest necessary to understand him truly. For example, we will be less likely to consider the possibility that Maimonides regards not only biblical teachings as problematic but Aristotelian teachings as well. We will thus fail to see the true complexity of the problems with which Maimonides may have had to deal, let alone how he may have dealt with them. (See "How to Begin," 145; H. Davidson, "Maimonides' Secret Position on Creation," in *Studies in Medieval Jewish History and Literature*, ed. I. Twersky [Cambridge, Mass: Harvard University Press, 1979], 16–40.)

29. "How to Begin," 145; "Literary Character," 44–46, 71.

30. "Literary Character," 44–46.

31. *Guide*, Introduction; "Literary Character," 46–48, 62–64, 68–70.

32. See the epigraph of "Literary Character," 38; "How to Begin," 142.

33. "How to Begin," 155, 168–171, 177.

34. For this and following see *Philosophy and Law*, 20, 23–58; also "Literary Character," 38.

35. "Quelques remarques," 143–4; "Le Lieu," 189, 195; *Philosophy and Law*, 60–78, 80–110.

36. The essays in question are, "Quelques remarques sur la science politique de Maimonide et de Farabi"; "Der Ort der Vorsehungslehre nach der Ansicht Maimunis"; "Maimonides' Statement on Political Science"; "Notes on Maimonides' 'Letter on Astrology.' "

37. "Quelques remarques," 147, 149 and "Farabi's Plato," 357–8.

38. "Quelques remarques," 144–7, 157–8, 168–70; "Le Lieu," 189; *Philosophy and Law*, 58, 98–110.

39. "Quelques remarques," 147; "Farabi's Plato," 357.

40. "Quelques remarques," 147–8; "Farabi's Plato," 358–9.

41. "The Attainment of Happiness," para. 58, trans. and ed. M. Mahdi in *Alfarabi's Philosophy of Plato and Aristotle* (Glencoe, Ill.: Free Press, 1962), 47; "Quelques remarques," 146, 156–7.

42. *Philosophy and Law*, 53–54; "Quelques remarques," 145, 159, 167.

43. "Quelques remarques," 144–5, 149–157 (esp., 157), 162–3 (esp., n. 59), 166, 170–1.

44. "Quelques remarques," 144, 156–7, 160 and "The Literary Character," 77 (n. 112).

45. It is implied in Strauss's characterization of the *Guide* as a Jewish book cited above, that Strauss adheres to a very strict notion or definition of what philosophy is. Strauss advances this view on the grounds that such was the manner in which Maimonides understood it. The evidence for this includes the fact that for Maimonides, Farabi was the "modern" authority for the character of philosophy. It may even be suggested that Strauss feels indebted to both Farabi and Maimonides for his own recovery of this understanding of philosophy. (See "Quelques rémarques," 160-1, 167.)

46. "How to Begin," 145-9; "Quelques rémarques," 157, 161 (n.54), 171-2; "Le Lieu," 189; "Farabi's Plato," 393.

47. "Le Lieu," 194-5.

48. Strauss's discussion of the interrelationship of these principles is very complicated. At a certain level, he traces their formal accommodation to the character of the typical addressee of the *Guide*. (See "How to Begin," 145-9; "Le Lieu," 194-5.)

49. "How to Begin," 140.

50. It is worth noting here that the *Guide* is not the only place in Maimonides' works where he stresses the question of literary order or the principles of literary composition. In the introduction to his *Commentary on the Mishnah*, Maimonides devotes a great deal of attention to the question of how the order of the Mishnah was determined. This is necessary because the author or compiler of that work, employed more than one principle of literary organization thus rendering its plan somewhat obscure.

Furthermore, Maimonides treats the organization of the law in very different ways in his two other major works. In the *Mishneh Torah*, Maimonides' code of Jewish law, he divides the law into fourteen parts. In his treatment of the commandments in the *Guide*, he also divides the law into fourteen parts. However, this division is quite different from the one employed in the *Mishneh Torah*. Maimonides then not only stresses the issue of order but also is a master of its various types. He is so masterful that he is capable of bringing about through the employment of order the appearance of disorder. (See "Literary Character," 61-62.)

51. *Guide*, Introduction; "Literary Character," 61.

52. "How to Begin," 142; "Literary Character," 61.

53. "How to Begin," 144.

54. Ibid., 149-54, 158; "Literary Character," 61-62.

55. "How to Begin," 149-52, 154-61, 172-8.

56. Ibid., 144-6.

57. Ibid., 149-50.

58. Ibid., 143.

59. Ibid., 155.

60. Ibid., 149-50, 156-7, 160, 164-5 (with 148, 152, 159); "Literary Character," 51-2.

61. "How to Begin," 150.
62. Ibid., 161, 163–4; see also, Maimonides' *Treatise on Resurrection*.
63. *Guide*, 3. 29 and 32.
64. "How to Begin," 159–65; "Literary Character," 66.
65. "How to Begin," 171; "Literary Character," 64, 87; "Quelques rémarques," 164–6; see also, Maimonides' *Commentary on the Mishnah*: Sanhedrin, chap. 10 (Heleq).
66. "How to Begin," 150–1, 169–70, 182–3; see also, "Literary Character," 75–6.
67. "How to Begin," 177; see also, 180–1.
68. Ibid., 162. Consider also the philosopher's speech concerning warfare in Judah Halevi's *Kuzari*, 1.2–4. It must be noted, however, that Strauss observes elsewhere that Farabi also deals with the theme of war in a manner somewhat different than his teachers, Plato and Aristotle. He attributes this to the impact of Islam.
69. As is well known, progress is an important theme in Strauss's reflections on the history and problems of philosophy. Hence, it is of some importance to know what he thought about the possibility that medieval philosophy, especially Islamic philosophy, might have thought that it constituted an advance beyond classical thought, an advance made possible through the rise of Islam and other revealed religions. It is also important to know what he thought about the relationship between any such "progress" and the progress that modern thought, beginning with Machiavelli, claimed to have made. The facts are rather complicated as is Strauss's treatment of them. In a number of places, Farabi and Maimonides following him offer an account of moral virtue that depreciates its status severely. Indeed, in the *Political Regime*, Farabi offers an account of liberality that resembles the famous critique of it offered by Machiavelli in the fifteenth chapter of the *Prince*. (See the discussion of the timocratic city in the *Political Regime*.) However, Farabi insists that his thought is the recovery of the thought of Plato and Aristotle. (See "Attainment of Happiness," para. 63, *Farabi's Philosophy of Plato & Aristotle*, 49–50.) He suggests, therefore, that his account of morality merely brings more clearly to light the true classical teaching on this subject.
70. *Philosophy and Law*, 20; "Quelques rémarques," 157.
71. "How to Begin," 154–7; "Literary Character," 65 and, esp., 70.

4

Maimonides' Conception of
Philosophy

Kenneth Seeskin

No one doubts that Leo Strauss's essay "The Literary Character of the *Guide of the Perplexed*" revolutionized the study of Maimonides.[1] Although Maimonides says that he wrote the *Guide* in order that the secret teachings of the Torah be "glimpsed and then concealed," few of Strauss's modern predecessors took this remark seriously.[2] If all one read were the commentaries of Guttmann or Wolfson, for example, one would come away with the impression that the *Guide* is a philosophic treatise comparable to Aquinas's *Summa Theologiae*. We owe Strauss a great deal for emphasizing that the *Guide* has a literary structure all its own: a letter written to a disciple named Joseph.[3] We learn from the introduction that Joseph is an observant Jew who is not sure whether to follow his intellect and renounce the foundation of the law or hold fast to the law and turn his back on intellect. But if the *Guide* is a letter written to a disciple, it is also a book intended for a wider audience, for Joseph's perplexity is hardly unique. Maimonides tells him in the introductory epistle that he wrote the *Guide* "for you and for others like you." Thus the *Guide* has two purposes: (1) to relieve the perplexity into which people like Joseph have fallen, and (2) to explain the meaning of obscure terms and parables in the Bible.

The most immediate problem Maimonides faced in writing such a book is that no one can guarantee that everyone who reads it will be as qualified and conscientious as Joseph. Whether we are talking about the twelfth century or the twentieth, the majority of Jews believe in a God who changes from one moment to the next, displays emotion, responds to special appeals, and intervenes in the natural order. Maimonides was well aware that if this view were challenged in too abrupt a fashion, people would lose faith in God and the results would be disastrous. Throughout the *Guide*, he cites the famous talmudic dictum that prohibits discussion of the secrets of the Torah in public, and in several passages suggests that even without this prohibition, it would be imprudent to present a beginning student with advanced material.[4] Just as we would kill a baby by giving it food intended for an adult, Maimonides argues we would damage the intellect by exposing it to divine science right away.

On the other hand, Maimonides was not content to let people wallow in ignorance. He knew, for example, that if people believe in a God who is corporeal, they violate the most sacred teaching of Judaism: that God is one.[5] His response is to seek a compromise. He admits that the majority of worshipers can be enlightened about God's incorporeality but argues that when it comes to more difficult matters, the best course of action is to keep the secrets of the Torah out of the public domain.[6] The question is: How secret does he have to be to accomplish this? If there are religious and philosophic reasons for writing an esoteric book, at what point would Maimonides have too much esotericism and begin to confuse even his most sophisticated readers?

According to Strauss, Maimonides' esotericism runs deep. Confronted by an esoteric book, a responsible interpreter must also be esoteric, lest the secrets of the original author fall into the wrong hands.[7] Since the Torah is esoteric, and the *Guide* is an imitation or repetition of the Torah, the *Guide* is an esoteric interpretation of an esoteric doctrine. To use one of Strauss's favorite images, it is a book with seven seals. But Maimonides was not the only author who faced the problem of how to deal with esotericism. In Strauss's opinion, the interpreter of Maimonides is in the same boat as Maimonides himself. So unless the interpreter wants to reveal a doctrine Maimonides labored to keep secret, he or she must write in an esoteric manner as well. The upshot is that a person who reads Strauss on Maimonides confronts an esoteric interpretation of an esoteric interpretation of a doctrine that is esoteric in its own right. In Platonic terms, the reader is three times removed from the truth. It should come as no surprise, then, that Strauss's introduction to the Pines translation of the *Guide* never takes up the question of what Maimonides' philosophic contribution amounts to. Since Maimonides' goal was to speak to trained readers while holding untrained ones at bay, Strauss argues that he had to become a master of the art of revealing by not revealing and of not revealing by revealing. What kind of art is this? According to Strauss, the need for esotericism is based on the "rigid division" of mankind into an inspired and intelligent minority and an uninspired and foolish majority.[8] This division raises the same question over again. Do we need seven seals to keep an uninspired majority in the dark, and at what point does esotericism keep even the inspired minority guessing about the real meaning of the text?

To answer these questions, I propose that we think of esotericism in two ways.[9] The first is what I will call *normal esotericism*. This applies to a book that deals with a complex and demanding subject and requires intense concentration to be appreciated. Although the uninspired majority may not be able to follow it, the book contains no booby traps, blind alleys, or concealed doctrines—at least none that the author has put there intentionally. One could say that the *Critique of Pure Reason* is esoteric in this sense because it is inaccessible to all but a technically trained audience. While it challenges the orthodox view of God, few people have been thrown into a religious crisis as a result of reading it.

By contrast, *deep esotericism* applies to a book in which the author hides the true meaning behind hints, clues, or cleverly constructed diversions. Maimonides alerts the reader that the *Guide* is a diffuse book in which one subject may be treated in a variety of places. So it will not do to read the chapter on *shema* (to hear) and think one has a good idea of Maimonides' view of divine/ human interaction. Strauss is right to say that the *Guide* is designed to reflect the give and take of oral instruction; but the same could be said of any number of books whose authors knew nothing about talmudic prohibitions against speech in public.

As Strauss would have it, Maimonides' predicament in writing the *Guide* was this. The Torah is an esoteric book written in parables. If Maimonides were to write the same kind of book, he would be trading one parable for the other and not be making any progress. Therefore, he had to find a way simultaneously to reveal the truth *and* hide it, a way that would fool one audience but make good sense to the other. The solution can be found in Maimonides' famous admission that he intends to contradict himself.[10] After all, asks Strauss, what better way is there to hide the truth than to say "a is b" and then say "a is not b"?[11] Since one of these claims must be true and the other false, the truth is revealed and concealed at the same time. But which statement is the revelation and which the concealment? Strauss proposes that of two contradictory claims, the one that occurs least frequently is the one Maimonides regards as true.[12]

In the introduction to the *Guide*, Maimonides lists seven types of contradiction found in prophetic and philosophic writing. Of the seven, he says he will avail himself of two. The first is unproblematic: a teacher speaking to introductory students may have to say something at the beginning of the inquiry that he or she intends to take back at the end. The second type is more interesting because it does involve a measure of concealment.

> In speaking about very obscure matters it is necessary to conceal some parts and to disclose others. Sometimes in the case of certain dicta this necessity requires that the discussion proceed on the basis of a certain premise, whereas in another place necessity requires that the discussion proceed on the basis of another premise contradicting the first one. In such cases the vulgar must in no way be aware of the contradiction; the author accordingly uses some device to conceal it by all means.[13]

It is regrettable that Maimonides' description of this type of contradiction is not only vague but extremely short. He does not say how often he intends to use it, so that Strauss goes beyond the text in claiming that contradictions are the "axis" of the *Guide* or that Maimonides makes contradictory statements on all important subjects.[14]

In fact, Maimonides limits the scope of this type of contradiction to *very obscure matters*. I take this to mean that he will use contradictions in those areas where there is no demonstration and little hope of finding one.[15] The reason is simple: if you demonstrate *P*, you will not conceal anything by going on to assert not-*P*. What Maimonides appears to say, then, is that when no demonstration is available, it is sometimes necessary for the discussion to proceed on the basis of contradictory premises. To take an example that Strauss does not say much about, Maimonides offers a standard Aristotelian account of cognition at *Guide* 1.68. This theory is based on an analogy between human cognition and divine. Earlier

(1. 52–59), he insisted that God bears no relation to anything in the created world and therefore God's wisdom is not analogous to ours.[16]

Though Maimonides does not connect this sort of contradiction with the philosophic tradition, it is nonetheless true that from a philosophic perspective, there is nothing startling in what he proposes. In areas where demonstration is impossible, many philosophers have turned to the aporetic method, which begins by showing that plausible arguments can be made on opposite sides of a question. In the *Meno* and *Protagoras*, for example, Socrates presents arguments to show that virtue is teachable and arguments to show that it is not. Rather than trying to conceal something from his respondents, he is trying to persuade them that they have to ask more fundamental questions about virtue, in particular what virtue is. In view of the confusion to which conflicting arguments may lead, we can understand why a philosopher might wish to reserve them for mature audiences. By the time he wrote the *Republic*, Plato came to see that the Socratic method could have harmful consequences if practiced on people with insufficient training in philosophy.[17] Socrates, it will be remembered, was willing to talk to young and old alike.[18]

Another way to look at this issue is to ask whether Maimonides has a doctrine that *could* be expressed in a straightforward way if he wanted to do so or whether his view of philosophy makes linear arguments and pithy conclusions all but impossible. In some passages, Strauss suggests that direct and plain communication of the secrets of the Torah is impossible by nature.[19] Yet this view, as Strauss himself admits, runs into an immediate difficulty. The Talmud prohibits direct and plain communication of these secrets. Why would the law prohibit something that is not within our power?[20] Strauss therefore takes the law to imply that direct and plain communication *is* within our power, and it is clear why. If Maimonides' way of communicating the secrets of the Torah is to contradict himself, then of necessity, one of two contradictory statements must hit the nail on the head. As Strauss puts it: "while the other devices used by Maimonides compel the reader to guess the true meaning, the contradictions offer him the true teaching quite openly in either of the two contradictions."[21] Thus, Strauss compares Maimonides' true teaching to an inscription in an unknown language that must be deciphered by an archeologist.

Against Strauss, I want to argue that the *Guide* does not contain *a* true teaching that is hidden from the reader but a patchwork of doctrines, conjectures, and observations dealing with speculative matters. It is esoteric because it is difficult to achieve certainty in a field where all we have are glimpses of the truth; but the *Guide* is not a book with seven seals, and there is no reason why an interpreter cannot discuss Maimonides' contribution in a forthright way.

The Aporia of Maimonides

We have seen that the *Guide* does not begin with a list of postulates but with an educated person pulled in two directions. In this respect, the opening pages are in keeping with Aristotle's claim that philosophy begins in wonder.[22] Wonder (*thaumadzein*) is another name for puzzlement (*aporein*); puzzlement makes one confess ignorance, and a confession of ignorance makes one a lover of knowledge. Unfortunately, the history of philosophy reveals that the path to knowledge is blocked because great thinkers do not always agree on what the first causes are or how they should be investigated. People then encounter a second level of puzzlement when they recognize that it is possible to advance arguments on opposite sides of important questions.[23] In metaphorical terms, reason finds itself tied in knots.

According to Aristotle, first philosophy is an attempt to untie these knots and point the mind in the right direction. An immediate consequence of this view is that first philosophy cannot be demonstrative. Since its premises are in doubt, it cannot move from premise to conclusion; its function is rather to scrutinize difficulties and resolve conflicts. Aristotle's general name for this type of argument is *dialectic*. In the *Topics* he lists three uses for dialectical argument, the last of which pertains to philosophy:

the ability to see puzzles on both sides of a subject will make us see more easily the truth and error in the points that arise. It is also useful in regard to the principles employed in the individual sciences. For it is impossible to discuss them on the basis of the principles proper to the particular science because the principles are prior to everything else. That is why we must deal with generally accepted opinions [*endoxa*]. This task belongs properly and most appropriately to dialectic, for dialectic is a process of scrutinizing opinions and holds the path to the principles of all investigations.[24]

It is clear that not every problem can be resolved in a dialectical fashion. If primary premises are already in place, it would be foolish to begin an investigation by turning to generally accepted opinions. Again in the *Topics* (104b1–18), Aristotle claims that dialectical problems involve situations where (1) people hold no opinion either way, (2) the mass of people hold an opinion contrary to the philosophers, (3) the philosophers hold an opinion contrary to the masses, (4) members of each group hold opinions contrary to other members, (5) arguments conflict with one another, or (6) the subject matter is so vast that it is difficult to give any arguments at all, for example, the eternity of the world.

The hallmark of dialectical reasoning is that the puzzle be genuine and that the arguments on both sides of the issue be such that reasonable people either can or do hold them.[25] The assumption is that if we examine the arguments in a systematic way, subjecting each side to criticism and revising our opinions as we go along, we can untie the knots in which reason has tied itself. The issue has nothing to do with trying to satisfy two sets of audiences; it is rather the conviction that the claims of great thinkers cannot be completely mistaken so that they are likely to have some bearing on the resolution of the problem.[26]

We can therefore appreciate Joseph Owens's remark that while Aristotle is often viewed as the prince of dogmatists and the patron of deductive reasoning, this impression is highly misleading.[27] The deductive methods discussed in the *Posterior Analytics* provide an idealized conception of a finished science; yet surely Aristotle is the last person on earth to argue that a method appropriate to one area of knowledge must be appropriate to all. In the *Metaphysics*, he begins by reviewing the history of the problems he wants to discuss, considers alternative accounts of important ideas, allows himself the liberty to return to the beginning of a problem and make a fresh start, and even raises the issue of whether first philosophy is possible.

Except for a short treatise on logic written at an early age, there is nothing in the Maimonidean corpus comparable to Aristotle's *Organon*. On the other hand, we have seen that the *Guide* begins with a predicament similar to the one described by Aristotle: the reader is perplexed by conflicting claims from reputable authorities. At first the puzzle seems obvious: the choice between Athens and Jerusalem; but as the book develops, the puzzle becomes more complex. It is *not* between philosophic demonstration, on the one

hand, and prophetic authority, on the other. Maimonides is enough
of a rationalist to see that in areas where demonstrations are
possible, no perplexity arises:

> For in all things whose true reality is known through demonstration
> there is no tug of war and no refusal to accept a thing proven—unless
> indeed such refusal comes from an ignoramus who offers a resistance
> that is called resistance to demonstration. Thus you can find groups
> of people who dispute the doctrine that the earth is spherical and that
> the sphere has a circular motion. These folk do not enter into our
> purpose. The things about which there is perplexity are very numer-
> ous in divine matters, few in matters pertaining to natural science,
> and nonexistent in matters pertaining to mathematics.[28]

For Maimonides, the classic example of demonstrably certain
knowledge is the existence and unity (incorporeality) of God.[29]
Throughout the *Guide*, he claims that his position on this matter
will be demonstrated, has been demonstrated, or demonstrates a
position about which there can be no doubt or dispute.[30] Faced with
scores of passages in the Bible that imply that God is corporeal, he
maintains that they cannot be interpreted literally and that anyone
who insists on literal interpretation is no better than an idolater.[31]
Recall that the incorporeality of God is an issue where even the
uneducated majority can be enlightened.

Not surprisingly, the question of what can and cannot be demonstrated is critical to Maimonides. At *Guide* 1.32, he argues that
knowledge of the difference is a mark of human perfection; later,
at 1.71, he criticizes the Mutakallimun for ignoring it. All of this is
of a piece with his insistence that logic is a prerequisite for divine
science.[32] It is significant, then, that once Maimonides gets beyond
the existence and unity of God, his mode of argument changes.
Instead of offering a straight proof of his position, he examines
competing arguments: three on creation (five if we include the
Epicureans and Mutakallimun), three on prophecy, and five on
providence. In regard to creation, he points out that even Aristotle
did not think he could demonstrate his position.[33] To know whether
the world is eternal or created, one would have to know whether
causes and principles that apply to the sublunar realm also apply to
the heavens. Since our knowledge of the heavens is extremely
limited, this question can never be answered with certainty. At
Guide 1.71, Maimonides points out that philosophers have been

debating the eternity of the world for three thousand years with no resolution in sight. Even among Maimonides' immediate predecessors, Saadia believed in creation *ex nihilo* while Ibn Ezra believed in creation from a preexisting material.

Once we leave the physics of the sublunar realm or the existence and unity of God, the tradition that derives from Athens was anything but monolithic. Two consequences follow. First, the job of *reconciling* physics (*ma'aseh bereshit*) and metaphysics (*ma'aseh merkabah*) with the Torah is more complicated than it first appears. If the philosophers themselves cannot agree on the application of sublunar physics to the celestial realm, the use of physics to explain the Torah is very much in doubt. Second, Maimonides does not contradict himself when he says at *Guide* 2.2 that he has no intention to write a treatise on natural science or to provide a summary of what others have said on divine science.[34] All the passage means is that he will take for granted results that have been demonstrated elsewhere. This leaves open the possibility that he will discuss and critically evaluate theories that have not been demonstrated.[35] In any event, it is safe to say that Joseph would have ample reason to be perplexed even if he had not been exposed to the prophetic tradition: no less an authority than Aristotle maintained that philosophy could tie a person in knots.

In regard to the prophets, many people have interpreted Maimonides as saying that prophetic awareness is superior to philosophic.[36] I agree with Strauss's later view that this interpretation overlooks one central point: there is for Maimonides no such thing as specifically religious cognition.[37] In other words, all cognition, whether prophetic or philosophic, stems from the human intellect and is subject to its limitations. According to Exodus 34: 23, even Moses could not see the face of God and had to settle for something less.[38]

There is, of course, one area in which prophets have superiority. Maimonides conceives of prophecy as an overflow from the rational faculty of the prophet's mind to the imaginative. It follows that prophets have all the abstract understanding of philosophers plus the dreams and visions to which that understanding gives rise. The problem is that the area in which prophetic understanding exceeds philosophic—the imagination—is tied to material things and is frequently the source of error. It is, after all, the imagination that is responsible for belief in a corporeal God. In some instances, for example, the *Guide*, Maimonides warns his readers not to solve philosophic problems by relying on the imagination alone. Unfortunately there is a strong tendency for people to regard material things as the only realities and to rely on the imagination when thinking about God. That is why the prophets use visual imagery to make themselves understood.[39] But prophetic literature cannot help but pose a problem: By what procedure can we take visual imagery and derive a metaphysical conclusion?

Obviously, no simple procedure exists. In the case of corporeality, the literal meaning of the prophets is exactly the opposite of their real meaning. As Maimonides points out, the sages who interpret the prophets also speak in parables and rely on visual imagery. Note, for example, that Maimonides himself admits to perplexity when trying to interpret the sayings of Rabbi Eliezer.[40] So no matter how much truth it contains, the prophetic tradition is hardly a model of clarity. It could be said, therefore, that even if Joseph had never studied philosophy, he could still be perplexed about his own religion. If Maimonides is right, many people are.

I suggest that the real perplexity Maimonides has in mind does not arise from being *between* traditions but of being *in* traditions each of which strain the limits of human understanding. The issue, then, is not the rivalry between Athens and Jerusalem as much as the speculative nature of the subject both of them address.

Maimonides on Creation

Consider the issue of creation. It is well known that the opening lines of *Genesis* are highly ambiguous. The verb *bara* (to create) is used only of God and raises the question of whether divine creation bears any resemblance to human. The words *tohu vavohu* (unformed and void) are grammatical nonsense whose meaning is open to a variety of interpretations. There is even a dispute on the parsing of the first sentence: although the usual translation is "In the beginning God created . . . ," according to a tradition that derives from Rashi, it should be "When God was creating . . . " Since the philosophic tradition has not produced a consensus either, Maimonides had no choice but to abandon demonstration and proceed dialectically.

The theory that Maimonides ascribes to Moses asserts that God created the world *ex nihilo* by a free act of will. Its advantages are two: (1) by making God the sole cause of the world, it avoids the dualism involved in positing two causes: God and an eternal formless matter; and (2) by allowing for free will, it upholds the foundation of the law.[41] The theory ascribed to Plato claims that God did create the world from formless matter. Its advantages are (1) it avoids the issue of how an immaterial source can create a material world, and (2) it, too, allows for free will and upholds the foundation of the law. The theory ascribed to Aristotle claims that the world comes to be by eternal emanation from a necessary and unchanging source. It has three advantages: (1) it holds that time is an accident attaching to motion, (2) it preserves our normal understanding of cause and effect, and (3) it holds that the world is eternal *a parte post*. What is more, the Aristotelian theory raises an important question: if creation involves novelty—a first instant in time—how can God initiate new activity? How can a perfect being who is pure actuality move from potency to act?

Even the theory of the Kalaam has something going for it. Although it rejects the normal understanding of cause and effect by ascribing all regularity in nature to the will of God, it points out that there are heavenly phenomena such as planetary orbits that cannot be explained by any known causal theory.[42] It, too, raises an important question: Why should we assume that the categories of act and potency apply to the will of God? Normally a thing moves from potency to act by responding to an external cause. But the will of God is completely autonomous so that if it initiates new activity, it would only be responding to itself. In short, there is no reason why intermittent activity is incompatible with divine perfection.

As noted above, the question of creation turns on the question of whether categories that apply to the sublunar world also apply to the celestial. The Aristotelians claim that since matter and form and act and potency are the basis of all scientific understanding, we have little choice but to apply them to heavenly phenomena and eventually to God. The other side claims that it is presumptuous to think that because these categories work on earth, they must also work in heaven. Maimonides raises a similar question about time. Why should we assume that the principles that explain the universe as it is at present also explain its origin?[43] None of these issues is the sort that allows one to reach a definitive conclusion. Thus, all Maimonides can do is point out that the application of earthly categories to the sublunar realm rests on a number of questionable assumptions. On the other hand, he is honest enough to admit that a questionable assumption could be true so that there is a chance that Aristotle is right. In Maimonides' words:

> It is possible that someone else may find a demonstration by means of which the true reality of what is obscure for me will become clear to him. The extreme predilection that I have for investigating the truth is evidence by the fact that I have explicitly stated and reported my perplexity regarding these matters as well as by the fact that I have not heard nor do I know a demonstration as to anything concerning them.[44]

This passage is significant because it shows that the author of the *Guide of the Perplexed* was not above admitting perplexity himself.[45]

There is, of course, a vast literature on Maimonides' view of creation, and I cannot treat every issue in the space provided here. But no matter which interpretation one prefers, it is undeniable that Maimonides' method is extremely flexible. After presenting the major alternatives, he delves into everything from astronomy to biblical criticism, from physics to psychology, from analysis of observable facts to speculation on unobservable ones. Like Aristotle, he even allows himself the liberty to start over.

What, then, is Maimonides' position? I agree with Marvin Fox that it is none of the theories in isolation but a construction based on insights from all three.[46] The Aristotelians are right about the sublunar realm and eternity *a parte post*. The Mutakallimun could be right about divine volition in the sense that nothing prevents us from thinking of God's will as they suggest. In the last analysis, the best alternative affirms that God created the world from nothing by a free act of will but that the world will continue to exist in its present form. Although Maimonides says that he does not accept the Platonic theory, he thinks it is permissible to believe it since it ascribes free will to God.[47] So interpreted, his treatment of creation is a classic case of dialectical reasoning as described by Aristotle. I grant that his discussions are not easy to follow and that judged by modern standards, his terminology is not very precise.[48] But given the vastness of the problem, the ambiguity of the biblical text, the lack of consensus among philosophers, and the paucity of scientific evidence at his disposal, we must ask whether a better method was available.

Suppose, for example, that the Talmud said nothing about discussing creation (*ma'aseh bereshit*) in public. And suppose that Maimonides could be assured that only the most sophisticated readers would have access to his book. Would his treatment of this issue be any different? I suggest it would not. The discussion we have is the clearest one Maimonides can give even if it proceeds in a slow, halting manner and looks at the issue from more than one perspective. The arguments he considers are foolish; neither are they completely convincing. Although many of Strauss's followers have argued that Maimonides was secretly committed to the Aristotelian position, Herbert Davidson is correct in saying that we can imagine a philosopher trotting out stock objections to a position he holds in order to trick unsuspecting readers, but we can hardly imagine someone taking the time to fashion new and interesting arguments to do the same thing.[49] The fact is that Maimonides' view of Aristotle is a thorough, well-reasoned critique—hardly what we would expect from a man trying to hide his sympathy behind a trail of hints, clues, and contradictions. I suggest, therefore, that Maimonides' position on creation is exactly what he says it is: the scales have been tipped in favor of a creating God but the issue is far from closed.

Human Knowledge and Its Limits

The discussion of creation is a paradigm for understanding Maimonides' conception of philosophy as a whole. On the question of how to resolve intellectual conflicts, his strategy is not to side with Athens *or* Jerusalem but to examine the issues on a case by case basis taking insights from whatever source he can. Julius Guttmann is therefore right in saying that for Maimonides, divine science cannot be given a rigorous formulation.[50] Instead of unified theory that describes its objects in precise detail, it is a series of insights that, in Maimonides' terms, we represent to ourselves in a loose vocabulary in order to point the mind in the right direction.[51] The reference to pointing calls to mind *Republic* 518, where Socrates claims the purpose of education is not to put sight in blind eyes but to turn the soul away from the world of becoming and toward that of being.

The reference to pointing is also significant because the talmudic dictum that prohibits discussing the secrets of the Torah in public does allow one to provide chapter headings to a student capable of learning on his or her own. Not surprisingly, Maimonides says that no one should expect him to do anything more than what the law allows.[52] The question is: What does the term "chapter headings" mean? Strauss appears to take it literally, pouring over the opening words of Maimonides' chapters for hidden clues. But in view of Maimonides' repeated warnings about the evils of literal interpretation, there is no reason why we have to take it this way. In fact, "chapter headings" may simply be his way of saying that he cannot resolve every issue or provide a complete account of every theory. As he says in the introduction, "A sensible man thus should not demand of me or hope that when we mention a subject, we shall make a complete exposition of it, or that when we engage in the exposition of the meaning of one of the parables, we shall set forth exhaustively all that is expressed in that parable."[53] In short, Maimonides assumes his readers can fill in many of the details and see for themselves what an argument presupposes. This is a long way from writing a book with seven seals.

How, then, should we interpret Maimonides' claim that his purpose is to see that the truth is glimpsed and then concealed? Although deep esotericism is a possible reading, it is by no means compelling. We do not have to imagine Maimonides like a poker player who shows his hand one card at a time, hoping to keep the audience guessing. In the introduction to book 3, he repeats the talmudic dictum about speaking in public but adds that it would be cowardly not to set down for others something he regards as clear.[54] He goes on to say that his understanding of these matters is not the result of a divine revelation but of following conjecture and supposition. Thus, anyone who examines the *Guide* with care will be in a position to know everything Maimonides knows.

The intellectual modesty expressed in this passage is in keeping with the sentiments expressed in the introduction to book 1, where Maimonides claims that a sensible person should not expect the *Guide* to remove every difficulty or to contain a complete account of every subject. The reason is that truth in these matters is never fully known to anyone.[55] I take this to mean that even the inspired and intelligent minority have no choice but to rely on conjecture and supposition. As he remarks elsewhere, earthly matter is a strong veil that surrounds us and prevents us from apprehending the true realities.[56] The best that we can see are flashes of light that appear from time to time. I suggest, therefore, that the reason truth is glimpsed and then concealed is that once we come to appreciate the difficulty of the subject, we will see that only a fool would claim to offer more than a partial vision. In Platonic terms, we may be able to get a few glimpses of the sun, but in the last analysis, we can never completely leave the cave.

The issue at stake here is not a talmudic prohibition nor a desire to keep unpopular views from falling into the wrong hands; it is rather the question of when human knowledge reaches its limits. As Maimonides points out, his view on the limits of human knowledge has nothing to do with the need to comply with Jewish law; it is something he thinks any philosopher should grasp.[57] But therein lies the problem. Religion is not a part-time endeavor; it asks for a total commitment to a way of life. If Maimonides could demonstrate that all of Judaism rests on a logically secure foundation, he would have nothing to hide: the uninspired majority would praise him for upholding tradition while the inspired minority would be won over by the force of his arguments. I have argued, however, that his message is much more sobering: beyond the existence and unity of God, very little of Judaism rests on a certain foundation or ever will. According to Maimonides, belief in creation is necessary to uphold the foundation of the law; but after twelve chapters of painstaking analysis, the most he can say is that the scales are tipped in that direction. Intellectuals might cheer this result, as Aquinas did, by pointing out that if creation is possible, one can believe in it without sinning against reason; but the majority of people are not likely to be so sanguine. If you cannot know for sure that the foundation of the law is true, why go to great lengths to obey it?

Maimonides' way of keeping the uninspired majority away from unsettling results was very simple: the book itself, which is to say a long, daunting, slow-moving exposition that presupposes technical training in several subjects and makes no concessions to popular tastes. He claims that even a beginner should be able to derive some benefit from reading his book, which is probably a reference to the sections on incorporeality.[58] But he also claims that a person who finds nothing in the *Guide* that is of any use ought to think of it as never having been written. As one who has taught the *Guide*, I can say with assurance that many readers have taken this advice to heart.

In short, normal esotericism is enough to insure that untrained readers will have no access to Maimonides' position on obscure matters. Note that the arguments dealing with creation, prophecy, and providence do not appear until the issue of corporeality has been discussed at length and detailed critiques of Aristotle and the Kalam put forward. In fact, it is difficult even for an advanced reader to work through the *Guide* without a profound sense of humility. So there is little reason to think Maimonides violated the talmudic prohibition about speaking in public, and even if he did, he was careful to provide himself with an additional defense: the issues on which he wrote were so important that he decided to take extraordinary action by writing a book.[59] On the general issue of putting pen to paper, it is well known that Maimonides took part in public controversies and was willing to challenge religious authorities when he thought they were wrong on scientific matters. So if persecution was a factor in his literary career, he did not show much sign of it. We must therefore ask why he needed a deeper level of esotericism. What goal would it serve that was not better served by something else?

In my opinion, not only is no purpose served but the literary integrity of the book is seriously compromised. It was, after all, Strauss who called attention to the fact that the *Guide* is a literary work that takes the form of a letter written to a student. Although the text says that Joseph is an observant Jew with a fine character and a good knowledge of philosophy, there is nothing to indicate that he is a genius or that he has been blessed with prophetic vision. On the contrary, he has come to Maimonides because he is perplexed. We must therefore ask what sort of book would clear up his perplexity and put him on the right track. We can imagine a demanding book that would require close attention to every word and turn of argument. But if the book is much more than demanding and the truth is buried so deeply that it is difficult to say what philosophic contribution the author is trying to make, it would hardly relieve Joseph of perplexity, since it would only trade one set of puzzles for another.

In fact, Strauss's argument for deep esotericism goes well beyond anything found in the *Guide*. Maimonides says he wants to resolve Joseph's perplexity, to show how an observant Jew can obey the commandments without renouncing his or her intellect. But what if no resolution is possible? What if the dichotomy between faith and reason is irreconcilable so that Strauss is correct in saying that Judaism and philosophy are incompatible? That Strauss himself was skeptical of attempts to resolve opposites is well known. In a famous passage from *Natural Right and History*, he claims that

"In every attempt at harmonization, in every synthesis however impressive, one of the two opposed elements is sacrificed, more or less subtly but in any event surely, to the other."[60]

If this view is right, or more important, if Maimonides regarded it as so, the *Guide* would have to be esoteric in the deepest possible sense. Contrary to what Maimonides says, his purpose in writing the book would be to convince Joseph that faced with a legal system based on divine revelation and a philosophic tradition based on rational inquiry, he has to pick one or the other. If the question is how to make the uninspired majority fear God and obey the law, Judaism is the only reasonable alternative; if it is how to formulate the most convincing arguments about God, philosophy is. One is entirely practical, the other theoretical; one is based on noble lies, the other on dangerous truths. If the choice between them is ultimate, then all the passages in the *Guide* that claim Judaism is not only compatible with philosophy but also requires it must be diversions intended to make the uninspired majority respect something it cannot understand.[61]

Unfortunately the uninspired majority is not the only problem. What about that part of the inspired minority who want a theory that unites moral and intellectual virtue, who believe that a Jewish understanding of God and creation is superior to the other options? If Strauss is right, they too would have to be kept in the dark, lest someone call attention to the fact that Maimonides' attempt at a unified theory was only a ruse. Thus, Maimonides' esotericism would have to be clever enough to fool all but a small band of followers.

It is clear, then, that Strauss's main motive for attributing deep esotericism to Maimonides is his own conviction about Jerusalem and Athens, a conviction he ascribes to Maimonides without the slightest hesitation: "Jews of the philosophic competence of Halevi and Maimonides took it for granted that being a Jew and being a philosopher are mutually exclusive."[62] "He [Maimonides] obviously assumes that the philosophers form a group distinguished from the adherents of the law and that both groups are mutually exclusive."[63] On the impossibility of a "synthesis" between faith and reason, Strauss is certainly right; but synthesis is not the only way of overcoming opposition. Neither philosophy nor Judaism speak with a single voice, and in Maimonides' opinion both call for a critical examination of existing views of God and human reason. Once we begin this examination, the global question "Which side is right?'' gives way to more limited ones like "What arguments need to be reworked?'' and "What insights need to be reformulated?''

Maimonides could be a Jew *and* a philosopher not because he had a grand synthesis but because he was able to take material from one tradition and shed light on the other. In that way, he did not leave either tradition exactly as he found it. If the sages of the Mishnah would have been puzzled by Maimonides' account of creation, Aristotle would have been surprised to learn that he was committed to a rigid determinism. But there is nothing startling in the claim that great thinkers extend the limits of a tradition by asking new questions and experimenting with new modes of thought. So, even if Judaism in its classical period is incompatible with philosophy in its classical period, there is no reason to think that Maimonides was stuck with a dichotomy he could not overcome. According to Maimonides, human perfection is both practical and theoretical, aware of what it can demonstrate and what it cannot.[64]

Of particular interest is Maimonides' use of the parable of the four rabbis who entered paradise (*pardes*).[65] According to the story, one died, one went mad, one became an apostate, and only Akiba entered and left in peace. Although the story easily lends itself to esoteric interpretation, that is not how Maimonides chose to read it. In his hands, it is a story about what happens when people are exposed to physics and metaphysics. Rather than emphasizing that Akiba left paradise with a secret that he could only divulge in cryptic ways, Maimonides chose to emphasize that of the four rabbis who entered, Akiba was the only one who knew his limits and stayed within them. In keeping with this parable, the central thrust of the *Guide* is not to hide a well-formulated but potentially dangerous doctrine but to offer a critique of any doctrine that deals with God and the origin of the world. In this way, Joseph's perplexity is resolved by showing him what counts as knowledge and what is only well-founded conjecture.[66]

Notes

1. Leo Strauss, "The Literary Character of the *Guide of the Perplexed*," in *Persecution and the Art of Writing* (Glencoe, Ill.: Free Press, 1952), 38–94. The question of how to read the *Guide* is as old as the book

itself. Maimonides' translator, Samuel Ibn Tibbon, argued that the *Guide* contained a doctrine that was so esoteric it eluded many of those who sought to defend Maimonides against allegations of heresy. We should keep in mind, however, that Ibn Tibbon was himself an Aristotelian. For the history of this problem, see A. Ravitsky, "Samuel Ibn Tibbon and the Esoteric Character of the *Guide of the Perplexed*," *AJS Review* 6 (1981): 87–123. Note, as Ravitsky does, that there is no clear evidence that Maimonides either approved of Ibn Tibbon's interpretation or disapproved of it.

2. *Guide of the Perplexed*, trans. Shlomo Pines (Chicago: University of Chicago Press, 1963), introduction, 6–7.

3. Note Strauss, *Persecution*, 20: "The first chapters of the *Guide* look like a somewhat diffuse commentary on a Biblical verse . . . rather than like the opening of a philosophic or theological work."

4. *Guide* 1, Introduction, 33–34: 8–9, 70–79. The talmudic prohibition is from B. Hagigah 11b, 13a.

5. Cf. Strauss, "How to Begin to Study *The Guide of the Perplexed*," in *Guide of the Perplexed*, xxi: "The necessity to refute 'corporealism' (the belief that God is corporeal) does not merely arise from the fact that corporealism is demonstrably untrue: corporealism is dangerous because it endangers the belief shared by all Jews in God's unity."

6. *Guide* 1.35: 79–81.

7. Strauss, "The Literary Character," 55: "It may fairly be said that an interpreter who does not feel pangs of conscience when attempting to explain that secret teaching and perhaps when perceiving for the first time its existence and bearing lacks that closeness to the subject which is indispensable for the true understanding of any book."

8. Strauss, "The Literary Character," 59.

9. Cf. Alfred Ivry, "Leo Strauss on Maimonides," in *Leo Strauss's Thought*, ed. A. Udoff (Boulder, Colo.: Rienner Publishers, 1991), 83. According to Ivry, the choice is between an esotericism in which Maimonides knows that his beliefs are founded on opinion rather than demonstration and an esotericism in which Maimonides does not believe what he seems to affirm.

10. *Guide* 1, Introduction, 20.

11. Strauss, "How to Begin," xv; "The Literary Character," 73.

12. Strauss, "The Literary Character," 73.

13. *Guide* 1, 18.

14. Strauss, "The Literary Character," 73–74.

15. For more on contradictions in Maimonides, see Marvin Fox, "Maimonides' Method of Contradictions" in his *Interpreting Maimonides* (Chicago: University of Chicago Press, 1990), 67–90. Fox points out that Maimonides introduces this subject by talking about contraries and contradictories; but when he discusses the works of philosophers, or his own

work, Maimonides introduces another term: divergences. According to Fox, *contradiction* has to do with the truth and falsity of statements, while *divergence* has to do with actions. Thus Maimonides' normal procedure is not to make contradictory statements but to make a statement and then do the opposite. As an example, Fox cites *Guide* 2.35, where Maimonides says he will not discuss the prophecy of Moses; the fact is, however, that he says quite a lot about it in the rest of the book. But it is difficult to know whether the distinction between contradiction and divergence is significant. In the passage from *Guide* 1, Introduction, 18, quoted above, Maimonides talks explicitly about contradictory premises. Moreover, even if we follow Fox, the same question arises: does Maimonides have a well-formulated doctrine he is trying to conceal? Fox responds by saying that given contradictory statements, we have to affirm one and deny the other; but when presented with a divergence, we experience a "dialectical tension" or balancing act. I agree that Maimonides presents the reader with dialectical tensions, but surely Maimonides does not leave the reader with tensions that are unresolved (cf. Fox, 23, 43, 79–81, 319). Fox needs to say what the resolution is or where it takes place. Is it systematically concealed or could it be discovered by a reader with adequate training? If the latter, Maimonides' procedure is no different from that of dozens of philosophers who use the dialectical method.

16. See, in particular, *Guide* 1.56: 130–1. For more on *Guide* 1.68, see Shlomo Pines, "The Limits of Human Knowledge according to Al-Farabi, ibn Bajja, and Maimonides," in *Maimonides: A Collection of Critical Essays*, ed. J. Buijs (Notre Dame: University of Notre Dame Press, 1988), 104–5. I agree with Pines that the doctrine espoused in 1.68 cannot be known to be true and is presented largely as a statement of what philosophers in the Aristotelian tradition believe.

17. See *Republic*, 518.

18. See *Apology*, 30a.

19. Strauss, "The Literary Character," 59–60.

20. For Maimonides' view on this matter, see *Commentary on the Mishnah*: Avot, introduction ("Eight Chapters"), esp., chap. 8.

21. Strauss, "The Literary Character," 74.

22. Aristotle, *Metaphysics*, 982b12–20, cf. Plato, *Meno*, 84B, and *Theaetetus*, 155D. For an excellent treatment of the aporetic nature of Aristotelian first philosophy, see Joseph Owens, *The Doctrine of Being in the Aristotelian Metaphysics* (Toronto: Political Institute of Mediaeval Studies, 1963), 211–9.

23. *Topics*, 145b17–20: "Likewise, the equality between contrary reasonings is generally thought to cause puzzlement. For whenever we reason on both sides of a question, and everything seems to follow from each side of the contrary arguments, we are puzzled . . ." (my translation).

24. *Topics*, 101a35–101b4 (my translation).

25. *Topics*, 104a-3–5.

26. *Nicomachean Ethics*, 1098b 27–29. There is a great deal of debate on the nature and scope of dialectic in Aristotle. Part of the problem has to do with the generally accepted opinions (*endoxa*) with which dialectic begins. According to *Topics*, 104a7–10, the claims taken up by dialectic range from opinions that are probable at best to the views of well known and authoritative sources. This ambiguity raises the question of whether to interpret dialectic in a strong or a weak sense: as establishing the first principles of a science or as indicating which of two opinions is most likely to be true. At *Metaphysics*, 1004b22–26, Aristotle compares dialectic to sophistic and opposes both to philosophy. Since first philosophy cannot demonstrate its own first principles, it is easy to sympathize with those who think Aristotle has a strong sense of dialectic as well. For a single volume laying out the main issues, see J. D. G. Evans, *Aristotle's Concept of Dialectic* (Cambridge: Cambridge University Press, 1977). On how to understand *endoxa*, see J. M. Le Blond, *Logique et Methode chez Aristotle* (Paris: S. Vrin, 1939), 77–85. On the need for a strong sense of dialectic, see Terence Irwin, *Aristotle's First Principles* (Oxford: Clarendon Press, 1988), 37–39, 174–5.

27. Owens, *Doctrine*, 214, n. 13.

28. *Guide* 1.31: 66.

29. There is a dispute on whether Maimonides denies that God's existence can be demonstrated at *Guide* 2.24: 327. According to Pines's translation, he does; but according to Ibn Tibbon's translation, he does not. Note that at *Guide* 2.35: 364, Maimonides says quite clearly that the existence and unity of God can be known by human speculation alone.

30. See, e.g., *Guide* 1.51: 113; 1.55: 129; 1.56: 130–1; 1.59: 137; 2.1: 248.

31. *Guide* 1.36: 84.

32. *Guide* 1.34: 75; 1.55: 129; 3.51: 619. Maimonides is very careful to distinguish strong proof or demonstration (*burhan/mofet*) from weak proof or persuasion (*dalil/re'ayah*). See, for example, *Guide* 2.18: 299, where Maimonides claims there is a demonstration that change in material things implies movement from potency to act but a persuasive argument that the Active Intellect can act at one time but not at another. For an excellent discussion of Maimonides' logic, see Arthur Hyman, "Demonstrative, Dialectical, and Sophistic Arguments in the Philosophy of Moses Maimonides," in *Studies in Philosophy and the History of Philosophy* 19 (Washington, D.C: Catholic University of America Press, 1989), 35–51. Although I am generally sympathetic with Hyman's argument, I take issue with his interpretation of creation. According to Hyman, there are two types of dialectical argument in Maimonides: one in which either of two alternatives is accepted, the other in which the strongest position is a combination of insights taken from different alternatives. Hyman takes Maimonides' discussion of creation as an example of the first; in the next section, I will argue it is an example of the second.

33. *Guide* 2.15: 289–293; 2.23: 322.

34. Cf. Strauss, "The Literary Character," 43–46.

35. See, e.g., *Guide* 2.24: 322–7, where Maimonides discusses the status of astronomy as a science. For more on Maimonides' view of astronomy, see Menachem Kellner, "On the Status of Astronomy and Physics in Maimonides' *Mishneh Torah* and *Guide of the Perplexed*," *British Journal for the History of Science* 24 (1991): 453–463.

36. Two recent examples are Fox, *Interpreting Maimonides*, 249 and Pines, "Limits," 100.

37. Strauss, "How to Begin," xxxvii. There are passages where Maimonides suggests that prophetic understanding exceeds philosophic, e.g., *Guide* 2.16: 294, but once again, we must keep in mind that prophetic understanding is expressed in the form of parables.

38. *Guide* 1.54: 123–5.

39. According to Strauss, "How to Begin," xxxvii, Maimonides appears to contradict himself at *Guide* 2.35–36 when he says that (1) Moses' prophecy was unique in being entirely intellectual, but (2) the record of Moses' prophecy, the Torah, is filled with similes and metaphors. Why do we have to take this as a contradiction? Even if Moses' awareness was intellectual, it could still be true that he had to introduce visual imagery to communicate with other people. The Torah, as Maimonides never tires of pointing out, speaks in the language of ordinary men and women. Note, in addition, that according to Maimonides, *Guide* 2.35: 363, not everything that reached Moses also reached the rest of Israel.

40. *Guide* 2.26: 330.

41. *Guide* 2.25: 328–9.

42. For Maimonides' discussion of this issue, see *Guide* 2.19–20: 24.

43. *Guide* 2.17: 297–8: "The essential point is, as we have mentioned, that a being's state of perfection and completion furnishes no indication of the state of that being preceding its perfection."

44. *Guide* 2.24: 327.

45. He also admits to it at *Guide* 2.24: 326, cf. 2.16: 330.

46. Fox, *Interpreting Maimonides*, 293.

47. At *Guide* 2.13: 283–4, Maimonides says he does not accept the Platonic view, but at 2.25: 328–9, he allows one to hold it. According to Herbert Davidson, "Maimonides' Secret Position on Creation," in *Studies in Medieval Jewish History and Literature*, ed. I. Twersky (Cambridge, Mass: Harvard University Press, 1979): 16–40, an esoteric reading of Maimonides favors the Platonic rather than the Aristotelian alternative. For a defense of the Platonic interpretation on grounds that have nothing to do with esotericism, see Norbert Samuelson, "Maimonides' Doctrine of Creation," *Harvard Theological Review* 84 (1991): 249–71. Samuelson's article contains an excellent critique of recent work by Kaplan, Harvey, Davidson, and Fox. In a nutshell, Samuelson's view is that Maimonides

adopted a Platonic interpretation of creation not because it is what reason demands but because it is the most literal reading of scripture. In reply, note (1) Maimonides normally rejects literal interpretation, (2) the text of Genesis is so ambiguous that "literal" interpretation is all but impossible, and (3) Maimonides warns the reader not to try to resolve this issue by relying on the imagination. Finally, since matter and form have connotations of gender (male and female), the Platonic interpretation presupposes an analogy between the creation of the world and the creation of a living creature within it. This contradicts the whole tone of Maimonides' negative theology.

48. On the imprecision of Maimonides' terminology, see Sarah Klein-Braslavy, "Maimonides' Interpretation of the Verb *Bara* and the Problem of the Creation of the World," (Heb.) *Da'at* 16 (1986): 39–55. Klein-Braslavy interprets the looseness of Maimonides' language as evidence of a skeptical *epoche*. For a more traditional reading, see Harry Wolfson, "The Meaning of *Ex Nihilo* in the Church Fathers, Arabic and Hebrew Philosophy, and St. Thomas," in *Studies in the History of Philosophy and Religion*, ed. I. Twersky and G. H. Williams (Cambridge, Mass.: Harvard University Press, 1973), 207–221. Once again, Samuelson, "Maimonides' Doctrine," provides a helpful survey of the available options.

49. Davidson, "Maimonides' Secret Position," 36.

50. Julius Guttmann, *Philosophies of Judaism*, trans. D. W. Silverman (New York: Holt, Rinehart & Winston, 1973), 177.

51. *Guide* 1.57: 132–3.

52. *Guide* 1, Introduction, 6–7.

53. *Guide*, 6.

54. *Guide* 3, Introduction, 416.

55. *Guide* 1, Introduction, 7.

56. *Guide* 3.9: 436–7.

57. *Guide* 1.31: 67.

58. *Guide* 1, Introduction, 15.

59. *Guide* 1, Introduction, 16. Jewish law allows one to circumvent many of the commandments in exceptional circumstances. On this issue, see M. Berakhot, end.

60. Strauss, *Natural Right and History* (Chicago: University of Chicago Press, 1953), 74.

61. See, e.g., *Guide* 1.34: 75; 2.11: 276; 3.51: 54. For a sustained criticism of Strauss's attempt to separate Maimonides the philosopher from Maimonides the talmudic expositor, see David Hartman, *Maimonides: Torah and Philosophic Quest* (Philadelphia: Jewish Publication Society of America, 1976). Also see Joseph Buijs, "The Philosophical Character of Maimonides' *Guide*: A Critique of Strauss' Interpretation," in *Maimonides*, 59–70. For the compatibility of philosophy and Judaism in the "Parable of the Palace," see Menachem Kellner, *Maimonides on*

Human Perfection (Atlanta: Scholars Press, 1990), chap. 6. Note that philosophic understanding must come in addition to, not in replacement of, talmudic training. For scholars sympathetic with the Athens/Jerusalem split, see Raymond L. Weiss, *Maimonides' Ethics* (Chicago: University of Chicago Press, 1991) and Kenneth Green, *Jew and Philosopher: The Return to Maimonides in the Jewish Thought of Leo Strauss* (Albany, N.Y.: SUNY Press, 1993), esp. chap. 3.

62. Strauss, *Persecution*, 19.
63. Strauss, "Literary Character," 43.
64. *Guide* 3.54: 637–8.
65. *Guide* 1.32: 68–9.
66. I would like to thank Kenneth Green, R. Z. Friedman, Menachem Kellner, and Josef Stern for comments on earlier drafts of this chapter.

5

Leo Strauss and Jewish Modernity

Allan Arkush

Leo Strauss was much more concerned with premodern Judaism than with modern Judaism. He wrote far more about modernity in general than about Jewish modernity in particular. His relatively sparse writings on the impact of modernity on the Jews and Judaism are nevertheless of considerable signficance. They can teach us many things about the ways in which Jews have responded to the challenges posed by the dominant trends of the last two centuries and by the recent changes in their position in the world. They address some of the most important questions that we can ask ourselves today in a searching and profound manner.

Strauss's most illuminating discussion of what we are calling (but what he did not describe as) Jewish modernity is found in the preface he wrote in 1962 to the English translation of his first book, *Spinoza's Critique of Religion*. In this essay, he reflects from a distance of more than thirty years on the evolution of his thought during a critical period of his earlier intellectual development, a period when Jewish matters greatly preoccupied him. He shows us the path that once led him from political Zionism through a consideration of various other Jewish teachings to an awareness of the untenability of all modern attempts to solve the Jewish problem. This road brought him to a juncture where he faced two positive alternatives: the unqualified reaffirmation of orthodoxy or the exploration of the possibility of a return to premodern Jewish rationalism. We all know where he went from there.

Strauss's path was, it must be said, an unusual one. Many Jews estranged from tradition have in recent decades returned, to be sure, to orthodox Jewish faith, and some have even pursued a course somewhat similar to his and looked to Maimonides for guidance. A much greater number have continued to adhere to the theologies and ideologies rejected by Strauss more than half a century ago as altogether inadequate solutions to the Jewish problem. Of these, the large majority, in all likelihood, have never heard of Leo Strauss. Even among the few who can be presumed to have heard of him, only a very small number have felt the necessity to grapple with his views on Jewish modernity.

What I plan to do here is to retrace some of Strauss's steps along the road that led him to reject so many of the existing forms of modern Jewish thought. After doing this, I intend to examine certain aspects of the very limited reaction to Strauss's views on the part of some other Jewish thinkers who continue to adhere to the positions that he abandoned, and then to explore some of the reasons why this reaction has been so limited. I hope I will also be able to shed some additional light on the matters with regard to which Strauss and these other thinkers were not in accord.

A Jew in Germany in the 1920s

I suppose I ought to begin where Strauss himself begins in his preface to the English translation of his Spinoza book, with his account of the predicament in which he found himself when he was a student in Germany in the 1920s. I would like to go back a little further and at least make mention of Strauss's upbringing during the years prior to World War I in an orthodox Jewish home in a rural district of Germany. The absence of any reference to this period in the aforementioned preface was perhaps one of the things on Gershom Scholem's mind when he complained to Strauss that in this essay, "you seem to leap over several stages in your autobiography."[1] One can only regret, along with Scholem, that Strauss did not tell us more about his early youth; but does this omission really matter?

Scholem himself wrote a whole book about this stage of his own life. His autobiography, *From Berlin to Jerusalem*, includes an account of his rejection as an adolescent of the assimilationist outlook of his parents and his awakening to the attractions of Judaism. Scholem had good reason to produce such a book. Knowledge of his youthful feelings with regard to the Jewish religion definitely assists us in understanding the sources and even the nature of his mature thought. In the case of Strauss, on the other hand, one may plausibly argue, as Allan Bloom has done, that "There is nothing in his biography that explains his thought."[2]

Without disagreeing with Bloom, we might still attribute some significance to the fact that Strauss grew up in a pious milieu. If we do so, we may find it easier to understand his feelings, if not necessarily his ideas, about Judaism. Strauss's writings on the Jewish religion seem to reflect a profound awareness, an awareness nurtured by memories, of what it is to live in a relationship of loving obedience to the Lord of the Universe. It is hard not to suspect that an unacknowledged desire to reclaim this lost relationship lay behind his search for an intellectually viable form of Judaism. In the absence of any direct encouragement from Strauss, however, we cannot make too much of this.[3]

The Theologico-Political Problem

The first thing that Strauss himself tells us in the preface to the Spinoza book is that the ensuing volume was written in the mid-1920s by "a young Jew born and raised in Germany who found himself in the grip of the theologico-political problem."[4] In elucidating the nature of this problem, as it appeared to him both at the time he wrote the book and, it seems, more than three decades later, Strauss highlights the failure of liberalism to take root in the Weimar Republic. Illiberal forces, which regarded the Jews as inadmissable aliens, remained powerful in post-World War I Germany and were evidently destined to obtain control of it. In the eyes of the people who would ultimately have the power to decide such things, Jews were not, and could not become, Germans.

Facing such hostility, the Jews of Germany could continue to insist that "they were no less German than the Germans of the Christian faith or of no faith," or they could choose the more honorable course of spurning those who had rejected them and turning to Zionism. The latter alternative was the choice, as Strauss reminds us, of only "a small minority of German Jews," albeit "a considerable minority of German-Jewish youth studying at the universities."[5] Strauss, it seems, implicitly criticized the majority of German Jews for failing to understand the true nature of their situation or for neglecting to take steps to regain their lost honor, but he did not explicitly condemn them for these things. By 1962, he seems to have felt it was too late for such recriminations.

Strauss himself belonged to the minority of German Jews that accepted Zionism. In the preface, he sketches the underlying principles of the political Zionism to which he was once attracted, distinguishing it carefully from the Jewish messianic tradition upon which it drew. In the course of doing so he restates with apparent approval the political Zionist critique of liberalism. Pinsker and Herzl, Strauss observes, "started from the failure of the liberal solution" to the Jewish problem. What this failure meant to the initiators of political Zionism was, in Strauss's words, "that Jews could not regain their honor by assimilating as individuals to the nations among which they lived or by becoming citizens like all other citizens of the liberal states: the liberal solution brought at best legal equality, but not social equality; as a demand of reason it had no effect on the feelings of non-Jews." Strauss does not observe that, in the opinion of the founders of political Zionism, these feelings would *always* be hostile and threatening and that anti-Semitism was a virtually ineradicable menace. What he does make completely clear is the solution these men proposed to the Jewish problem: the restoration of the Jews' "honor through the acquisition of statehood and therefore of a country."[6]

Strauss goes a long way toward endorsing the ideology of political Zionism. He speaks of "the truth proclaimed by Zionism regarding the limitations of liberalism."[7] He acclaims Zionism's crowning achievement, the establishment of the State of Israel, as "a blessing for all Jews everywhere regardless of whether they admit it or not."[8] There are, however, significant differences between the classical Zionist analysis of the Jewish problem and the views espoused here by Strauss. While Strauss agrees with these Zionists that liberalism cannot solve the Jewish problem and approves of the alternative they supply, he does not reiterate their contention that the anti-Jewish feelings of non-Jews will always and everywhere (even in the best liberal democracies) be so severe as to require all Jews, or nearly all Jews, to turn to Zionism in order to recover their dignity, honor, and pride. Nor does he believe that political Zionism provides an adequate solution to what he calls the Jewish problem.

Strauss recalls the failure of liberalism in Germany in the 1920s and identifies the changes it portended for German Jews. He attributes this failure not to the intrinsic fragility of liberalism or to the innate unassimilability of the Jews but, at bottom, to the particular heritage of the German people, which was deeply inimical to liberal ideas. Even so, liberalism had a real chance to succeed in Germany following World War I. Strauss writes that in the aftermath of Germany's defeat, "liberal democracy had become ever more attractive." What caused it to fail was, in a manner of speaking, an accident: "at the crucial moment the victorious liberal democracies discredited liberal democracy in the eyes of Germany by the betrayal of their principles through the Treaty of Versailles."[9]

History might have proceeded differently. If the victors in World War I had conducted themselves in a wiser and more principled fashion, liberalism might really have taken root in Germany in the 1920s, and at least one young Jew born and raised there might not have found himself so inescapably locked in the grip of the theologico-political problem that he felt compelled to become a Zionist. Unless I am mistaken, nothing in Strauss's writings indicates a belief that the liberal democracy of which he was a citizen when he wrote the preface was one in which the situation of the Jews was so unsatisfactory as to necessitate a turn to Zionism.[10] It is possible that he believed that the establishment of the State of Israel in 1948 had made a decisive difference, that this achievement had restored the honor not only of those Jews who became its citizens but of all other Jews as well. This, indeed, seems to be what he meant when he wrote that Israel constituted a "blessing for all Jews everywhere regardless of whether they admit it or not." Still, it does not seem to me that in 1962 he would have gone so far as to say that if a Jewish state were not already in existence, it would be incumbent upon self-respecting American Jews to attempt to create one.

It is in any case clear enough that Strauss, while sympathetic to political Zionism, was convinced of its basic inadequacy. It could not, he said, solve the Jewish problem. When he made this statement, however, he was using the term "Jewish problem" somewhat idiosyncratically. Normally it refers to the problem the Jews confront in securing their existence in this world. Strauss employs it to refer, in addition, to the problem that they face in interpreting the significance of being Jewish. He uses it, in other words, to encompass what Ahad Ha'Am, the founder of cultural Zionism, identified as two distinct problems: (1) the problem of the Jews and (2) the problem of Judaism. However successful political Zionism may be in addressing the first of these two facets of what Strauss calls the Jewish problem, it was, in his opinion, incapable of addressing the latter.

The first reference in the preface to *Spinoza's Critique of Religion* to the spiritual difficulties faced by modern Jews pertains to the Jews of Germany alone. As Strauss puts it, they "opened themselves to the influx of German thought, the thought of the particular nation in the midst of which they lived—a thought which was understood to be German essentially: political dependence was also spiritual dependence. This was the core of the predicament of German Jewry."[11]

When Strauss discusses, a little while later, the incapacity of political Zionism to provide a solution to the spiritual problem of the Jews, he does not allude again to this dimension of the German Jewish problem. Nevertheless, even though he is speaking at this point of Jews in general, he seems to have in mind primarily the situation of the Jews of Germany, even those of them who were drawn to the Zionist movement. For these people, shaped as they had been by German thought, political Zionism was too narrowly conceived. "This narrowness," he writes, "was pointed out most effectively by cultural Zionism." Its spokesmen charged that political Zionism "lacks historical perspective," and fails to build "a community of the mind." The Jewish state it aims to create "will be an empty shell without a Jewish culture which has its roots in the Jewish heritage." The founders of cultural Zionism were not German Jews, but they clearly addressed a need that German Zionists, who were becoming detached from their German roots, felt with particular urgency.

They addressed it, but they could not, at least as far as Strauss was concerned, even begin to satisfy it. He dismisses the ideology of cultural Zionism in only a few sentences. It is based, he writes, on a previous interpretation

of the Jewish heritage itself as a culture, that is, as a product of the national mind, of the national genius. Yet the foundation, the authoritative layer, of the Jewish heritage presents itself, not as a product of the human mind, but as a divine gift, as divine revelation. Did one not completely distort the meaning of the heritage to which one claimed to be loyal by interpreting it as a culture like any other high culture?

Cultural Zionism is, in Strauss's opinion, an incoherent doctrine. When it "understands itself, it turns into religious Zionism. But when religious Zionism understands itself, it is in the first place Jewish faith and only secondarily Zionism."[12]

What would the founder of cultural Zionism have said in response to this? As someone whose maternal grandfather came from the same Ukrainian town as Ahad Ha'Am (Skvira) and was slightly acquainted with him, I believe I can say with some confidence (if not necessarily any authority) that Strauss's remarks here would by no means have sufficed to persuade him that he was misguided. Strauss does not, after all, present a comprehensive refutation of Ahad Ha'Am's doctrine of a distinctive Jewish national mind that had produced, over the centuries, a culture that authentic Jews ought to preserve. And while Ahad Ha'Am himself was certainly aware that his teaching involved a radical reorientation with regard to traditional Judaism, he was nonetheless prepared to argue that it amounted not to a distortion of Jewish tradition but to a revision of it, one that would enable it to survive with its moral essence intact in a world increasingly devoid of faith in God.

What Strauss says in the preface concerning cultural Zionism does not, then, dispose of it as a viable alternative, but neither does it reveal the ultimate basis of his rejection of it. In *Natural Right and History*, he articulates his fundamental views on pertinent matters much more fully. "The historical school," he writes, "assumed the existence of folk minds, that is, it assumed that nations or ethnic groups are natural units, or it assumed the existence of general laws of historical evolution, or it combined both assumptions." What the historical school has obscured is "the fact that particular or historical standards can become authoritative only on the basis of a universal principle which imposes an obligation on the individual to accept, or to bow to, the standards suggested by the tradition or the situation which has molded him." Since "no universal principle will ever sanction the acceptance of every historical standard . . . all standards suggested by history as such proved to be fundamentally ambiguous and therefore unfit to be considered standards."[13] One need only contrast this strong affirmation of an individual's prerogative to discard his or her own past with Ahad Ha'Am's essay "The Spiritual Revival" in order to get a notion of how far apart the two men stood.[14]

When cultural Zionism really "understands itself," Strauss writes, "it turns into religious Zionism." Why, we may ask, does this have to happen? Why can't it turn back into political Zionism? The weakness of political Zionism lay in its lack of "an historical perspective," but if such perspectives are in the final analysis dispensable, political Zionism may be a satisfactory position after all, and not merely an empty shell. If it is an empty shell, it is one that might perhaps be best filled through recourse not to the supposed products of the Jewish national mind but to an acceptable universal standard. Political Zionism might then provide something close to a complete answer to both aspects of the Jewish problem as Strauss has delineated it, that is, the modern Jews' vulnerability to Gentile enmity and their loss of spiritual moorings.

This, however, is not the direction that Strauss's ruminations take. He relates, instead, how the collapse of cultural Zionism into religious Zionism, or, at bottom, into Jewish faith, induces the "Jewish individual who or whose parents severed his connection with the Jewish community" and who is disenchanted by the failure of liberalism to consider once again the possibility of *teshuvah*, a return to Judaism.[15] The Judaism to which such a person first turns her attention consists, in the nature of things, of those new interpretations of the Jewish religion that purport to have confronted and overcome the challenges posed by modernity.

Philosophy and Law

Strauss's first summation of his understanding of these newer versions of Judaism is found in his book *Philosophy and Law*, first published in 1935. He subsequently dealt with them in the preface to *Spinoza's Critique of Religion* and in a number of other short pieces. On all of these occasions, he characterized the different versions of modern Judaism as constituting, in essence, unsuccessful attempts to develop a synthesis of Orthodoxy and the Enlightenment. All of them, he maintained, sacrificed indispensable elements of Jewish tradition in order to arrive at untenable compromises with modern thought. This was true of the representatives of the "old [rationalist] thinking" and, to a lesser but still decisive degree, of the initiators of the "new [existentialist] thinking" as well.

The rationalists operate on the assumption that it is impossible to prove, and therefore impossible to affirm, what Strauss never ceased to regard as the basis of the Jewish tradition: "belief in the creation of the world, in the reality of biblical miracles, in the absolute obligation and the essential immutability of the Law as based on the revelation at Sinai." These thinkers, of whom Hermann Cohen is the greatest representative, may continue to speak of creation, miracle, and revelation, but they no longer understand these terms literally. They have "internalized" them, in ways that rob them of their meaning.[16] Their Judaism is one in which, in Strauss's words, "the content of revelation is seen to be rational, which does not necessarily mean that everything hitherto thought to be revealed is rational."[17] What it means, in fact, is that everything in the tradition that they do not consider rational is utterly dispensable.

Strauss repudiates this method of "internalization." He says, for example, that "if God did not create the world in an 'external' sense, if He did not really create it, if Creation thus cannot be maintained even in its theoretical content as simply true, as the fact of Creation, then, for the sake of probity, one must deny the Creation or at least avoid talking about it." Those who employ internalizations of the kind he deplores do so, according to Strauss, because they are "wholly under the spell of the way of thought created by the Enlightenment and fortified by its successors or opponents."[18] They may think that what they are doing amounts to a remaking of the tradition, but what they are really doing is repudiating it.

The representatives of the "new thinking" are not similarly guilty of rejecting at the very outset the basic premises of Jewish tradition. Their point of departure is, instead, their own experience of, in Strauss's words, "something undesired, coming from the outside, going against man's grain."[19] They are moved by the awareness of something absolute, "the experience of God as the Thou, the father and king of all men."[20]

This is an experience that Strauss treats respectfully, but it is also one that he is wary of misconstruing. He writes:

The very emphasis on the absolute experience as experience compels one to demand that it be made as clear as possible what the experience by itself conveys, that it not be tampered with, that it be carefully distinguished from every interpretation of the experience, for the interpretations may be suspected of being attempts to render bearable and harmless the experience which admittedly comes from without down upon man and is undesired.[21]

The interpretations placed upon the absolute experience by the principal representatives of this Jewish "new thinking," Martin Buber and Franz Rosenzweig, are quite dubious, as far as Strauss is concerned. He dismisses Buber as someone who has reduced everything "the Biblical authors say" (even when they are reporting God's own words) to nothing more than a "human expression of God's speechless call."[22] The failure of Rosenzweig Strauss sees mainly as the result of his inconsistent application of his own principles. Despite his rejection of the "old thinking," he allows rationalist scruples to interfere with his response to the absolute experience and to bar him from accepting without hesitation what his ancestors had once accepted, namely, the reality of biblical miracles and the absolutely obligatory character and essential immutability of the law as based on the revelation at Sinai. While they may continue to speak of creation, miracles, and revelation, Buber and Rosenzweig are, in the end, just about as thoroughly mired in "internalization" as are the rationalists.

Thus, the Jew seeking to do *teshuvah* can obtain no guidance from the thought of the most celebrated Jewish thinkers of recent generations. These thinkers have all stopped short of affirming the unalterable basis of Jewish tradition. They have been deterred from doing so by their firm or lingering allegiance to ideas rooted in the Enlightenment, ideas that cannot be blended with Judaism without turning it into something new and fundamentally different. The inquirer who finds their thought unsatisfactory may still feel impelled to wonder, however, "whether an unqualified return to Jewish orthodoxy was not both possible and necessary." Such a return could only be achieved, the young Strauss determined, if it would prove possible to refute decisively the thinker who had issued, centuries earlier, the greatest challenge to orthodox Judaism: Spinoza.[23] With a view to answering this question, Strauss undertook his study of Spinoza's writings.

After completing this study, Strauss reached the conclusion that Spinoza had achieved a great deal. He *had* demolished orthodoxy's claim to *know* the truth of its basic doctrines. Even so, however, he did not destroy the possibility of a full return to Jewish orthodoxy. He had not succeeded in *disproving* the fundamental premise of orthodoxy, that is, the existence of a mysterious, omnipotent God. In spite of Spinoza, then, one could return to orthodoxy, but only if one was prepared to believe, to accept on faith, what one could not know for sure. This is something Strauss himself was not prepared to do. He sought, instead, to determine whether a solid foundation for what he called an "enlightened Judaism," that is, a rationally supportable Judaism, could be found in the thought of Maimonides. But now, we must continue to focus our attention on Strauss's understanding of Jewish modernity.

Non-Orthodox Responses to Strauss's Critique

What we must consider next is the nature of the Jewish response to Strauss's critique of the various types of modern Jewish thought. How have political Zionists, cultural Zionists, modern Orthodox Jews, and other Jewish modernists reacted to what Strauss had to say about them? To what extent have they felt compelled to contend with the difficulties with which he has confronted them?

It would be futile, I think, to search among the spokesmen of political Zionism for evidence of any response on their part to Strauss's reiteration of the cultural Zionist argument that their movement risks becoming "an empty shell" unless it retains close links to Jewish tradition. Figures much closer to their own ideological home than Strauss have repeatedly and insistently voiced such warnings. In responding to them, the political Zionists have not needed to pay any particular attention to Strauss's formulation of what are to them very familiar difficulties.

Strauss, as we have seen, not only echoed the cultural Zionists but subjected them to criticism as well. But in this camp, too, it would make little sense to search for a response to his arguments. If cultural Zionism exists at all today, it is less as a coherent ideology than as a mood or a program for action. There are people who attempt to follow in Ahad Ha'Am's footsteps, but there is virtually no one seeking to perpetuate his teachings concerning the innate identity of the Jewish people. Strauss's critique of the ideological basis of cultural Zionism has consequently evoked no perceptible opposition.

In fact, the only real response to Strauss's view of Jewish modernity is to be found among those Jewish scholars and thinkers who are more or less the heirs of Hermann Cohen, Martin Buber, and Franz Rosenzweig. Even among people who share this general orientation, concern with Strauss has been very limited, but it has not been insignificant. Perhaps the best place to begin a consideration of the views of thinkers of this stripe would be with what is, to the best of my knowledge, the most recent work on Strauss to appear in print in Israel, an article written by Ehud Luz, a professor of Jewish thought at the University of Haifa, entitled "Leo Strauss's Judaism."

Luz analyzes and criticizes, among other things, Strauss's treatment of Cohen, Buber, and Rosenzweig. In his view, Strauss has erred in denying the legitimacy of these thinkers' attempts to reinterpret Judaism. His mistake results chiefly, Luz says, from his misguided reaction to what he perceived to be the dangers inherent in historicism. Fearful of the anarchic consequences of all efforts to relativize the significance of ancient texts, Strauss insisted that the only way to approach such writings was to seek to understand them *not* better than their original authors understood them but *just as* they understood them. In our attempt to comprehend the Jewish tradition, Strauss felt that we "are obligated to speak its language and not to force upon it concepts which are foreign to it."[24]

Yet this is precisely what he considered Cohen, Buber, and Rosenzweig guilty of doing. They fully accepted the historical-critical approach to the Bible but this did not prevent them from attempting to compose a kind of modern *midrash* on it. Strauss's criticisms of these thinkers raise, according to Luz, the question of "whether abandonment of a 'naive' approach to the biblical texts necessarily eliminates the possibility of relating to them as holy scriptures. Is it possible, even after Spinoza, to create a modern *midrash*?"[25] This, Luz says, "is the great theological problem of our generation. The response to the challenge posed by Strauss depends on the solution of it."[26]

Luz himself solves this problem by arguing that the creation of such a modern *midrash* is indeed possible. "Historicism," he maintains, "does not obligate us to argue that we understand the past better than it understood itself. It only obligates us to recognize that we are part of a process of development which perpetually advances toward the future on the basis of a previously formulated outlook."[27] The need for a new *midrash* arises, Luz writes, as a result of

the contradiction between the transcendent character of the sources and the historical world in which we live. It is this need that gives birth to a new method, one which enables the believing thinker, who regards himself as obligated by the sources, to uncover within the sources themselves a truth relevant to his era. Because this *midrash* is based on faith, it aspires to overcome historicism, and does not call for an absolute relativization of the sources.[28]

Believing thinkers, Luz says, contribute to the ongoing development of the *Torah she-be-al-peh*, the "oral Torah," a process whose significance Strauss fails to appreciate. They operate on the assumption that, as the nineteenth-century Jewish thinker Nachman Krochmal put it, "He who at the outset established all of the generations alters, in his goodness, the modes of understanding and research in each and every age."[29] In this interaction with the traditional texts, they may even have recourse to philosophy as a tool of interpretation, as did Cohen, Buber, and Rosenzweig.[30]

What can one say in response to all of this? Is it correct to characterize Strauss as someone whose fear of anarchism led him to an excessively rigid delimitation of the bounds of legitimate interpretation of sacred texts? Did Strauss needlessly exclude the possibility of a new kind of "oral Torah," one that would give Judaism the ability to update itself, and did he for this reason fail to appreciate the true merits of the greatest religious thinkers produced by German Jewry?

I do not find it possible to answer these questions affirmatively, along with Luz. His basic mistake, I believe, is to place too much emphasis on Strauss's objections to the hermeneutical methods of the modern Jewish thinkers he criticizes. What was unacceptable to Strauss was not primarily the procedures employed by these men in their interpretation of traditional texts but the essential content of their thought. They may have believed that they had not abandoned any part of the substance of the Jewish faith, but, in his opinion, they had indeed done so. Not one of them continued to uphold unreservedly a belief in the creation of the world, in the reality of biblical miracles, and in the absolute obligation and the essential immutability of the law as based on the revelation at Sinai. These things constituted, as far as Strauss was concerned, the very foundation of the Jewish tradition. He could therefore not acknowledge the legitimacy of an "oral Torah" that negated or circumvented them, as did the teachings of Cohen, Buber, and Rosenzweig.

The real challenge posed by Strauss, then, is not to determine whether a modern *midrash* is possible but whether he is correct in his identification of the indispensable foundations of the Jewish religion. Most contemporary non-Orthodox Jewish thinkers are unutterably remote from sharing any such notion and are therefore disinclined to pay much heed to Strauss's thoughts on modern Judaism. This is true, I think, of everyone except Emil Fackenheim.

Fackenheim first became acquainted with Strauss's Jewish writings in the 1930s, during his days as a student in Berlin. In 1987 he remarked that they impressed him greatly when he first encountered them and that they still impressed him.[31] A number of Fackenheim's writings include some almost reverential references to Strauss. He has dedicated what he calls his own "major and definitive work in the field of Jewish thought" to the memory of Leo Strauss.[32]

What I have noted so far are merely some of the outward signs of a deep, spiritual kinship. Of greater importance is the evidence of a strong intellectual affinity to Strauss that one finds in Fackenheim's work. His overall understanding of the problematic character of modern Jewish existence bears many resemblances to that of Strauss. There is evidence for this throughout his writings, especially in the attention he gives to the profound gulf separating believing from nonbelieving Jews, in his recognition of the importance of Spinoza, and in his critique of liberal Judaism. He himself seems to feel, strangely enough, that he is basically in accord with Strauss when he maintains that Rosenzweig's "new Jewish thinking" is "in decisive respects destined to remain ours."[33]

What Fackenheim means by this is, above all, that modern Jews must take their bearings from "present experience" of the divine incursion into this world. The principal problem with Rosenzweig, however, from Fackenheim's point of view, is his contention "that not until the Messianic age could anything happen that would affect the Jewish faith."[34] Fackenheim himself, as everyone knows, is very much of the opposite opinion.

Fackenheim's student, Michael Morgan, also criticizes Strauss for failing to give appropriate consideration to recent Jewish history in *his* Jewish thought. Strauss, he says, wrote his preface to *Spinoza's Critique of Religion* "in the early 1960s, in a Jewish world defined by the twin realities of Auschwitz and the rebirth of the Jewish state. Yet neither of these events seems to influence how he, in the 1960s, views the theologico-political predicament which 'gripped' him in the waning days of Weimar. There is, however, good reason to think that they should have."[35] Even though he refrains from giving voice to it, we must presume that Fackenheim himself shares this opinion.[36] We ought to note, finally, one other difference between Strauss and Fackenheim. While Strauss regards the gulf between Orthodoxy and secularism as an impassable one, Fackenheim sees it as one that may someday be bridged—especially in Israel. He commends such groups as *Gesher*, which devotes itself to accomplishing this task. These groups are, he writes, "the hope of the Israeli and indeed the whole Jewish future." His purpose in writing *To Mend the World*, the book he regards as his own definitive work in the area of Jewish thought, and which he has dedicated to the memory of Strauss, is, he says, to supply "the theoretical basis of the *Gesher*-practice."[37] In order to do so, to mediate the conflict between religious and secular Jews in the Jewish state, Fackenheim does what Strauss does not do; he takes what he calls a "plunge into history."[38] Where he lands, or whether he lands at all, are not questions with which we need to concern ourselves at the moment.

Orthodox Responses to Strauss's Critique

Having completed our survey of some of the non-Orthodox Jewish responses to Leo Strauss's thoughts on Jewish modernity, we must now turn our attention to the world of Orthodox Jewry. By Orthodox Jews, I really mean the modern Orthodox, that is, those who participate in the modern world enough to be aware of and concerned with the ideas that are circulating among people besides themselves. While Orthodox Jews of this stripe are perhaps no less certain of the validity of their fundamental principles than the separatist, ultra-Orthodox Jews to their ideological right, many of them have, it seems to me, a desire to obtain some measure of recognition from the secularist camp. This they do receive from Leo Strauss. Strauss's announcement that Orthodoxy stands unrefuted and his declaration of the bankruptcy of all non-Orthodox modern forms of Judaism would seem, in fact, to be music to their ears. To the best of my knowledge, however, no prominent representative of modern Orthodox Judaism has taken any special delight in what Strauss has said or made a practice of adducing him as a witness against modern interpretations of Judaism that differ from his own.

Part of the explanation for this situation lies no doubt in the notoriety that Strauss has acquired, in some Orthodox quarters, on account of his unpalatable views concerning the secret teaching of Maimonides. Part of it lies, perhaps, in the fact that he is not well known, even in academic circles. He has never been, and in all likelihood will never be, so well known as to be of obvious use in the way that I have been suggesting. Still, one can imagine that things might have developed differently. If, say, cultural Zionism and liberal versions of Judaism were now proceeding from strength to strength, and if modern Orthodoxy were constantly losing ground to such forces, then Orthodox apologists might now be feeling the need to seek out Leo Strauss as an ally. But this is not the way things are. It is not on its left but on its right that modern Orthodoxy currently faces a serious challenge; and in meeting this challenge, Leo Strauss cannot offer it any useful assistance.

It should not be forgotten, finally, that Strauss constitutes, besides a possible source of support, something of a challenge to modern Orthodoxy. Even when he comes closest to affiliating himself with Orthodoxy he indicates his wariness of any "unenlightened" Orthodoxy. He points to the need for rational confirmation of the grounds of religious belief, the kind of confirmation that modern Orthodox thinkers, no less than contemporary non-Orthodox thinkers, have by and large come to regard as unattainable. And who wants to listen to a man who insists on the need to locate something that you do not believe can be—or even needs to be—found? It is, therefore, not surprising that modern Orthodox thinkers have paid scant attention to what Leo Strauss has had to say about Jewish modernity.

Strauss and Jewish Post-Modernism

Mostly heedless, then, of what Strauss thought and wrote about them, the various camps through which he himself passed more than half a century ago continue to perpetuate themselves. But something new has appeared on the scene, something that Strauss vaguely anticipated as early as 1935. In one of the last paragraphs of his introduction to *Philosophy and Law*, he succinctly restated his basic position: "If in the end there are only the alternatives of Orthodoxy or atheism, and if, correspondingly, the desirability of an enlightened Judaism cannot be rejected, then one is forced to question whether enlightenment must necessarily be modern enlightenment."[39] We are obliged to turn for help to the medieval

Enlightenment, "unless we can know in advance what cannot be known in advance, namely, that only new, unheard of, ultramodern thoughts can help us out of our predicament." Since Strauss wrote these words, postmodern thinkers, thinking such "ultramodern thoughts," have indeed arisen and seem to promise some sort of help. A number of them have discovered Leo Strauss's writings on Judaism and have some things to say about them. But these are matters that are beyond my competence to discuss, and— fortunately—beyond the boundaries of my assignment as well.

Notes

1. Quoted in Kenneth Hart Green, *Jew and Philosopher: The Return to Maimonides in the Jewish Thought of Leo Strauss* (Albany, N.Y.: SUNY Press, 1993), 148.
2. Allan Bloom, *Giants and Dwarfs* (New York: Simon & Schuster, 1990), 236.
3. Strauss not only fails to encourage such notions, he actively discourages them. In "A Giving of Accounts" (with Jacob Klein), *St. John's Review* 22 (1970), he very briefly reminisces about his upbringing in a strictly observant home. He then proceeds to describe how, as an adolescent, he furtively read Schopenhauer and how "without being aware of it, I had moved rather far away from my Jewish home, without any rebellion" (p. 2). This is, to the best of my knowledge, his lengthiest public statement with regard to his youthful loss of faith. It seems somewhat less than candid. One has difficulty imagining Strauss, of all people, sliding away from religious observance in an unthinking manner.

It should be noted that these remarks occur in the context of a statement where Strauss expresses strong reservations about making personal revelations of any kind. "Is it proper," he asks, "for people to talk about themselves in public? The general answer is: no" (ibid.). He proceeds to ask, "Why then speak of one's life at all?" To this question he provides the following answer: "Because the considerations at which I arrived are not necessarily true or correct; my life may explain my pitfalls" (ibid.). Perhaps he did not think that a more detailed discussion of his loss of religious faith would serve any such purpose.
4. Leo Strauss, *Spinoza's Critique of Religion*, trans. E. M. Sinclair (New York: Schocken Books, 1965), 1.
5. Ibid., 4.
6. Ibid., 5.
7. Ibid., 6.
8. Ibid., 5.

9. Ibid., 2.

10. Michael Morgan speaks of Strauss's a priori argument for the "homelessness of the modern Jew in liberal democracies" in his *Dilemmas in Modern Jewish Thought* (Bloomington, Ind.: Indiana University Press, 1992), 42. This, I think, constitutes an overstatement. Strauss himself, at any rate, felt sufficiently at home in the United States in 1950 to decline Martin Buber's offer to sponsor his appointment (as his successor) as professor of social philosophy and general sociology at the Hebrew University (Cf. *The Letters of Martin Buber: A Life of Dialogue*, ed. Nahum N. Glatzer and Paul Mendes-Flohr, trans. Richard Winston, Clara Winston, and Harry Zohn [New York: Schocken Books, 1991], 548).

11. *Spinoza's Critique of Religion*, 3.

12. Ibid., 5–6.

13. *Natural Right and History* (Chicago: University of Chicago Press, 1953), 17–18.

14. Ahad Ha'Am, *Selected Essays*, trans. Leon Simon (Philadelphia: The Jewish Publication Society of America, 1912), 265ff.

15. *Spinoza's Critique of Religion*, 7.

16. *Philosophy and Law: Essays toward an Understanding of Maimonides and his Predecessors*, trans. F. Baumann (Philadelphia: Jewish Publication Society of America, 1987), 5.

17. *Spinoza's Critique of Religion*, 8.

18. *Philosophy and Law*, 6.

19. *Spinoza's Critique of Religion*, 8.

20. Ibid.

21. Ibid., 11–12.

22. *Spinoza's Critique of Religion*, 11.

23. Unlike a considerable number of modern Jewish writers who have regretted Spinoza's excommunication, Strauss never sought to welcome him back into the Jewish fold, symbolically, by restoring to him his original first name, Baruch. But neither did he make a habit of resorting to the name chosen by Spinoza himself following his departure from the Jewish community, Benedict. It is interesting to note, however, that on the one occasion when he needed to make a choice between Spinoza's two first names (i.e., in the title of the chapter on Spinoza, written by Stanley Rosen, in the *History of Political Philosophy*, which Strauss coedited with Joseph Cropsey), he apparently consented to the use of Benedict. (See p. 43.)

24. Ehud Luz, "Yahaduto shel Leo Strauss," *Da'at* 27 (1991): 57–58.

25. Ibid., 57.

26. Ibid.

27. Ibid., 58.

28. Ibid.

29. Ibid., 59.

30. Ibid.
31. *What Is Judaism?* (New York: Summit Books, 1987), 26.
32. Ibid., 306.
33. *To Mend the World* (New York: Schocken Books, 1982), 92. Strauss, Fackenheim notes, has offered

the most searching account of Rosenzweig's shift from the "old" to the "new" thinking. He has also argued powerfully for a return, after and despite Rosenzweig's new thinking, to the old, i.e., to the authoritativeness of the Torah. Yet in an unpublished lecture given just prior to his death, Strauss not only argued for the irrefutability and moral nobility of traditional Orthodoxy (in its Mizrachi-Zionist form) but also admitted his inability to regard it as more than a noble illusion. Thus the most powerful Jewish philosopher since Rosenzweig came to testify that the new thinking is intellectually inescapable. (Ibid., 89)

Fackenheim does not specifically identify the lecture in question, but both the content of his comment and his reference to a further comment (on p. 264) seem to indicate that he has in mind Strauss's lecture on 4 February 1962 at the University of Chicago, entitled "Why We Remain Jews: Can Jewish Faith and History Still Speak to Us?" (where he does speak of Judaism as a noble illusion). If so, it is rather difficult to understand why he would describe it as a lecture Strauss gave "just prior to his death" (He died, after all, in 1973). The lecture is, in fact, contemporaneous with the "searching account" (in the preface to *Spinoza's Critique of Religion*) beyond which Fackenheim seems to regard it as constituting some kind of advance. In any case, whichever came first, the preface or the lecture, the view expressed in the lecture that orthodoxy is, in the end, but a "noble illusion" is fully compatible with the argument in the preface for the superiority of the "old" to the "new" thinking. There is, therefore, no reason to conclude from anything Strauss says in the lecture that he arrived at the conclusion that the new thinking is inescapable.

Fackenheim stands on firmer but rather different ground when he maintains that Strauss may have considered his return to the "old" thinking of Plato and Aristotle to be itself an act of "new" thinking, since it was rooted in an "ultimately unarguable commitment" (*To Mend the World*, 264). But even if this is the case, it shows Strauss to be infinitely remote from Rosenzweig's brand of "new thinking."
34. Ibid., 64.
35. Morgan, *Dilemmas in Modern Jewish Thought*, 50.
36. Fackenheim does credit Strauss (*To Mend the World*, 262–63) with having pondered deeply "the Hitler regime and all its works," but he notes that he wrote about such subjects with "characteristic prudence and restraint," confining himself "at least in print, to a few terse statements."

From Fackenheim's point of view, it would seem, Strauss's restraint was at the very least questionable.

37. *To Mend the World*, 146.
38. Ibid., 101.
39. *Philosophy and Law*, 19.

6

Leo Strauss and the Fourth Wave of Modernity

Frederick G. Lawrence

Leo Strauss articulated the "crisis of Western culture" to motivate serious men and women to radical "return"—either a return with all its religious connotations or a return to the classical or premodern rationalism of Platonic political philosophy.[1] For Strauss as a Jew, religious return was, as I understand, an open option not taken. But the need for return to standards of human achievement—as enacted by the premodern rationalism of Moses Maimonides—was not in question. The novelty and radicality of that return rested on the pivotal realization that the modern liberal horizon set by modern rationalism, with its potentiality or even tendency toward self-destruction of any human or reasonable standard, had to be surmounted. Strauss taught that the critique of the present was "the necessary beginning, the constant accompaniment, and the unmistakable characteristic of the quest for truth that is possible in our time."[2]

Strauss had the benefit of the phenomenological movement's revolt from the neo-Kantianism then dominant in the German academy and of Husserl's and Heidegger's fulfillment of the slogan, "Back to the things themselves!"[3] This return made possible Husserl's and Heidegger's analyses of the phenomenon of "horizon." In their own distinctive ways, each demonstrated that it is one thing to consider a possible range of diverse objects within an already established horizon, and quite another to envisage thematically or to transcend that horizon. The reversal of obnubilation and the

131

transcendence of horizon epitomizes what is meant by the truly radical. Strauss, in setting forth the *status quaestionis* regarding the possibility of a return to Jewish Orthodoxy, as well as the reasonable grounds for deciding against such a return in favor of the philosopher's way of life (as itself keeping alive the awareness of the alternative solutions to the concrete problem of living), presupposes such radicality.

Both Heidegger and Strauss pushed the movement "back to the things themselves" and to the foundations. Heidegger as a former Catholic and Strauss as a Jew were each haunted by Nietzsche's posing of the God question. Recently Hans-Georg Gadamer has written to me that Heidegger often said in his last years that "Nietzsche has finished me." This statement has all the ambiguity which Heidegger invested in such incantations as "Only a god can save us!" Even so, I cannot help wondering if something like the same utterance could have been meant, if never literally spoken, by Leo Strauss. Isn't this at least suggested by his own account of being concerned, from his earliest days, with two questions—God and politics—if we put them together with what he openly admitted to Karl Löwith about Nietzsche's sway over him during his most formative years?[4]

Strauss's radicality, in contrast to both Husserl and Gadamer, is shown again in his construal of the "things themselves" in phenomenology's slogan. Actions (*pragma*) in Strauss's view can be handled adequately neither in terms of mere objects of perception, such as mail boxes and gateposts favored by Husserl, nor in terms of such objects of sheerly instrumental or technical concern, as dominate Heidegger's analysis of what is "beforehand" (*Vorhandenheit*) in *Being and Time*.[5] For Strauss the *pragmata* are objects of practical and political concern. So Aristotle's that-for-the-sake-of-which everything else is chosen and done or the Gospel of Luke's necessary being (*unum necessarium*) is at stake in the theological-political problematic. In a manner that was made possible by Heidegger, Strauss, as a Jew in Weimar Germany, becomes more radical than even Heidegger. In the end one wonders if Heidegger ultimately lacked such proximate models of authentic religious life as Strauss found in his fellow Jews Hermann Cohen and Franz Rosenzweig in spite of the fact that Strauss discovered their rationales of return were insufficiently radical because their thought was still too conditioned by the modern liberal horizon. I find it significant that Strauss's wonderful story of clarification by contrast in which Heidegger revealed Max Weber to be an orphan child, was confided first to Rosenzweig, who was clearly judged to be a kindred spirit.[6]

Strauss's return to Maimonides embodies all his radical emphases: the role of the esoteric, the guidance provided by the Arabic predecessors, the importance of Plato's *Laws* for the interpretation of prophecy, the centrality of law in Judaism and Islam, the model of the philosophers (*falasifa*), and the rigorous separation of reason and faith, philosophy and theology, nature and nature, Athens and Jerusalem.[7] The radicalism built into premodern rationalism turns the "Maybe it's true" punch line of Martin Buber's Hasidic tale about the holy rabbi and the notorious skeptic into a defense of Orthodoxy against modern rationalism, as well as of the philosopher's decision not to return to Orthodoxy.

Strauss's radicality therefore outstrips that of the "orphan-child" Weber who was, by his own admission, religiously tone-deaf; but it also surpasses the God-haunted Heidegger, because Strauss did not restrict himself to oracular sayings about some gods or other, ringing down the changes on Nietzsche's salvaging of respectability for "the sacred." No, Strauss can take a place in the ranks of those who know profoundly, and so are capable of expounding with great appreciation, the teachings of Judaism, and even of exposing from this point of view the serious shortcomings of both political and cultural Zionism.[8] Strauss offered us not vague, ambiguous thought about "the gods" or "the sacred," or the importance of myths and symbols in tandem with "religious experience," but a detailed account of the moral and intellectual grandeur of a particular religion or faith and its most important tenets.

Strauss's writings about Judaism—in contrast to those of Heidegger about the earth, sky, men, and gods—seem to possess the power that comes from having tried to understand that religion or faith and its authoritative books and commentaries as their authors themselves understood them. Though he writes with passion, it does not strike me that Strauss speaks of Judaism with the romanticism of the "fallen away." It is rather the respect or reverence of one who has not refuted that "Maybe it's true." In an age when most theologians treat religious matters with either historicist distancing and condescension or with romantic nostalgia, Strauss's writing about the Jewish faith is a breath of fresh air. Strauss on *teshuvah* helps me understand the Jewish idea of repentance more than many a biblical scholar.[9] This is due in part to Strauss's incredible power as a writer, but I believe also that such eloquence results from personal knowledge of the realities discussed more than from a mastery of the art of saying things well.

As a Catholic theologian, I come from a tradition in which political sense or awareness has been weak of late. The philosophy that predominated in scholasticism was based on a "kept Aristotle." Justly we might describe it in terms used by Strauss in *The City and Man* as a philosophy that had lost its character of "ascent."[10] The loss of awareness that philosophy's root motivation is the question of the right or best way to live meant that Roman Catholic attention to philosophy has been too complacently attached either to premodern philosophy as responding to the question about being (that is, as metaphysics or ontology) or to modern philosophy as responding to the epistemological question about knowing: how do we know we know? Thomism, or any of the schools, was institutionalized in a tradition expressed quintessentially in the manuals or handbooks of post-Tridentine seminaries and Catholic colleges. In that tradition the horizons of the originating geniuses of the tradition, such as Augustine or Aristotle or Thomas Aquinas, were collapsed into the mode of the *philosophia perennis*, which my own main mentor, Bernard Lonergan, characterized as "passing from book to book without passing through the mind of anyone." At its worst, this tradition embodied what Heidegger criticized as "onto-theology" and indicted as "forgetful of Being." At its worst, it presented the hermeneutic absurdity of a huge set of answers to questions no one was asking, or had never asked in quite those terms. Perhaps Heidegger's concern for the truth about God and religion helped him when it came to making his radical critiques of the philosophic traditions of Cartesianism, neo-Kantianism, and *Weltanschauungsphilosophie*. Like the Catholic tradition that Heidegger had called "the system of Catholicism," these typical modern deformations of philosophy all operated within the horizon of *Vorhandenheit*, with assumptions about either objectivity or subjectivity, or both, which represent derailment into forgetfulness of Being.[11]

Having demolished all extrinsic criteria for truth, Heidegger was open to mystery in an uncritical manner that was beyond good and evil, incapable of discerning the difference between the vicious circle of the demonic and the vicious circle of the divine, nonetheless.

In his lack of political awareness, Heidegger remained preoccupied with the traditional philosophic questions about being and knowing (albeit in his own unique way). However much he tried to radicalize philosophy in his procedure of *Destruktion* that anticipated the deconstructionists, his approach amounts to a massive dedifferentiation of properly philosophic competence.[12]

Strauss, on the other hand, maintained the traditional definition of philosophy as replacing opinions about what is highest and best with true and certain knowledge of the whole. He invoked the rationalist criteria of sense evidence and the logical idea of episteme set forth in Aristotle's *Posterior Analytics*. If for Strauss there is a history of the decline and fall of philosophy, it certainly did not start with Plato and Aristotle, as it did for Heidegger, but with modernity's "three waves."[13] And it was Strauss's heightened preoccupation with the political that permitted him to grasp what almost no one—except his own followers—has seen so clearly, namely, the paramount role played by Machiavelli in the origins of modernity. Not just the collapse of theory into technical expertise, but the underlying moral and theological rebellion against the Great Tradition beginning with Plato is what separates Strauss's analysis of modern derailment from all the other accounts. The modern project into which specifically modern science was co-opted by the propaganda of thinkers such as Descartes, Bacon, Spinoza, and Hobbes was grounded in the moral revolution of Machiavelli. He, Machiavelli, is the initiator of the "first wave" of modernity.[14]

Strauss's insight into the pervasive influence of Machiavelli represents almost a quagmire for contemporary Christian philosophers and theologians who in general have been intent on being liberal while maintaining an innocence or ignorance about liberalism's Machiavellian roots. Strauss's hypothesis of the three waves of modernity overshadows even the analysis of thinkers whose concerns overlap his own—people such as Heidegger, and Strauss's fellow students including Karl Löwith, Gerhard Krüger, Hans-Georg Gadamer, Jacob Klein, and other contemporaries like Helmut Kuhn, Carl Schmitt, and Eric Voegelin—because of the way it combines detailed analysis with explanatory comprehensiveness. His hypothesis is only possible because he was able to transcend the modern horizon. It not only makes clear the discontinuity with the premodern horizon of the ancient and classic authors, but it also shows how the progressive radicalization of modernity, especially by Rousseau and Nietzsche, the founders of the succeeding waves, was enabled by a partial and incomplete return to premodern ideas.

To my knowledge there is only one great contemporary thinker who, on his own terms, agrees essentially with Strauss in this matter—Bernard Lonergan, a Roman Catholic theologian. His analysis is based on his own appropriation of the intrinsic criterion for judgments of truth and value thematized by the ancients in what he named "the pure, detached, disinterested, and unrestricted desire to know."[15] The application or actuation of the pure desire occurs primarily in acts of direct understanding that yield guesses or hypotheses in response to "What is?" questions, and in acts of reflective understanding that issue in judgments or acts of verification in which the sufficiency of evidence for the validity of possibly relevant answers to "What is?" questions is ascertained in response to "Is it so?" questions.[16] As enactments of the pure and unrestricted desire to know, such acts of human understanding are normative. The problem is that ascent toward correct understanding can be blocked or distorted by different kinds of blind spots and biases.[17] Lonergan analyzes these as dramatic, individual, group, and general biases.[18] His treatment of commonsense bias comes quite close to Strauss. "Common sense" is used by Lonergan to mean, not the virtue of prudence or practical wisdom, but a specialization of human intelligence for dealing with the particular and concrete.[19] Common sense is untheoretical, the home of opinion, proverb, and maxim. But the commonsense (or general) bias is antitheoretical, and so intent upon the short-term effectualness that it is willing to trim true theory in order to conform with unintelligent, unreasonable, irresponsible, and so bad practice.[20] In other words, the bias of common sense excludes anything but what Machiavelli called "effective truth" (*veritá effettuale*).[21]

Lonergan shows common sense's inherently uncritical nature (but not thereby that common sense is unintelligent). Fully critical reflection is only realized from a theoretic or contemplative standpoint (beyond the reach of common sense), because it lets the human being operate in an intellectual pattern of experience.[22] This analysis recalls Plato's teaching about the Cave, and Strauss's retrieval of the Platonic teaching about the role of the philosopher in relation to the city and the political life.

According to Lonergan, commonsense bias is so destructive because the renunciation of intelligence it entails leads to what he calls "the longer cycle of decline," in contrast to the dramatic, egoistical, and group biases that bring about shorter cycles of decline.[23] The renunciation of the normativity of intelligence in the name of practicality, thereby bringing theory into line with bad human performance, has a pervasive and cumulative effect. One set of rationalizations or compromises sets the conditions for the evil social consequences that for anyone intent upon effectual truth alone would justify more radical rationalizations and compromises. In the social and cultural spheres, these are apprehended as ideologies or cover stories.[24] I believe that Strauss's construction of successive waves mounting up to the "crisis of our time . . . the crisis of the West" is a verification and filling in of Lonergan's notion of the longer cycle of decline.

Similarly, there is the breakthrough by the German Roman Catholic theologian Johann Baptist Metz, the leading student of Karl Rahner whom many consider to be the most important Catholic theologian of the twentieth century.[25] Rahner wrote his foundational work, *Geist in Welt*, under the influence of his teacher at Freiburg, Martin Heidegger. Metz was prompted to reconceive fundamental theology as political by noticing the almost total neglect of the Holocaust by leading Catholic theologians in the post-World War II period, including his dear mentor Karl Rahner. You might justly say that Metz is the counterpart for Catholic thought of Emil Fackenheim in Jewish theology. Metz later shifted from speaking of the modern age as the history of liberation to a much more profound level. In an essay entitled "Redemption and Emancipation"[26] Metz called into question the Enlightenment thesis of progress as based on an illusory anthropogeny. The Enlightenment notion of thinking things through practically and politically as if one could not speak of God is in reality a gambit for human refusal to take responsibility for the evil that people cause in the world, while at the same time vaunting their superiority to premodern times in the name of "ideologies of winners": the liberal capitalist ideology based on Locke's differential rights or on Kant's idea of a civilization inhabited by devils; or the communist ideology of the revolutionary proletariat.

Metz's indictment of modernity's "no-fault" humanism reminds us of Strauss's agreement with Nietzsche and Heidegger that the universal and homogeneous state is populated by "the Last Man," or *das Man*.[27] Strauss's question, also expressed in the title of his famous essay "Progress or Return?" basically agrees with Lonergan and Metz on the problematic character of progress.[28] The question of return as posed by Strauss is more general than the alternatives posed by Lonergan and Metz. Whereas the latter believe that the human crisis is such that it can only be radically solved by a return to Jerusalem, Strauss believes the return may be *either* to Jerusalem *or* to Athens.

One of the great conundrums regards where Strauss himself really stood. Most agree that he could not actually return to Jewish Orthodoxy, because for him, unlike Cohen or Rosenzweig, it had to be all or nothing. One question is whether as a philosopher Strauss returned to Athens or remained a Nietzschean, which has certainly been plausibly suggested of late.[29] Still, some would agree that the subtlety of Strauss's way of characterizing Maimonides dictates that it would be rash to settle on any of these three options as Strauss's own position. At least we can say that Strauss has debunked early modern rationalism and the new probity as obstacles to decent intelligent people's choosing to return to Jerusalem.[30] I believe Strauss's statement, "I shall not for a moment forget what Jerusalem stands for."[31] I think he makes it a duty for any honest searcher for wisdom not to forget it either. I believe Strauss's singular retrieval of the question about Athens or Jerusalem to be his greatest achievement.[32] It is also an achievement that goes beyond the limits of the choice to return to Athens alone, because the choice for human wisdom is really a choice that goes beyond human wisdom. For as apodictically as Strauss stated his belief that "philosophy in the Platonic sense is possible and necessary," and that "the classics demonstrated that truly human life is a life dedicated to science, knowledge and the search for it," he also said that "a philosophy based on faith is no longer a philosophy."[33]

I suggest, then, that as far as we can tell, either this is as far as Strauss got, or Strauss has the distinction of being the founder of "the fourth wave of modernity."

Strauss and the Tension between Athens and Jerusalem

After the immense success of *The Closing of the American Mind*, when one of Strauss's greatest students, Allan Bloom, returned to Boston College for a talk, there was the traditional after-dinner discussion with the Boston-area students of political theory— teachers and doctoral students—many of whom had themselves been students of Strauss and of Bloom. Having been taught by

Bloom at many weekend and several daylong sessions in connection with our perspectives program, I consider myself fortunate to have been one of his students. At this particular discussion I reminded Bloom that Strauss had judged the tension between Athens and Jerusalem to be at the heart and core of the vitality of Western civilization and thought, and that Strauss always kept the tension vividly present in his work. I asked Bloom why that tension—and especially the Jerusalem side of the tension—was almost entirely absent from his excellent book. Bloom's answer was a forthright statement. He spoke with warmth and esteem of how much Strauss meant to him; of how Strauss was present to him constantly in his work and in his daily thoughts; and of how he was simply not up to retrieving adequately the horizon of Jerusalem and the Bible in which Strauss had been able to live and be at home; and that this was, alas, a genuine shortcoming.

Bloom's response that night was not exactly a "giving of accounts." It did incarnate the meaning and value of the sort of friendships that are based on a common esteem for learning and for the great books about which he had written so eloquently in *The Closing*. This is the great gift Strauss offered his students, and I shall always be grateful to Bloom for that powerful witness to what Strauss had dedicated his life to achieving.

At the same time, the truth of the objection as conceded by Allan Bloom points to something problematic in Strauss's explicit position. I believe we need to examine more closely the aspect of rationalism because rationalism is a mistaken position even for philosophy. I believe for a number of reasons that Strauss performatively went beyond rationalism. Some of his students, however, have not been able to get beyond rationalism, and to the extent that this is true they have not been able to keep alive in themselves the vital tension between Athens and Jerusalem. So either they attempt a genuine return to premodern rationalism in forgetfulness of "what Jerusalem stands for," or they take the Nietzschean route with more or less skill in the arts of esotericism. Playing a dangerous game, their game is as sterile as any scholasticism for which philosophy has lost its character of ascent.

The Straussian Alternatives: Beyond Rationalism
or the Fourth Wave

Strauss was utterly impressed with the seriousness with which Heidegger read the books of the ancients in the conviction that they could teach us truth as valid for today as ever it was. He also followed the pioneer of the phenomenological movement, Edmund Husserl, in an aspect of his thought that Heidegger himself rejected, namely, the ideal of philosophy as a rigorous science.[34] Heidegger criticized the logical ideal of apodictic knowledge from Aristotle to Descartes and Husserl as party to the forgetfulness of Being, because it operates in the horizon of *Vorhandenheit* with which beings or entities may come at least partially to sight, but Being as such must necessarily remain concealed. Instead of just granting to science and theory whatever legitimacy Aristotle, the original theorist of *episteme*, rightly associated with exactness (*akribia*), as well as in his philosophical practice of diverse investigations, Heidegger virtually obliterated the normative criteria of logical rigor.[35] For most of his career, Husserl pursued the goal of discovering apodictic grounds for all knowledge and especially of philosophy as a science, by means of a phenomenology of perception and a transcendental reduction. In contrast, Heidegger's radicality caused him gradually to shed all traits that might be connected with what he called the "subjective objectivism" of *das Vorhandene*, and to take up the phenomenology of language that concentrated its sights chiefly on poetic utterances. Here Strauss followed Husserl and not Heidegger.

As Thomas Pangle stresses in his commentary on the Strauss/ Voegelin correspondence, and as Strauss himself seems to suggest, he never gave up the orientation of the early Husserl which he believed to be a genuine revival of classical rationalism: "Husserl has seen with incomparable clarity that the restoration of philosophy or science . . . presupposes the restoration of the Platonic-Aristotelian level of questioning."[36] Clearly for Strauss the alternative to arguing logically on the basis of empirical evidence or beginning with commonsense opinion—either in the form of dialectic or in the (essentially unattainable) form of the scientific treatise in which all presuppositions are made explicit, all rules of derivation are stated, and all terms and axioms are defined implicitly—is to submit our human operations of reasoning and choosing to the arbitrariness of fateful dispensation as Strauss says of Heidegger.[37] If nothing else, Heidegger's misadventures with national socialism would point to the preferability for reasonable persons of "precise observation and rigorous analysis."

It remains that for Strauss precise observation and rigorous analysis as carried out under the auspices of modern rationalism and intellectual probity are one thing: and precise observation and rigorous analysis as performed in the light of "the old love of truth" are quite another.[38] The skepticism of the former is based on dogmatic assumptions motivated by the "prejudice against prejudice." The latter is based on questions in the classic sense that arise when there are two or more alternative and contradictory answers to a *What is?* question that seem plausible at first sight.

Strauss begins to transcend rationalism in this very discrimination of the contexts or orientations within which precise observation and rigorous analysis occur. Even so, Strauss's rationalism gives an emphasis to the question that is tendentious. If Thomas Pangle is right in the way he highlights questions for Strauss as chiefly motivated by doubt, then we see a tendency to regard something as questionable precisely in so far as it implies doubt and therefore demands not just a possibly relevant or verifiable answer, but a certain answer based on knowledge of things by their absolutely necessary causes.[39] This really has to do with a failure on Strauss's part to distinguish between two different kinds of questions:

1. "What is?" questions, which are responded to by insights that grasp the possibly relevant intelligibilities of things that may or may not be actually relevant depending on whether the conditions specified by understanding do or do not happen to be fulfilled; these are questions for understanding that of themselves do not demand the truth, but only possibly relevant understanding. Once such understanding is attained, then there arise *Is it so?* questions.

2. "Is it so?" questions, which are responded to when one returns to the data to check out whether the evidence is sufficient to warrant the assertion that the possibly relevant understanding already attained is actually relevant; such warrants involve not the demonstrable elimination of every possible alternative except the one under consideration, but rather the grasp of the virtually unconditioned, which is the ascertaining that the conditions required for the occurrence or existence of the intelligibility in question are actually fulfilled.

Rationalism of any kind conflates the experiential and normative criteria of sensing and understanding with the absolute criteria of judgment.[40] As a result, it is held that insights have to grasp in sense data or the reality under discussion in dialectic the absolutely necessary intelligibility at stake: The intelligibility in question must be such and so, and could not be otherwise; this intelligibility has to hold true so universally that it excludes contingency. Such an exigent standard of intelligibility is practically unachievable for human acts of understanding. This stringent standard is something that Strauss respected conscientiously. In defense of Strauss, Nathan Tarcov has put the moderation of Strauss's interpretative claim to marvelous use.[41] Fully aware that his interpretations of famous authors' difficult texts could in no wise be exhaustive, Strauss did not manifest the dogmatism of which he and Straussians are sometimes accused. In cases of positive construction, Strauss offered possibly relevant interpretations more or less well supported by the texts he adduced as evidence in producing his interpretations, although the possibility of certainty was greater when it came to eliminating demonstrably false or wrongheaded interpretations. The care with which Strauss made limited prospective judgments in interpreting goes beyond rationalism.

In the important footnote of *Philosophy and Law* in which Strauss showed the bias of "the new intellectual probity," he quoted Père A. Gratry on how critique motivated by probity or modern rationalism excludes the supernatural, while the real "essence of criticism is attentiveness."[42] Strauss's attentiveness in interpreting is incomparable, and his best students have learned this from him. Being attentive in this fashion goes beyond rationalism.

Strauss seemed to insist upon the classic demonstration by Plato and Aristotle of the theoretic or contemplative life as the absolutely most choiceworthy for human beings as such. Wouldn't a demonstration of the necessity of this rank-ordering of ways of life imply the prior demonstration of the complete intelligibility of the universe? Yet Strauss admits that classical philosophy did not demonstrate the complete intelligibility of the universe, but only that people as people have an awareness of the whole, which is by no means demonstrative proof of the intelligibility of the whole.[43]

One does sense that for Strauss the life of free insight, unrestricted inquiry, and human wisdom alone is more choiceworthy than the life of faith, reverence, obedience, and piety. At times he comes close to arguing the superiority of the philosophic life over the religious one, but at the end of the day, Strauss says straight out that "philosophy itself is possibly not the right way of life. It is not necessarily the right way of life, not evidently the right way of life, because this possibility of revelation exists."[44] As Strauss pursues this train of thought, we begin to hear explicitly how beyond rationalism he himself is: "But what then does the choice of philosophy mean under these conditions? In this case, the knowledge rests itself on an unevident premise. And it seems to me that this difficulty underlies all present-day philosophizing, and that it is this difficulty which is at the bottom of what in the social sciences is called the value problem: the philosophy or science, however you might call it, is incapable of giving an account of its own necessity."[45]

Revelation is not impossible and so possible; therefore, philosophy as a way of life is not self-evident, and cannot be made so. Still, people in this life must choose, in the very serious sense that they cannot get out of choosing, since "not to choose" would also be a choice. Moreover, as Aristotle does make evident in both the *Metaphysics* and the *Nicomachean Ethics*, such choosing involves a settling of the issue of happiness, the that-for-the-sake-of-which everything else is chosen.[46] Built into the structure of this human choice is the necessity of taking a stand on the rationality of the whole of one's life, which, the more deliberate and so fully human it is, entails a stand on the intelligibility of the whole.[47]

In one of his most beautiful writings, one of the great essays on liberal education, Strauss said:

> Philosophy, we have learned, must be on guard against the wish to be edifying—philosophy can only be intrinsically edifying. We cannot exert our understanding without from time to time understanding something of importance; and this act of understanding may be accompanied by the awareness of our understanding, by the understanding of understanding, by *noesis noeseos*, and this is so high, so pure, so noble an experience that Aristotle could ascribe it to his God. . . . By becoming aware of the dignity of mind, we realize the ground of the dignity of man and therewith the goodness of the world, whether we understand it as created or uncreated, which is the home of man because it is the home of the human mind.[48]

The truth of this statement goes beyond the limits of rationalism, for its focuses not on "thought thinking itself," as so many have rendered Aristotle's *noēsis noēseos*, but on the understanding of understanding. I believe that here Strauss uses understanding in perhaps three senses: the first time, as the intellectual capacity or as the dianoetic habit or excellence called *nous*; next, as the act or operation of understanding; and third, in the phrases "awareness of understanding" and "understanding of understanding," it covers the act, the habit, and the human potency.

In the essay on the mutual influence of theology and philosophy already cited above, Strauss stated:

> The philosophers transcend the dimension of divine codes altogether. . . . Instead they embark on a free quest for the beginnings, for the first things, for the principles. And they assume that on the basis of the knowledge of first principles, of the beginnings, it will be possible to determine what is by nature good, as distinguished from what is good merely by convention. This quest for the beginnings proceeds through sense perception, reasoning, and what they called *noesis*, which is literally translated by "understanding" or "intellect," and which we can perhaps a little bit more cautiously by "awareness," an awareness with the mind's eye as distinguished from sensible awareness. But while this awareness has certainly its biblical equivalent and even its mystical equivalent, this equivalent in the philosophic context is never divorced from sense perception and reasoning based on sense perception.[49]

In this passage I want to underline how *noesis*, or intelligent awareness, goes beyond and is irreducible to sense perception and reasoning based on sense perception, even if its actuation in our coming to know occurs necessarily by means of them.

In our experiences of understanding, the natural desire to understand from which they arise is defined, as Thomas Aquinas remarked in the first section of his *Commentary on the Posterior Analytics*, by the questions "if it exists" (*an sit*) and "what is it" (*quid sit*).[50] Whenever we understand something, we grasp the intelligibility—the form or *eidos* or *quod quid est*—in the sensible or imaginable matter. This happens because "what is?" questions express a desire to know the cause or formal cause. Strauss's point about sense perception and reasoning based on sense perception has to do with the truth realized so clearly by Aristotle that by nature the proper fulfillment of the human desire to understand is by the reception in our intelligence of the intelligible forms or species of material things.[51] Thomas Aquinas in all clarity told us that the proportionate object of our intelligence in this life is the "whatness of material things" (*quidditas rei materialis*).

What Strauss has indicated in his descriptions of the philosophic life is that the human desire to know is in principle without limit, since to set any limit upon it would be irrational, arbitrary, and obscurantist. Where Maimonides emphasized the incomprehensibility of God, Thomas Aquinas stressed that just because the proper fulfillment naturally attainable by human intelligence is limited by the proportionate object as either intrinsically or at least extrinsically conditioned essentially by matter, this does not necessarily mean that the fulfillment naturally desired is limited in the same fashion. In fact, as Lonergan wrote, "we are not content to ask *quid sit* solely with regard to material things, and we are not content with merely analogical knowledge of immaterial things. We keep on asking why and we desist not because we do not desire, but because we recognize our impotence to satisfy our desire."[52] Maimonides might not have disagreed.

Aquinas boldly claimed that the question *quid sit Deus?* expresses a desire that arises naturally as soon as anyone hears about God's existence, because "the desire of our intellects is natural in origin and transcendental in its object."[53] The adequate fulfillment of the question would be proper knowledge of God in virtue of an infinite form, neither intrinsically nor extrinsically conditioned by space and time. This attainment is beyond the natural proportion of any possible finite intellect, and so is the strictly supernatural. The upshot of this is that natural reason can go no further than to acknowledge "the paradox that the desire to understand arises naturally, that its object is the transcendental *ens*, and that the proper fulfillment that partially is attainable is restricted to the proportionate object of finite intellect," namely, beings intrinsically or extrinsically conditioned by space and time.[54]

In the passage cited above on understanding understanding, Strauss implies that one can move from the grasp of partial intelligibility in understanding things, important and trivial, to an explicit understanding of understanding; and that one can move from understanding to the affirmation of the ultimate goodness of the world. This is Strauss going beyond rationalist presuppositions, for the world can only be good if the real is completely intelligible. To my knowledge, Strauss never says this in print.

Indeed, the only person I know who has fully explicated the core structure of this argument, which had already been sketched by Aristotle in *Metaphysics*, Book XII, is Bernard Lonergan in chapter 19 of *Insight*.[55] There Lonergan makes explicit what Strauss at most implies and then only with extreme caution: the philosophic apprehension of the universe is to be reached only by way of an exigence for complete intelligibility.

Strauss pointed rationalism beyond itself toward its basis in the infinite desire to know, which is the nerve of all inquiry, learning, reflection, judgment, deliberation, and reasonable choice. But in his profound awareness that the Greeks did not reach a clear and precise affirmation of divine transcendence and hence of the complete intelligibility of the world, and in his rationalism, Strauss suggested that the decision to make the philosophic desire to understand the universe as intelligible normative in one's living is ultimately an act of faith whose premises are not evidently reasonable.[56] Performatively, this is not consistent with himself; and in his statements about understanding understanding, Strauss disagrees with this. In his rationalism Strauss also opens the door to the fourth wave of modernity that exoterically uses what Athens and Jerusalem ostensibly hold in common against the moderns as a support for liberal democracy, the freedom of philosophers, and the instrumentalization of religion in the service of the morality of the vulgar, while it esoterically suspects or perhaps even opts for the ultimate unintelligibility of the whole. Then there follows a failure to reprobate every obscurantism that lies at root of the regularity with which politics and God are discussed without any genuine interest in the question *quid sit Deus?* but rather just the contrary.

Strauss also opens the door for the fourth wave in his insistence upon the independence of the dianoetic virtues of the philosopher from all moral virtue save the moderation that saves his skin.[57] He also does it in the oft-quoted passage from his famous debate with Alexandre Kojéve:

Philosophy as such is nothing other than the real consciousness of the problems, that is to say, of the fundamental and comprehensive problems. It is impossible to think about these problems without being attracted toward a solution, toward one or the other of certain rare typical solutions. However, as long as there is no wisdom, but only the search for wisdom, the evidence of all these solutions is necessarily smaller than the evidence of the problems. As a result, the philosopher ceases to be a philosopher from the moment that his "subjective certitude" of the truth of a solution becomes stronger than the consciousness that he may have of the problematical character of this solution. At this moment the sectarian is born.[58]

This is taken to mean that the philosophic approach is superior because nonsectarian by definition, and those who opt for a different, especially supernatural, solution are mere sectarians with no possible universalist claims. Liable to forget that the philosopher's holding the fundamental and comprehensive problems in suspense also assumes a stance based on premises that are not self-evident, he or she may set out "to show to his own satisfaction and that of others that he has, not a definitive, but a fuller account of the moral experience to which the pious point as their most significant experiences," in little doubt that he or she is the most subtle and open-minded expert in erotics.[59]

In Strauss's statement on understanding understanding cited earlier, I omitted a section where he said that that experience "leads us to realize that all evils are in a sense necessary if there is to be understanding. It enables us to accept all evils which befall us and which may break our hearts in the spirit of good citizens of the city of God." This idea of evil as a necessary condition for knowledge comes up in Strauss's interpretation of the second Genesis story of Adam and Eve in the Garden of Eden.[60] It has to do with his conception of the needed moderation about human expectations taught by Plato in the *Republic* and elsewhere.[61] But it also may have to do with Strauss's conception of the God of Judaism, Islam, and Christianity as mystery, not simply in the sense of being beyond the capacity of human intelligence properly to understand, but in the sense of being incomprehensible because of an unpredictability grounded in arbitrary will.[62] Strauss does not discuss the intellectualist rather than the voluntarist concept of God; nor does he tell us why not, except for the fact that he is Jewish. We can understand this in the case of Strauss, and we can concede how the neglect of intellectualism may be due to the shallowness of glib theists and neo-Thomists, who turn it into a form of obscurantism.[63]

It remains that the consolation of the philosophic appropriation of understanding in the face of the world's evils may also be a failure to come adequately to terms with the rootedness of moral evil in the bipolar tension between (1) attachment and self-interest-edness of the sensitive and intersubjective element in ourselves, which furnishes the point of departure for state of nature theories, and (2) the detachment and disinterestedness of the pure desire to know and live as it has unfolded concretely in history.[64] If the lower, sensitive, and intersubjective level has in fact so interfered with the unfolding of inquiry and reflection, of deliberation and decision as to bring about the obvious lack of intelligibility in human situations, then there mounts up an increasing irrelevance of intelligence and reasonableness to the real problem of human living.[65] Then it may be needful for the philosophic humanism that only contemplates the problems to acknowledge its lack of primacy and to transcend itself by becoming open to an absolutely supernatural solution to the problem of evil, in spite of the fact that so many "who profess the solution . . . live it imperfectly or not at all."[66] As Lonergan has argued:

> The humanist viewpoint loses its primacy, not by some extrinsicist invasion, but by submitting to its own immanent necessities. For if the humanist is to stand by the exigencies of his own unrestricted desire, if he is to yield to the demands for openness set by ever further questions, then he will discover the limitations that imply man's incapacity for sustained development, he will acknowledge and consent to the one solution that exists and, if the solution is supernatural, his very humanism will lead beyond itself.[67]

Strauss has seen the need pointed out precisely by Machiavelli for exercising a toughness in the political sphere that cannot be precisely reconciled with morality for the sake of the overarching good of the polity. Lonergan, too, agrees in a certain way with Machiavelli that the "limitations that imply man's incapacity for sustained development" have created a situation in which, if "man would be only a man, he has to be less."[68] This is Machiavelli's point about the efficacy of taking people's bestiality seriously in terms of force and fraud, which Strauss said was the basis of the three waves. Strauss's three waves are an account of the implication of trying to handle people's sinful performance by engineering in Hobbes and Rousseau, and by people's bestowal of grace upon themselves in Nietzsche.

However, the waves are also an account of the exacerbation of the dialectic between love of what is near and love of what is highest and best caused by the demand of the absolutely supernatural that humanism transcend itself in spite of the scandalous character of religions. In light of the longer cycle of decline as implemented by the three waves of modernity, the explicit refusal to be open to the supernatural solution based on an exoteric pretended fidelity to the ancient's love of truth may be the foundation of a fourth wave of modernity in our time.

Notes

1. On "the crisis," see Leo Strauss, *The City and Man* (Chicago: University of Chicago Press, 1964), 1–12; and Strauss's "The Crisis of

Our Time" and "The Crisis of Political Philosophy" in *The Predicament of Modern Politics*, ed. Harold J. Spaeth (Detroit: University of Detroit Press, 1964), 41–54 and 91–103. On "return," see "Progress or Return?" in *The Rebirth of Classical Political Rationalism: An Introduction to the Thought of Leo Strauss*, ed. Thomas Pangle (Chicago: University of Chicago Press, 1989), 227–270.

2. Leo Strauss, *Philosophie unde Gesetz: Beitrage zum Verständnis Maimunis und seine Verlaüfer* (Philadelphia: Jewish Publication Society, 1935), 13.

3. See Hans-Georg Gadamer, "The Phenomenological Movement," *Philosophical Hermeneutics*, trans. David E. Linge (Berkeley: University of California Press, 1976), 130–181.

4. See "Correspondence Concerning Modernity" (Exchange of Letters with Karl Löwith beginning 1 October 1946), *Independent Journal of Philosophy* 4 (1983): 105–19.

5. Leo Strauss, "A Giving of Accounts," with Jacob Klein, *St. John's Review* (Annapolis, Md.) 22 (1970): 1–5: and "An Unspoken Prologue to a Public Lecture at St. John's," *Interpretation: A Journal of Political Philosophy* 7 (1978): 1–5.

6. Ibid.

7. See Remi Brague, "Leo Strauss and Maimonides," in *Leo Strauss' Thought: Toward a Critical Engagement*, ed. Alan Udoff (Boulder, Colo.: Rienner Publications, 1991), 93–114, which is replete with bibliographical references both to the unfolding of Strauss's work on Maimonides and to scholarship's responses to that work. See, also, Eve Adler, "Leo Strauss's *Philosophie und Gesetz*," ibid., 183–226.

8. Leo Strauss, "Preface to the English Translation" of his *Spinoza's Critique of Religion*, trans. E. M. Sinclair (New York: Schocken Books, 1965), 1–31, esp., 1–8. Also "Progress or Return?," 227–41.

9. Ibid., 227–30.

10. *The City and Man*, 29.

11. Heidegger said he "was driven onto the path of thought especially about the question of the relationship between the Word of Holy Scripture and theological-speculative thought" (*Unterwegs zur Sprache*, 7th ed. [Pfullingen: Neske, 1982], 96, my translation). After moving from the Theological Faculty to the Philosophical Faculty, he wrote in a letter to the theologian Engelbert Krebs on 9 September 1919: "Epistemological insights encroaching upon the theory of historical knowledge have made the system of Catholicism problematic and unacceptable to me—but not Christianity and metaphysics (though the latter in a new sense)." Cited by Bernhard Casper, "Martin Heidegger und die theologische Fakultät Freiburg 1909–1923," *Kirche am Oberrhein*, eds. R. Bäumer, K. S. Frank, H. Ott (Freiburg: Herde, 1980), 534–41 (my translation).

12. See Frederick Lawrence, "The Fragility of Consciousness: Loner-

gan and the Postmodern Concern for the Other,'' *Theological Studies* 54 (1993): 55–94.

13. Leo Strauss, "The Three Waves of Modernity," *Political Philosophy: Six Essays by Leo Strauss*, ed. Hillel Gildin (Indianapolis: Pegasus, 1975), 81–98.

14. Leo Strauss, *Thoughts on Machiavelli* (Glencoe, Ill.: Free Press, 1958), *passim*.

15. Bernard Lonergan, *Insight: A Study of Human Understanding* (London: Longmans, 1957), xi, xiv, 4, 9, 74, 220–2, 348–350, 380–1, 528, 550, 596, 599–600, 623–4, 636–9, 642, 682, 701–2, 738.

16. On the structured dynamism of human knowing according to Lonergan, see his "Cognitional Structure," *Collection: Papers by Bernard Lonergan*, ed. F. E. Crowe (New York: Herder and Herder, 1964), 221–39.

17. See Lonergan, *Insight*, 235.

18. Ibid., xiv, 191–203, 218–22, 222–5, 225–42.

19. On "common sense," see ibid., 173–244; on common sense's concern with the particular and the concrete, see ibid., 171–6, 287–9, 296–7.

20. See ibid., 225–42.

21.

22. See Lonergan, *Insight*, 420–1; on the critical limitations of common sense, see ibid., 225–8; on the intellectual pattern of experience, see ibid., 185–6.

23. On the "longer cycle of decline," see ibid., 228–36.

24. On ideology as the justification or rationalization of alienation, see Bernard Lonergan, *Method in Theology* (New York: Herder and Herder, 1972), 357–8; on ideology as cover story, see Lonergan, "Reality, Myth, Symbol," in *Myth, Symbol and Reality: Boston University Studies in Philosophy and Religion* 1, ed. Alan M. Olson (Notre Dame: University of Notre Dame Press, 1980), 31–37.

25. For an overview of the political theology of J. B. Metz, see Frederick Lawrence, "Transcendence as Interruption: Theology in a Political Mode," *Boston University Studies in Philosophy and Religion* 2, eds. A. M. Olson and L. Rouner (Notre Dame, 1981), 208–225.

26. See Johann Baptist Metz's article, "Erlösung und Emanzipation" in *Stimmen der Zeit* 191 (1973): 171–84. It set the tone for his last major work to date, *Glaube in Geschichte und Gesellschaft: Studien zu einer praktischen Fundamentaltheologie* (New York: Seabury Press, 1980), and his smaller work on religious orders, *Zeit der Orden? Zur Mystik und Politik der Nachfolge* (Freiburg, 1971). Metz's earlier more naive stance toward the Enlightenment is apparent in his books *Christliche Anthropozentrik* (Munich: Kosel-Verlag, 1962) and *Zur Theologie der Welt* (Mainz: M. Grunewald, 1968).

27. Leo Strauss, "A Restatement on Xenophon's *Hiero*," in *On Tyr-*

anny (Ithaca: Cornell University Press, 1963) 211–5, 223, 226; *The City of Man*, 4–6.

28. See Strauss, *The Rebirth of Classical Political Rationalism*, 227–70.

29. See S. B. Drury, "The Esoteric Philosophy of Leo Strauss," *Political Theory* 13 (1985): 315–37.

30. See "Preface to the English Translation" of *Spinoza's Critique of Religion*, 28–31. And see his *Philosophy and Law*, trans. Fred Baumann (Philadelphia: Jewish Publication Society of America, 1987), 113–4, n. 12.

31. *What Is Political Philosophy?* (Glencoe, Ill.: Free Press, 1959), 12.

32. "Jerusalem and Athens: Some Preliminary Reflections" (The Frank Cohen Public Lecture in Judaic Affairs), *The City College Papers*, 6 (New York,1967); now, also, in Strauss, *Studies in Platonic Political Philosophy*, ed. Thomas L. Pangle (Chicago: University of Chicago Press, 1983), 147–73.

33. Letter to Eric Voegelin, 4 June 1951, no. 19, in *Faith and Philosophy: The Correspondence between Leo Strauss and Eric Voegelin*, trans. and eds. P. Emberley and B. Cooper (University Park, Penn.: Penn State University Press, 1993), 91; No. 37 [Strauss to Voegelin, 15 February 1949], ibid., 78; on philosophy and faith, see "Machiavelli," in *History of Political Philosophy*, ed. L. Strauss and J. Cropsey (Chicago: University of Chicago Press, 1987), 296–7.

34. Leo Strauss, "Philosophy as a Rigorous Science and Political Philosophy," *Interpretation* 2 (1971): 19, now, also, in Strauss, *Studies in Platonic Political Philosophy*, 29–37.

35. See *Nicomachean Ethics* 1094b12ff.

36. Pangle, "Platonic Science in Strauss and Voegelin" in *Faith and Philosophy*, 341–5; Strauss, "Philosophy as a Rigorous Science and Political Philosophy," *Studies in Platonic Political Philosophy*, 37; comment on Husserl in Letter to Eric Voegelin, 9 May 1943, in *Faith and Philosophy*, 17.

37. See *Studies in Platonic Political Philosophy*, 31–32, 33–34, 36; "An Introduction to Heideggerian Existentialism," *The Rebirth of Classical Political Rationalism*, 27–46.

38. *Philosophy and Law*, 113, n. 12.

39. "Platonic Science in Strauss and Voegelin," *Faith and Philosophy*, 334–5.

40. On criteria as experiential, normative, and absolute, see Lonergan, *Insight*, 377–83.

41. See "Philosophy and History: Tradition and Interpretation in the Word of Leo Strauss," *Polity* 16 (1983), 5–29. Also, in the same vein of decaricaturing Strauss but on a different topic, see N. Tarcov, "On a Certain Critique of 'Straussianism,' " *Review of Politics* 53 (1991): 3–18.

42. *Philosophy and Law*, 113, n. 12. I am indebted to Christopher Bruell for pointing out this important note in "A Return to Classical Political

Philosophy and the Understanding of the American Founding," *Review of Politics* 53 (1991): 185, n. 44.

43. *The Rebirth of Classical Political Rationalism*, 260, 262.

44. "The Mutual Influence of Theology and Philosophy," *Faith and Philosophy*, 232–3.

45. Ibid.

46. See *Metaphysics* 1072a26f; 1072b27–31; 1073a3–5; *Nicomachean Ethics*, 1097a15–1097b9.

47. "Philosophy is essentially a quest, because it is not able ever to become wisdom (as distinguished from philosophy), philosophy finds that the problems are always more evident than the solutions. All solutions are questionable. Now, the right way of life cannot be fully established metaphysically except by a complicated metaphysics, and therefore the right way of life remains questionable. But the very uncertainty of all solutions, the very ignorance regarding the most important things, makes quest for knowledge the most important thing, and therefore a life devoted to it the right way of life" (*The Rebirth of Classical Political Rationalism*, 260).

48. "What Is Liberal Education?" *Liberalism Ancient and Modern* (New York: Basic Books, 1968), 8.

49. *Faith and Philosophy*, 219.

50. The following argument is dependent basically on the article by Bernard Lonergan, "The Natural Desire to See God," *Collection*, 84–95.

51. See Aristotle, *De Anima*, 417b20ff. Thomas Aquinas's commentary states that "no man can learn anything in the way of newly acquired knowledge, nor know anything in the sense of using knowledge already acquired, without sense impressions. No: when a man is actually thinking speculatively, he must at the same time form for himself some phantasma or sensible image. . . . It is plain that Avicenna was wrong in laying it down that the intellect has no need of sense after acquiring knowledge" (Translation by Robert Fitzgerald, "Robert Fitzgerald on the Creative and Discursive," *Enlarging the Change: The Princeton Seminars in Literary Criticism 1949–1951* [Princeton, N.J: Princeton University Press, 1985], 129.)

52. *Collection*, 86.

53. Ibid.

54. Ibid., 87.

55. *Insight*, 634–86.

56. See Thomas Prufer, "Juxtapositions: Aristotle, Aquinas, Strauss," *Recapitulations: Essays in Philosophy* (Washington, D.C., 1993) 35–43; Robert Sokolowski, *The God of Faith and Reason: Foundations of Christian Theology* (Notre Dame: University of Notre Dame Press, 1982), 157–64; see also *The Rebirth of Classical Political Rationalism*, 269.

57. See *Natural Right and History* (Chicago: University of Chicago Press, 1953), 161.

58. *On Tyranny*, 210.

59. Thomas L. Pangle, Introduction to *Studies in Platonic Political Philosophy*, 22.

60. "Jerusalem and Athens: Some Preliminary Reflections," *Studies in Platonic Political Philosophy*, 154–8.

61. See Strauss, "On Plato's *Republic*," *The City and Man*, 119–20; and "Plato, 427–347 B.C.," *Political Philosophy: Six Essays by Leo Strauss*, 177–8.

62. See Strauss, *The City and Man*, 162–3, 165–6, 169–70; *The Rebirth of Classical Political Rationalism* , 256–7; *Faith and Philosophy*, 219–21.

63. Strauss himself noted that this is what Gershom Scholem had done for the medieval Jewish philosophers. See *The Rebirth of Classical Political Rationalism*, 212–6.

64. See Lonergan, *Insight*, 688–93.

65. Ibid., 728.

66. Ibid., 729.

67. Ibid.

68. Ibid.

7

Athens and Jerusalem or Jerusalem and Athens?

Werner J. Dannhauser

Addressing an issue as weighty as this one, I am compelled by simple considerations of honesty to preface my thoughts with an identification of myself as a student of Leo Strauss, now dead for more than twenty years. I bring to my task the rare advantage of having been his student for seventeen years, and the rare disadvantage of being old enough to have been his student for seventeen years.

What is more, I am a follower of the teaching of Leo Strauss, so that I am called a Straussian, and even call myself one. I should also confess that I am a Jew who has never been an atheist but who has had his share of trouble in choosing Jerusalem over Athens.

Strauss on occasion analyzed things in the light of the opposition between the high and the low. He deserves full credit not only for teaching me to identify the high but for teaching me to love it insofar as the low in me permits.

Attempting to do justice to the thought of Leo Strauss on Jerusalem and Athens, I face a daunting but easily identifiable task. First, I must try to establish as precisely as possible what he meant when referring to "Jerusalem and Athens." My second task grows naturally out of my understanding of the first. I will try to show that Strauss thought that no thoughtful neutrality was possible between Jerusalem and Athens. Their juxtaposition always raises the question of the old union song: Which side are you on? Which side did Strauss choose? I intend to venture an answer to that question, but a tentative one. My third and final task is the most daunting one of all. It consists of raising the question of whether Leo Strauss was right in choosing the side he chose. My answer to that final question, however, will be a model of clarity and decisiveness: I do not know. That may sound like a profession of ignorance that would constitute my closest possible approach to Socrates, but it is more plausibly understood as an admission of incompetence. Only rarely does incompetence ever stop anybody from anything, and it will not stop me, but let the reader beware.

The Three Great Tensions

We begin our inquiry safely enough when we observe the fact that Leo Strauss was given to articulating his thoughts in terms of fundamental tensions or opposites. I have already referred to the opposition between the high and the low; one could also add the tensions between nature and convention as well as other pairs.

It is easy enough to identify the three greatest tensions explored by Leo Strauss: (1) the quarrel between the ancients and moderns, (2) the quarrel between poetry and philosophy (so ancient that the ancient Socrates called it ancient,) and (3) the relationship between Jerusalem and Athens. As far as I know, Strauss never referred to that tension as a quarrel; I do not know why.

One can venture some generalizations about all these opposites or oppositions. Strauss resisted any glib resolutions for these tensions and perhaps he resisted any resolutions for them whatsoever. In this respect, Strauss resembles Søren Kierkegaard. In *Concluding Unscientific Postscript*, the latter writes that in a Hegelian age given to making things easier and finding all sorts of solutions, "I conceived it as my task to create difficulties everywhere."[1] He certainly thought that tensions were potentially more productive and vitalizing than resolutions.

Before advancing in the course of my argument, I would like to confront a point made most ably by Thomas Pangle and others close to the thought of Leo Strauss, according to which Strauss really thought in terms of two, rather than three, fundamental tensions. If I understand the argument correctly, it asserts that however weighty the opposition between Jerusalem and Athens may be, it must basically be seen as merely a subdivision of the quarrel between poetry and philosophy. Pangle and others reason that the latter quarrel is ultimately about the status of reason, and religion is the most prominent alternative to reason. Moreover, our leading if not exclusive source of information about the gods is the poets. The weighty authority of Herodotus, in his remarks about Homer and Hesiod, lends credence to this point.[2]

The above argument fails to persuade me completely. If it were simply true, Leo Strauss would not have had to investigate the relationship between Jerusalem and Athens at all. He could have investigated "Athens versus Athens": the Athens of Plato and Aristotle versus the Athens of Homer and Hesiod. One can, to be sure, deny that contention, on the ground that an investigation of "Athens versus Athens" would of necessity be totally different. That is because one can plausibly maintain that the authors of Greek poetry did not believe in the gods they depicted, but one cannot plausibly maintain that the author (or even authors) of the Bible did not believe in God.

Some people among the Greeks believed in the Greek gods, and one can find more or less reliable reports on that. I must be permitted for once and once only to draw on something Leo Strauss said to me personally. I heard him say several times that upon retirement (a time that never came for him), he wanted to study local motion in the Bible. I never heard him say, nor has anyone, as far as I know, that he intended to spend his retirement years studying Homer.

The full argument about faith as an alternative to reason simply cannot be teased out of studying the great books we have inherited from Athens, if only because in Athens there is no equivalent to *revelation*. It must be considered possible that what we know about the God of Abraham, the God of Isaac, and the God of Jacob has only the status of poetic myth—a way of saying that it is not the truth, and perhaps a way of saying that Athens is superior to Jerusalem. It does not follow from this that all poetic myths are equal, or equally distant from the truth. Even when understood as poetic myth, the Bible has a powerful claim to be understood as the most profound and beautiful myth humanity possesses. As Jews, we can also claim that this myth is our own—and that the way to the good necessarily passes through one's own.[3]

Jerusalem and Athens: For What Do They Stand?

I shall begin the inquiry with the surface of things, asking simple questions. How does Leo Strauss present the juxtaposition of

Jerusalem and Athens? What terms does he use? In using this procedure, one is faithful to the spirit of Leo Strauss, who wrote, "The problem inherent in the surface of things, and only in the surface of things, is the heart of things."[4] The mere construction of two columns labeled "Jerusalem" and "Athens" and collecting the relevant words under them, would go a long way in introducing his thought on this topic clearly.

In the thought of Strauss, Athens stands above all for philosophy. He occasionally speaks of "science" or "Greek philosophy" or "theory" or "Greek thought" but most frequently simply of philosophy (the Greekness of Greek philosophy did not for him belong to its essence). Strauss links "philosophy" with such terms as "nature" and "regime," terms conspicuously absent from the Bible. Occasionally, he also associates philosophy with atheism, though he is fully aware of the fact that in the *Euthyphro* and elsewhere Socrates protests his piety and though he writes in his own last book that Plato's last book is his most pious book. One should note that a person who professes piety is not necessarily a pious person, and that in the guarded and careful way of the writing of Leo Strauss, a person's most pious book is not necessarily a pious book.[5]

The mention of atheism brings us naturally to the other pole, Jerusalem, which stands above all for the Bible and the biblical God. Sometimes, when he articulates the *problem* of Jerusalem and Athens, Strauss is more specific. Jerusalem stands for traditional Judaism, for Judaism simply, for Jewish Orthodoxy. In turn he equates the religion of the Bible with revelation (and once even with "the brute fact of revelation"), with belief in the mysterious and omnipotent God, with the life of obedient love (versus the life of free inquiry), and with *faith*.[6]

The mere collection of terms used by Leo Strauss suggests that he views the gulf between Athens and Jerusalem to be absolutely unbridgeable. One can buttress this contention with a few short quotations from Strauss's writing.

He states that for both Maimonides and Halevi—thinkers from whom he has learned a great deal and whom he obviously admires—"being a Jew and being a philosopher are mutually exclusive."[7] That language recurs when he declares that "Maimonides obviously assumes that the philosophers form a group distinguished from the group of adherents to the Law and that the two groups are mutually exclusive."[8]

The thought of mutual exclusivity pervades much of the writing of Leo Strauss. Discussing Maimonides' *The Guide of the Perplexed*, he remarks, "Its first premise is the old Jewish premise that being a Jew and being a philosopher are two incompatible things." Strauss is also the author of the following two categorical remarks: "A genuine philosopher can never be a genuine convert to Judaism or any other revealed religion." "Philosophy is invincibly ignorant of divine wisdom."[9]

The boldest and baldest statement by Leo Strauss on the conflict between Jerusalem and Athens occurs in his chapter on *The Kuzari* in *Persecution and the Art of Writing*. It merits, along with one of the footnotes attached to it, quotation:

> A merely defensive attitude on the part of the philosopher is impossible: his alleged ignorance is actually doubt or distrust. As a matter of fact the philosophers whom Halevi knew, went so far as to deny the very possibility of the specific experiences of the believers as interpreted by the latter, or, more precisely, the very possibility of Divine revelation in the precise sense of the term. That denial was presented by them in the form of what claimed to be a demonstrative refutation. The defender of religion had to refute the refutation by laying bare its fallacious character. On the level of the refutation and the refutation of the refutation, i.e., on the level of "human wisdom" the disputation between believer and philosopher is not only possible, but without any question the most important fact of the whole past.[10]

The uncompromising intransigence with which Leo Strauss articulates the tension between philosophers and believers (including Jews) is accentuated by the footnote he appends to the above passage. "One cannot recall too often this remark of Goethe (in the *Noten and Abhandlangen zum besseren Verständnis der West - ostichen Divans*): the characteristic, sole, and deepest theme of world and human history, to which everything else is subordinated, remains the conflict of unbelief and belief."[11]

In light of the depth of the gulf between Jerusalem and Athens, of the magnitude of the tension between belief and unbelief, one must conclude that if Leo Strauss is right in his analysis, then the term "Jewish philosopher" is a misnomer, an oxymoron.

An Energizing Tension

It is reasonable to assume that all the readers and writers of this volume, are to some degree, in one way or another, the products of the tension between Jerusalem and Athens. That is by no means simply a bad thing, for that tension has energized and vitalized Western civilization. In fact, it is very hard to imagine life without it. Presumably we would have to choose between the flatland of modern science, especially social science, and the fanaticism of the kind of Jewish Orthodoxy one finds in the Mea Shaarim section of Jerusalem (incidentally, I would prefer the latter). The superiority of Western civilization is inextricably linked to the tension between Jerusalem and Athens that has produced it.

That becomes evident when one considers the arguments one so frequently hears on behalf of multiculturalism. According to the latter, education in one culture is necessarily parochial, provincial, narrow, confined, and confining; but because of its dual ancestry, an education in Western civilization is truly a liberal education. It involves an introduction to both dogmatism and skepticism, to the rigors of mathematics as well as the charm of poetry, to the ironies of philosophers as well as the loftiness of prophets, to mysticism as well as analytical rigor, to the salutary warmth of Pascal as well as the bracing coldness of Spinoza.

The glories connected with the tension between Jerusalem and Athens cannot blind us to the fact that this deepest of tensions is necessarily experienced as painful to individuals, who expend considerable energy in trying to overcome it. One way to do so, obviously, is to opt for one of the sides. The choice of Jerusalem was advocated passionately by the Jewish thinker Lev Shestov (1866–1938). Shestov's final book, published the year of his death, *Athens and Jerusalem*, argues fervently that one should think in terms of a decision for Athens *or* Jerusalem and the author passionately picks Jerusalem:

> Within the "limits of reason" one can create a science, a sublime ethic, and even a religion; but to find God one must tear oneself away from the seductions of reason with all its physical and moral constraints, and go to another source of truth. In Scripture the source bears the enigmatic name "faith", which is that dimension of thought where truth abandons itself fearlessly and joyously to the entire disposition of the Creator: "Thy will be done!"[12]

Shestov's choice is effected so intensely that he even accuses human reason of laziness and cowardice.[13]

Few thinkers emulate Shestov's bold, extreme forthrightness. A more typical move by those who deal with the problem of Jerusalem and Athens is to construct a synthesis between them. But one is true to the spirit of the thought of Leo Strauss if one stops at speaking of an *attempt* at synthesis.

A vein of deep skepticism as to the very possibility of a synthesis between Jerusalem and Athens runs through the thought of Leo Strauss; in fact it intends to the idea of synthesis in general. In a letter of 25 February 1951, Strauss writes to Eric Voegelin that every synthesis is actually an option either for Jerusalem or Athens.[14] One might dismiss this as the kind of over-stating in which he sometimes indulged when trying to provoke his correspondents; at any rate, the letter was not published by Strauss himself. In his celebrated debate with Alexandre Kojève, Strauss makes a wonderfully sarcastic remark about syntheses in general in a rejoinder he did not hesitate to publish: "Syntheses effect miracles. Kojève's or Hegel's synthesis of classical and Biblical morality effects the miracle of producing an amazingly lax morality out of two moralities both of which made very strict demands on self-restraint."[15]

Strauss, then, can be said to argue that even if a synthesis between Jerusalem and Athens were possible, it would be undesirable because it would be decisively lower than both its thesis or antithesis. However, the main thrust of his thought is directed against the very possibility of synthesis. In arguing this, to be sure, one does well to be cautious, for Leo Strauss made only passing references to St. Thomas Aquinas, who is held up as the most prominent example of a synthesis between faith and reason.

Notwithstanding this notable omission, Strauss's disbelief in reconciling Jerusalem with Athens and thus attaining a higher plane remains clear. He thought that Hegel in his consecration of modernity was decidedly secular and had thus chosen Athens over Jerusalem. He speaks with great respect, but not with an evident agreement of the efforts of Hermann Cohen to find the truth as a synthesis between Plato and the prophets.[16] He writes of Heidegger's attempt to understand being (*Sein*) as a synthesis of the impersonality of Platonic ideas and the elusiveness of the biblical God, but he combined an appreciation of Heidegger's depth with deep distrust of his whole teaching.[17] He studied Nietzsche closely and with a great deal of admiration but he can scarcely be said to have bought into Zarathustra's teaching of the superman or of Nietzsche's seeing that superman as the Roman Caesar with the soul of Christ.[18] Wherever he looked, Leo Strauss saw would-be synthesizers, unsuccessful synthesizers, secret or not-so-secret advocators of Jerusalem over Athens or Athens over Jerusalem, but no genuinely successful synthesis.

Appealing from one part of Nietzsche's fertile thought to another part, Leo Strauss can be said to have subscribed to the desirability of maintaining, instead of synthesis, a "magnificent tension of the spirit" that stimulates human life in general and human thought in particular. The phrase comes from the preface of *Beyond Good and Evil*, a work admired by Leo Strauss as Nietzsche's most beautiful book.[19] Nietzsche thinks the fight against Platonism is in a way salutary because it energized Western civilization. He is against all "unstringing of the bow" and thus takes the side of Pascal against the Jesuits who would be all things to all people, even as he himself combats the democratic enlightenment of the eighteenth and nineteenth centuries. In a kind of imitation of Nietzsche, Leo Strauss takes the field against those who would unstring the bow between Jerusalem and Athens: the synthesizers, the dogmatic atheists, and the various forces of the marketplace dedicated to harmony.

At this point a serious question arises. If the tension between Jerusalem and Athens drives one to make a choice, doesn't everybody "unstring the bow" at least on a personal level? Didn't Leo Strauss? Once one does make a choice, what replaces "the magnificent tension of the spirit"?

Athens and Jerusalem: The Interaction

Keeping these questions in mind, we seek progress by taking a closer look at the tension between Jerusalem and Athens and by shifting our angle of approach. We then notice that the two sides do not simply talk past each other; they argue and they are able to argue because they share certain things in common. First of all, Athens does not simply and solely stand for reason, at least not in the sense of the kind of modern rationalism most prominently associated with the name of Descartes. Rationalism is associated with the treatise as a form of expression, and Plato wrote dialogues instead of treatises. Those dialogues are full of myths and their leading character, Socrates, is greatly influenced by a daimon in his soul. The more systematic Aristotle writes treatises, to be sure, but he also treats intuition as an intellectual virtue. The very name "philosophy" means "love of wisdom" and love of wisdom is not synonymous with the possession of wisdom. The Socratic profession of ignorance, not repudiated by Aristotle, does not sit easily with a rationality one naturally associates with a triumphant march to definite conclusions.

Second, just as Athens is not rigidly rational, Jerusalem is not rigidly irrational. In appreciating that, Leo Strauss was given to pointing to the following biblical passage:

> Behold, I have taught you statutes and ordinances, even as the Lord my God commanded me, that you should do so in the midst of the Law whither ye go in to possess it. Observe therefore and do them; for this is your wisdom and your understanding in the sight of the peoples, that, when they bear all these statutes, shall say: "surely this grand nation is a wise and understanding people." (Deuteronomy 4:5–6)

In these words, Moses, speaking on behalf of God, assures the people of Israel, that the law they are commanded to follow will strike the nations to whom it was not revealed as wise. By the unassisted use of their reason, they will see the rationality of God's revelation. Surely that corroborates to a significant extent the dictum that "the fear of the Lord is the beginning of wisdom" (Psalms 111:10).

The story of God's creation of the world also shows forth the element of reason in the Bible. It is nowhere near as wild and incomprehensible as the various myths of creation to which it is frequently compared. It does suggest creation out of nothing, but the "Big Bang" theories of the world's origin have made modern people less incredulous than previous generations about that, given the immense authority of physics. Moreover, the whole process of creation from the first through the sixth day turns out to be amazingly intelligible when an unassisted human approaches them sympathetically. Nowhere has this been demonstrated more dazzlingly than in the exegetical comments on Genesis by Leo Strauss.[20]

Because of the great rationality one discovers in the Bible and in a Judaism grounded on the Bible, one can well become skeptical of the project of modern religious existentialism. Following Kierkegaard, that project involves a justification of a leap of faith because of the insufficiencies of human reason. One oversimplifies but one does not entirely distort existentialism when one understands it as the self-destruction of reason *by* reason, but that self-destruction secures only a most dubious victory of Jerusalem over Athens. Rather, it tends to secure a triumph for any and all *commitment*, for any orthodoxy rather than Jewish Orthodoxy. At worst Judaism may be at a disadvantage because it contains too great an element of rationality; at best one justifies an option for Babylon or Constantinsate or Mecca fully as much as a choice of Jerusalem.

Since Jerusalem is no stranger to rational argument, it can summon up an argument against Athens. It is worthwhile to summarize that argument as articulated in the thought of Leo Strauss, who was completely familiar with the way leading thinkers before him—especially Pascal—had presented it.

One may object to this procedure because the willingness or even eagerness to consider the claims of faith is all by itself a victory of Athens over Jerusalem. It attests to a kind of Athenian breadth one does not find in Athens. The lovers of reason are polite to the faithful, but the faithful simply tend to scorn the achievements of reason. In other words, our very openness to the issue of Jerusalem or Athens constitutes a victory for Athens. Perhaps it does, but it is a victory that involves the possibility of a final Athenian surrender to Jerusalem, so the case is worth stating anyhow.

The question central to Jerusalem concerns the right way to live and in one sense it is quickly and definitively answered:

> It hath been told thee, O man,
> What is good,
> And what the Lord doth require
> Of thee:
> Only to do justice, and to love
> Mercy and to walk
> Humbly with thy God. (Micah 6:8)

The pious Jew receives a firm answer to his question because he accepts divine guidance, though the full answer is not that short, because it is recorded, as it were, with the law, the Torah. Athens, too, has an answer to this question, and the answer is not a totally different one, but it comes from a different source. It is an answer that has at its source not the word of God, but the dictates of unassisted human reason.

However, it only seems that way. If one keeps asking "why" in response to all the answers offered by reason, one comes sooner or later to statements that are no longer grounded in reason. One reaches fundamental axioms that cannot themselves be proven, though they provide the proof for all that follows them. The search for a philosophy without presuppositions is futile, so that Athens as well as Jerusalem builds on faith.

When one ponders the power of reason, one comes to see the limits of reason. Reason cannot prove everything and it cannot absolutely disprove very much. It cannot, for example, disprove a negative, and it is rationally bound to acknowledge its own limits. To be most specific, reason must admit that revelation is possible, and this bare admission is all that revelation needs. One can picture reason and revelation as two boxers, with Joe Louis playing the role of revelation. It is said that before his fight with Max Schmeling, Louis was warned that Schmeling would give him very few openings. He replied: "One opening is all I need." Philosophy must grant that revelation is possible, and that is the one opening for Jerusalem.

Belief in revelation is a belief in miracles. Believers can point with some satisfaction at the failed efforts of a very great philosopher to prove the impossibility of miracles. Spinoza undertook to do that in his *Theologico-Political Treatise*, a book on which Leo Strauss has commented extensively and incisively. It is a magnificent book, but what did Spinoza succeed in demonstrating? He may have proved that it would be a miracle if there were miracles—but that is exactly what the party of Jerusalem contends. Given the greatest of all miracles, the existence of God, the belief in all other miracles is easy enough for the believers.[21]

Since reason is unable even to show that miracles cannot occur, revelation has nothing to fear from reason. In the argument between Jerusalem and Athens, Jerusalem wins by not losing and Athens loses by not winning. At first sight it might seem that by arguing one concedes a victory to reason, for to argue is to reason and when one reasons one meets reason on its home ground. But that first sight is deceiving. Reason is honor-bound to be respectful to any attempts to establish a rational limit to reason. It therefore is honor-bound at some point to say to believers, "You may be right," and at that point the believers can claim to know they are right by the grace of God.

Is this argument against reason and for revelation a conclusive one? Did Leo Strauss subscribe to that argument? Its most concise and eloquent exposition occurs toward the end of chapter 2 of *Natural Right and History*, a chapter entitled "Natural Right and the Distinction between Facts and Values." In that chapter, Leo Strauss considers the challenge to natural right posed by the thought of Max Weber, "the greatest social scientist of the century."[22] Strauss treats Weber with respect, but the latter is scarcely the hero of the book. That honor belongs to Socrates, whose thought Strauss articulates in two chapters immediately following the argument recorded above. Strauss obviously dissociates himself from Weber. Never to my knowledge does he dissociate himself from Socrates. Not Weber but Socrates is the hero of *Natural Right and History*. Socrates in a way stands for philosophy; but if philosophy stands for atheism, as we have seen, and Socrates stands for philosophy, then Socrates stands for atheism. Nothing of which I know in the thought of Leo Strauss contradicts that bald assertion, and a great deal lends it weight. In turn, we must give the utmost weight to a counterargument explicit in the words and deeds of Socrates to the above explicated argument on behalf of revelation over reason. In trying to understand Strauss, it is urgent for us to do so, for we can reasonably assume him to be a follower of Socrates in this regard.

Philosophy and Atheism

Leo Strauss opposed and even denounced dogmatic atheism.[23] I tend to follow Hannah Arendt in the assumption that *all* atheism is dogmatic: an atheist is somebody who claims to know what cannot be known, hence he or she is a dogmatist. Before assenting to this assumption, however, we do well to examine the possibility of a Socratic undogmatic atheism. The Athenians may have been right in their insistence that Socrates was in fact an atheist. Let us assume so. But coming from a man who repeatedly professed ignorance, who knew only that he knew nothing, the atheism of Socrates would not, could not be dogmatic atheism. It eschews the criterion of Cartesian certainty.

According to a line of argument we can provisionally call Socratic, we do not have certain knowledge of the nonexistence of God, but uncertain knowledge can nevertheless be real knowledge. We may be unable to develop a strict proof that we are not dreaming when we are awake, but the tiny residue of uncertainty does not affect our actions or even have any noticeable effect on the landscape of our mind. We cannot prove that weightless and invisible goblins do not hover over us and attempt to impede our actions, but there is no discernible difference between acting as though they do not exist and knowing they do not exist.

Socratic atheism does not deny that we must assume certain things the existence of which we are unable to prove. It denies instead that God is one of those things. It proceeds by way of a dialectical examination of opinions. It then rejects the opinions it finds wanting. Belief in God turns out to be one of those opinions (for example, many events ascribed to divine agency can be better understood as chance events). The gulf between the philosopher and believer can never be bridged because the philosopher doubts what she can and believes what she must, while the believer believes what he can and doubts what he must.[24]

Philosophy and Happiness

This line of argument may or may not be compelling; in either case it is important to realize the extravagant claims it involves. It assumes that all believers are on some level subject to a fundamental delusion. It therefore necessarily involves the claim that one understands believers, who do not consider themselves subject to delusions, better than they understand themselves, a claim that nobody considered more problematical than did Leo Strauss. Nobody doubts that some people must be understood better than they understand themselves; anybody except Napoleon who has ever fancied himself to be Napoleon. But do we really, can we really, understand Moses better than he understood himself? What about Abraham?

Second, the argument sketched above obviously involves the claim that philosophy is the best way of life, but it is impossible to divorce considerations of superiority from considerations of happiness. Is philosophy the happiest way of life? One can plausibly argue that Socrates was a genuinely happy man, graced by an altogether enviable combination of wisdom, serenity, gentleness and playful wit.[25] Yet, while Socrates may have been *the* philosopher for Leo Strauss, he was not the only philosopher. One should consider the case of two modern philosophers whom Strauss studied with the greatest assiduity, Rousseau and Nietzsche. It is easier to see that they were great men than that they were happy men. One need not indulge in biographical trivialization to learn about their great suffering; one has only to read their own words to know they suffered. Their pain, as far as we can tell, was not always due to inevitable external circumstances.

I cannot here deal with the intriguing possibility that Leo Strauss might argue that modern philosophers are significantly less happy than were ancient philosophers. It must suffice that Strauss did advance the "greater happiness" claim when writing about Judah Halevi; at least he came very close to it. He states that in "the case of a man such as Halevi . . . the influence on him consists in a conversion to philosophy; for some time, we prefer to think for a very short time, he was a philosopher."[26]

The whole discussion on this point is shrouded in ambiguity because Strauss immediately goes on to state that Halevi "returned to the Jewish fold." How is it possible to cease being a philosopher? Perhaps one can return to the Jewish fold by remaining a philosopher and writing esoterically. We must remind ourselves that this whole discussion occurs in a book whose overriding theme is "writing between the lines."

I have become convinced of what in previous study of Strauss I could not accept, that Leo Strauss was of the party of Athens and not of the party of Jerusalem.[27] What makes the conclusion difficult for me, and not only me, and what makes it provisional for me is the exorbitant claim for philosophy tied to it. The philosopher does not just claim that philosophy can in effect prove a negative, but also that it knows that divine revelation is an impossibility for all time to come. Leo Strauss begins *The Argument and the Action of Plato's Laws* with the following quotation from Avicenna: "the treatment of prophecy and the Divine Law is contained in the *Laws*."[28]

Nothing following this quotation allows one to suggest that Leo Strauss differs from Avicenna's lavish assessment. The philosopher, Plato in this case, claims to know in a decisive way what can and cannot happen in human history even in the future. He knows by the power of his own thought that divine revelation is impossible. Evidently this is the final position of Leo Strauss; at least the book on Plato's *Laws* is his final book.

If Leo Strauss chose Athens over Jerusalem, and I think he did, one must add at once that this choice did not lead to the "unstringing of the bow." Perhaps he would have argued that philosophy has its own built-in "magnificent tension of the spirit." It is locked in an invigorating combat against an enemy over whom there is no final and conclusive victory. That enemy is ignorance.

Strauss's Choice

Did Leo Strauss make the right choice? I have already telegraphed my answer to this final question: I do not know. On the one hand, I am unable to refute his preference for Athens. On the other hand, the preference does not completely satisfy me. The position Leo Strauss espouses, that of undogmatic atheism, seems to me either indistinguishable from the wishy-washiness of agnosticism or else so full of *hybris*—given its claim that revelation is false—that it becomes indistinguishable from dogmatism.

Not knowing, I turn to another question, to which I will hazard an answer. If Leo Strauss chose Athens over Jerusalem why didn't he just come out and say so? To explain that one has finally to claim that Leo Strauss himself wrote esoterically: he did so by writing between the lines, so that only a few, the "happy few," would understand him. That may well be the case, but what is the point of writing esoterically so late in the twentieth century? It is easy to justify the esotericism of previous times by arguing that while religion was false it was also useful to decent life. But the utility of religion necessitates belief in its truth, and that confidence in its truth had been eroded by Feuerbach, Marx, Nietzsche, and others in the nineteenth century: why continue to be secretive about one's atheism when the truth of atheism has been let out of the bag?

Some great love and loyalty to the Jewish people are in evidence in the life and works of Leo Strauss. Even after the cat has been let out of the bag, the reticence of Maimonides remains preferable to the boldness of Spinoza, who was a good thinker but not a good Jew.

Leo Strauss *was* a good Jew. He knew the dignity and worth of love of one's own. Love of the good, which is the same thing as love of the truth, is higher than love of one's own, but there is only one road to the truth, and it leads through love of one's own. Strauss showed his loyalty to things Jewish in a way he was uniquely qualified to do, by showing generations of students how to treat Jewish texts with the utmost care and devotion. In this way he turned a number of his Jewish students in the direction of becoming better Jews. I know this for I am one of them.

Notes

1. *Concluding Unscientific Postscript*, trans. D. F. Swenson and W. Lowrie (Princeton: Princeton University Press, 1968), 166.
2. The argument I criticize is succinctly expressed by Thomas L. Pangle in his introduction to *Leo Strauss: The Rebirth of Classical Political Rationalism*, ed. T. L. Pangle (Chicago: University of Chicago Press, 1989), vii–xxxvii.
3. Strauss discusses the relationship between love of one's own and love of the good in various places. The best introduction to the subject is chapter 3, "The Origin of the Idea of Natural Right," of *Natural Right and History* (Chicago: University of Chicago Press, 1953), 81–119.
4. *Thoughts on Machiavelli* (Glencoe, Ill.: Free Press, 1958), 13.
5. See the following writings of Strauss: *The Argument and Action of Plato's Laws* (Chicago: University of Chicago Press, 1975), 2; *Studies in Platonic Political Philosophy* (Chicago: University of Chicago Press, 1983), 147–73; *What Is Political Philosophy? and Other Studies* (Chicago: University of Chicago Press, 1988), 9–55.
6. "Brute fact of revelation " is from a letter to Karl Löwith of 10 Jan 1946, reprinted in *Independent Journal of Philosophy* 4 (1980): 108. This letter should be read cautiously as evidence, as indeed should all private communications by Strauss, until one determines his relationship with the given correspondent.
7. See *Persecution and the Art of Writing* (Glencoe, Ill.: Free Press, 1952), 43, 95–141.
8. Leo Strauss, Introduction to Maimonides, *Guide of the Perplexed*, trans. S. Pines (Chicago: University of Chicago Press, 1963), xiv.
9. *Persecution and the Art of Writing*, 106–7.
10. Ibid. The essay on Halevi repays the closest possible study for illumination of our theme.
11. Ibid. Strauss quotes Goethe in German. The translation here is mine.
12. *Athens and Jerusalem*, trans. B. Martin (New York, 1968), 67–68. For the origin of the use of "Athens" and "Jerusalem" as symbolizing the differences between reason and revelation, see Tertullian, *De Praescriptione Haereticorum* 7; also, H. A. Wolfson, *The Philosophy of the Church Fathers*, 3d ed. rev. (Cambridge, Mass.: Harvard University Press, 1970), 102ff.
13. *Athens and Jerusalem*, 375.

14. *Faith and Political Philosophy: The Correspondence of Leo Strauss and Eric Voegelin, 1934–1964*, trans. and ed. P. Emberley and B. Cooper (University Park, Penn.: Penn State Press, 1993), 78. See note 6 above.

15. *On Tyranny*, rev. exp. ed. with the Strauss-Kojève correspondence (Ithaca, N.Y.: Cornell University Press, 1968), 205.

16. See *Philosophy and Law: Essays toward the Understanding of Maimonides and His Predecessors*, trans. F. Baumann (Philadelphia: Jewish Publication Society of America, 1987), 107–10; also, *Studies in Platonic Political Philosophy*, 233–47.

17. See *The Rebirth of Classical Political Rationalism*, 27–46.

18. *Studies in Platonic Political Philosophy*, 174–191.

19. *Beyond Good and Evil: Prelude to a Philosophy of the Future*, trans. W. Kaufmann (New York: Macmillan, 1966), 3; see also *Studies in Platonic Political Philosophy*, 174.

20. *Studies in Platonic Political Philosophy*, 152–63.

21. *Tractatus Theologico-Politicus*, trans. R. H. M. Elwes (New York: Dover, 1951), 81–97. See Strauss's *Spinoza's Critique of Religion*, trans. E. M. Sinclair (New York: Schocken Books, 1965).

22. *Natural Right and History*, 36.

23. See Strauss's epilogue to *Essays on the Scientific Study of Politics*, ed. H. Storing (New York: Holt, Rinehart & Winston, 1962).

24. I have learned a great deal about the argument from my friends: Nasser Behneger, David Bolotin, David Leibowitz, Thomas Pangle, and others. I should also record my general indebtedness in this respect to my beloved friend of blessed memory, Allan Bloom.

25. See Xenophon, *Memorabilia*, 1.6.14.

26. See *Persecution and the Art of Writing*, 109.

27. See my "Leo Strauss as Citizen and Jew," *Interpretation* 17 (1990): 433–47.

28. *The Argument and Action of Plato's Laws*, 1.

8

Philosophy and the Possibility of Revelation: A Theological Response to the Challenge of Leo Strauss

David Novak

There are three basic ways that one can hear or read the words of a particular thinker: one, as a disciple; two, as a student; and three, as an opponent. The disciple believes that everything (or almost everything) this thinker says and writes is the truth. What the disciple does not understand is what is not *yet* true for him or her; the present lack of understanding is his or her own problem, and it is hoped that it will be only temporary.[1] The student, on the other hand, believes that some of what the thinker says and writes is true and some of it is not true. Even what the student does not believe is true in the words of the thinker is still respected as a challenging alternative that calls for a respectfully reasoned response. Finally, there is the opponent who believes that nothing or almost nothing that thinker says or writes is true. The response of the opponent is usually one of dismissal, often involving personal ridicule or contempt.

Leo Strauss, *zikhrono li-vrakhah* (may his memory be blessed), has certainly inspired disciples, students, and opponents. And, at least among the disciples and the students, there are internal disputes.

Among Strauss's disciples, both those who learned from Strauss

himself and those who have learned from them or, by now, from
their disciples—those who either call themselves or are called by
others "Straussians"—there are disputes over what the master
really *meant*. Among those who have learned from Strauss, there
are disputes over what exactly is true in Strauss's teaching and can
be accepted, and what is not true in it. As for Strauss's opponents,
who are most often the opponents of *both* Strauss's disciples and
students, the usually categorical character of their dismissal of him
does not seem to admit enough doubt for there to be internal
disputes among them.

I would classify myself as a sympathetic student of Leo Strauss,
one who learned much from his lectures that I was privileged to
hear as an undergraduate at the University of Chicago, much from
the few personal conversations I was honored to have had with
him, and much from his writings that seem to be always at hand in
my own research and thought. Therefore, unlike Strauss's opponents, I am not here to either refute him or—God forbid—dismiss
him. Unlike his disciples, I am not here to explicate what Strauss
himself *really* meant, what his own point of view *truly* was. Frankly,
I am unclear about that; in fact, greater clarity on that is something
I have long hoped to learn from Strauss's disciples in their ongoing
intramural disputes.[2] For what Strauss *himself* really meant, what
his *own* point of view really was, is far from clear and evident. If it
were, there would be much more unanimity among his disciples
than there currently is. So, in the interim anyway, what I want to
do is to respectfully respond to the challenge to theology Strauss
seems to present, specifically to the challenge to the traditionalist
Jewish theology I espouse—although Christians and Muslims might
well respond to this challenge to their theologies similarly. In fact,
I believe that responding to the challenge Strauss seems to present
might well be one of the most powerful stimulants available to
Jewish theology today.[3]

Strauss's Challenge to Theology

Where might we find the *locus classicus* of Strauss's challenge to
Jewish theology? In first preparing myself for these reflections, I
needed the counsel of someone who knew Strauss far better than
I. So, I consulted my friend Joseph Cohen of St. John's College in
Annapolis, who had been a graduate student of Strauss for a

number of years at the University of Chicago, and who had enlightened me before about other aspects of Strauss's work. He wisely suggested that this locus is found in Strauss's little known essay from the early 1950s, "The Mutual Influence of Theology and Philosophy."[4] (Let be remembered that this essay began as a lecture Strauss gave in Jerusalem, a city—and not just an idea—he loved.[5]) After studying it, I agree with Professor Cohen's judgment, although as in all of Strauss's statements, it is difficult to locate Strauss's own opinion. But, since that is not my concern, I will only take some of the statements made there and respond to them. If what I am quoting is not what Strauss himself really meant, it is still an insightful presentation of what someone else meant, someone else worth responding to.

At the beginning of this great essay, Strauss writes about "the philosopher [being] open to the challenge of theology or the theologian [being] open to the challenge of philosophy."[6] At the end of the essay, Strauss writes that "philosophy must admit the possibility of revelation."[7] My questions are: What is the challenge of philosophy to theology? And, what can it mean for theology that philosophy admits the possibility of its prime datum, which is revelation? Let me begin my response with the second question, the one about the possibility of revelation, and conclude with the first question, the one about philosophy's challenge to theology. I can only hope that my responses will be worthy of the greatness of the thinker who has elicited them.

The Possibility of Revelation

The insistence that philosophy must admit the possibility of revelation implies that there are philosophers who would deny any such possibility. Who are they? Strauss, who sees philosophy as a way of life, states that "the right way of life cannot be fully established except by an understanding of the nature of man, and the nature of man cannot be fully clarified except by an understanding of the nature of the whole."[8] Then, speaking of Socrates as the paradigm of one who lived the philosophical life, Strauss says that Socrates was one "who knew he knew nothing, who therewith admitted that the whole is not intelligible, who merely wondered by saying the whole is not intelligible we do not admit to have some understanding of the whole."[9] So, in other words, philosophers who deny the possibility of revelation are those who are convinced, unlike Socrates, that they do have understanding of the whole and that revelation could not possibly be part of it, let alone the apex of the whole as the theologians usually assert. However, after Hegel, I am unaware of any philosopher who seems to have thought that he or she could explain the whole.[10] Moreover, even Hegel, who seems to have made such a claim in his later thought, did not dismiss the possibility of revelation; he like Spinoza before him only denied its ultimacy, reserving that distinct honor for philosophy alone.[11]

It seems, therefore, that it is not the case that some philosophers deny the possibility of revelation since the only impossibility one can cogently deny is logical impossibility. Yet there is nothing inherently illogical about the doctrine of revelation. What most philosophers do deny, however, is revelation's importance. Even if the possibility of revelation is admitted—which means it *could* occur—such an occurrence would make little or no difference to the quest for truth that animates authentic philosophers. Revelation could easily be relegated to the realm of the accidental, where it would be as far as possible from the realm of the essential. If the matter, then, is left at this impasse, philosophy and theology could not have any mutual influence at all. To cite two prominent modern examples, what influence could a philosopher like Bertrand Russell have on a theologian like Karl Barth and vice versa? Accordingly, the question is not just one about the possibility of the event of revelation, rather it is one about the possibility of the authority of revelation. Is that something a philosopher could authentically admit? It is the authority of revelation that challenges everybody, philosophers included.

Now when one speaks of authority, one is in the realm of political philosophy, the realm where Leo Strauss did his work as a scholar and a thinker; and the Hebrew Bible, the record of revelation accepted as authoritative by traditional Jews (and Christians *mutatis mutandis*), is a consummately political book. (So is the *Quran*.) The Bible is the constitution of a covenant between God and the world, and particularly between God and the people of Israel. The question, then, is: What philosophical understanding of authority admits the possibility that its ultimate truth could only come from revelation? Only a question like this could indicate why theologians should be open to the influence of philosophy. Without a question like this, there is simply no commonality in which influence, either way or both ways, could possibly take place.

Revelation and Political Authority

If the common nexus between philosophy and theology lies in the question of political authority, then we must ask just what philosophical understanding of political authority causes the philosopher not only to admit the possibility of revelation, but also to actually desire it. Revelation's importance as a ground of human action presupposes that it is desired as good, indeed the *summum bonum*.[12] So the Psalmist says, "As for me, the nearness of God is good for me" (Psalms 73:28). That nearness of God is the nearness of God's authoritative word. So the Deuteronomist says, "For the Word is very close to you, in your mouth and in your heart to be done" (Deuteronomy 30:14).

Modern discussions of political authority usually see the main issue as being that of autonomy versus heteronomy. However, only when we get ourselves out of this modern dichotomy can we see a real nexus between philosophy and theology. Nevertheless, we must first work our way through and out of this dichotomy because it is ours.[13]

Autonomy recognizes the self as the ultimate authority. It holds that the only commands having moral validity are those that the self issues to itself. Minimally, autonomy means independence. The mode of society that autonomy posits is that created by *contract*—that is, morally valid political standards are those that are or can be agreed upon by equally independent selves as authoritative for all. Heteronomy, on the other hand, recognizes the self as being part of a larger structure and thus having to conform to commands not of its own making but to those of an external authority. Minimally, heteronomy means dependence. The mode of society that heteronomy posits is one having preexistent hierarchy—that is, morally valid political standards are ones that assign to a person his or her rightful *status* in a society, a status existing prior to one's individual entrance into it. This distinction between autonomy and heteronomy underlies a number of important modern theories about society and its institutions such as Sir Henry Maine's distinctions between ancient and modern law, and Ferdinand Tönnies' distinctions between *Gemeinschaft* and *Gesell-*

schaft.[14] Nevertheless, despite the modern preference for this distinction, its roots are surely ancient.

The most cogent philosophical defense of heteronomy was made by Plato and his student Aristotle. Plato regarded the very notion of "self-mastery"—later understood as "autonomy"—to be absurd because it violates the distinction between subject and object that is presupposed by any coherent notion of transitive action. Therefore, he emphasizes that rule must be by the better part over the worse part, be those parts of the soul or of the city.[15] In order for rule to be beneficial, reason must rule over what is not rational. In the soul, reason must rule both the passions and the appetites. In the city, more rational persons must rule less rational persons. In both realms, that relation is inherently unequal.[16] Aristotle argues on both empirical and normative grounds that "to rule (*archein*) and to be ruled (*archesthai*) is both necessary and beneficial."[17] As such, hierarchy is inevitable (pure anarchy being in the human world as much a phantom as a pure vacuum in the physical world). The only question is what form of hierarchy is best. However, in contrast to what we shall be examining next, this hierarchy does not terminate in the human subject; rather, the human soul orients itself toward an end above itself, and by that criterion it rules what is below it.[18]

The most cogent philosophical defense of autonomy comes from Kant although, as we shall soon see, its roots long predate him. He emphasizes that it is the "law-making" power of the rational will "which determines all value."[19] That power is the ability to make rules that could apply to oneself as well as any other rational person in the same situation. Since, for Kant, great philosophical ability is not required to make rational moral judgments, one can assume an inherent equality among all persons having at least ordinary mental ability.[20] This is because Kant makes moral action more important in the human world than speculation about the basic structures of nature. By doing this he inverts 180 degrees the priorities of Plato and Aristotle.

This emphasis of Kant can be better understood by looking at the very etymology of the word *autonomy*. It comes from two Greek words: *autos* meaning "self," and *nomos* meaning "law." The problematic term is *autos*. Does it means "self" in the sense of "self-identity" as in A = A, or does it mean "self" in the sense of "self-awareness"? In other words, is "self" a point of reference, or is it a person who refers? If it means the former, that is, "the rule of law *it*self," then are we not back to the classical natural law position that asserts that reason is itself inherently normative?[21] It seems that Kant means something more radically innovative than that. He seems to mean that the self is capable of constructing a rational order in which it is both sovereign and subject. Accordingly, it seems that when Kant speaks of the rational human person as *Zweck an sich selbst*, the word "selbst" refers both to the irreducible selfhood of the human subject of the act as well as to the irreducible selfhood of the human object of the act, which begins by being located within the same person. Hence, suicide is the first moral situation Kant deals with in both the *Groundwork of the Metaphysics of Morals* and *Metaphysics of Morals*.[22] That oscillating role of sovereign/subject is the condition that makes for human equality in Kant's ideal democracy.[23] It is the ideal condition of every normal person. Authority, which is of course required by the division of labor in any society, even an ideal one, is relative and not absolute as it is for Plato and Aristotle. Every person, being primarily an end-in-himself/herself, is always to transcend any use of his or her labor as a means.

Nevertheless, attempts to constitute society on exclusively heteronomous grounds or exclusively autonomous grounds are subject to serious philosophical critique. The philosophical notion that individual human persons are to find their total fulfillment in an all encompassing, heteronomous, social order, the root of which comes from Plato (the Plato of the *Republic*, that is) has most recently been the target of Karl Popper.[24] Popper sees this notion as the most original philosophical justification of the totalitarianism of ideologues, which has brought such mind-boggling suffering to humankind in our own century especially. But, if Popper's critique is too colored by modernist prejudices for some, let me remind them that Aristotle had similar suspicions. For Aristotle, unlike Plato, the person's relationship with family is something the state must honor with restraint.[25] Furthermore, for Aristotle, also unlike Plato, the true metaphysician is able to transcend even the best society by becoming godlike, never to be morally obligated to serve any society again.[26]

The philosophical notion that an adequate human society can be constituted on the basis of autonomy alone has also been the target of philosophers since Hegel.[27] Most recently, philosophers such as Mary Ann Glendon and Michael Sandel have argued against John Rawls's view of autonomous justice, pointing out that the coherent survival of society requires that society be able to make claims on its citizens that are not themselves reducible to the individual right to contract—even to contract a social contract.[28]

So it seems that the best order philosophers can constitute for society is a mixture of heteronomy and autonomy—for autonomy alone seems to lead to anarchy, and heteronomy alone seems to lead to tyranny. Autonomy alone does not bring with it enough society; heteronomy alone brings with it too much society. Thus in democratic societies, which are the only places in the world where such debates can be conducted in public, philosophical debates (in the broadest sense of the term) are generally about how the rights of the majority are balanced by the rights of minorities and vice versa, the most basic minority being the individual person. The rubric of these debates is essentially the same not only for positivists, but also for adherents of natural law.[29] As Charles Taylor has recently demonstrated so powerfully, moral discourse in our society becomes almost unintelligible if not conducted with a vocabulary in which human selfhood is central.[30]

So far, the level of political philosophy that we have been examining does not seem to have any opening for theology at all. For the subject of theology, who is God, specifically the God of biblical revelation, is certainly neither a majority nor a minority, neither a society nor an individual. This God is not a majority because God is One (*ehad*) whereas a majority is many. This God is not a minority because God is Unique (*ehad*) and thus could not become part of any society as an individual can and must become.[31] Where, then, does political philosophy provide an opening for the God of biblical revelation, whether it is aware of it or not? I think that for this opening we must return to the ancients (who were so preferred by Leo Strauss), especially to Plato, the Plato of the *Republic*.

It will be recalled that at the beginning of this work, Socrates shows the inherent inconsistencies of three views of justice, those of Cephalus, Polemarchus, and Thrasymachus. However, when he is confronted by the view of Glaucon, he has no such logical refutation. For Glaucon basically presents the social contract theory that Socrates himself had accepted as the argument of the laws of Athens in the *Crito*.[32] The argument is that society can make claims on individuals who have already given their tacit consent to that society's authority. In Socrates' particular case, this meant that he would restrain himself from escaping from the death sentence of the Athenian court because by remaining in Athens of his own free choice he thereby accepted the authority of Athenian legal institutions. These institutions, nevertheless, could not make unconditional, total claims on him or any citizen. They could not stop him from being a philosopher.[33] Thus, his life and those of his fellow Athenians were involved in a delicate balance between personal rights and communal duties. In a somewhat different context, Freud called the balance of psychic demands made by what he called the pleasure principle and the reality principle the "economics of the libido," and sadly concluded that this is the best that civilization and its *discontents* could come up with.[34]

Unlike the first three views of justice, the view of Glaucon is not one that is necessarily false, it is only one that is humanly insufficient. It is insufficient because it sees the human person as essentially schizoid, unable to devote himself or herself to anything or to anyone with a full soul. At this level though, the human soul is restless, a restlessness that only a fool would deny.[35] Plato's constitution of his philosophical polity is his answer to this restlessness of the human soul. Theology cannot accept his constitution as the solution as we shall presently argue, but the very recognition of the question is the only opening that theology needs. At this level, philosophy and theology can at long last truly take each other seriously. Both philosophy and theology now believe that the solution to the human predicament lies in humans being properly related to that which surpasses them but which cannot itself be surpassed, or as Anselm unforgettably put it: "that which nothing greater can be conceived" (*id quo maius non cogitari nequit*).[36] And *that* certainly surpasses humans whether they are taken individually or collectively. The difference between theology and philosophy lies in whether the relationship with that greatest reality originates from below (as in philosophy) or from above (as in theology).

Creation and Revelation

Let us now see why theology can share Plato's question while simultaneously rejecting his answer. In the *Mishnah*, which is the second most authoritative book in Judaism after the Bible, we find a principle that appears in numerous rabbinic discussions thereafter. It is: "One may benefit another person without their

consent (*zakheen l'adam she-lo bi-fanav*), but one may not obligate
(*ein haveen*) another person without their consent."[37] An example
of this would be: I may accept money on your behalf without your
consent, but I may not pledge money on your behalf without your
consent. My right to benefit you without your consent assumes that
I know what is beneficial to you, a benefit you yourself acknowledge in principle. However, if it turns out that what I thought was
beneficial to you is not acknowledged by you in principle, then my
assumed benefit for you is in fact a detriment, which may be
refused. (In rabbinic Hebrew, *hov* is the same word for detriment
and obligation.[38]) The reason behind this formulation is that I have
more authority over my own life than you do because I have more
knowledge and concern for my own interests than you do. The
converse is equally true, that is, you have more authority over your
own life than I do because you have more knowledge and concern
for your own interests than I do.

    If left at this level alone, we seem to have the epistemological
foundation of moral autonomy, namely, I am transparent to myself
just as you are transparent to yourself. However, there are times
when you are required to act for my benefit even without my
consent, even contrary to it. Such action is required when I am in
danger of harming myself. When this is the case, then "you shall
not stand idly by the blood of your neighbor" (Leviticus 19:16).
When this is the case, I do not know what my benefit truly is; I am
not transparent to myself.[39] Furthermore, the other in the person
of society itself is authorized to enact rules for the common good
of which I am a part, even if that part is an unwilling minority. In
other words, society is at times authorized to act heteronomously.
The balance of heteronomy and autonomy is based on the assumption that no one is totally transparent, even to themselves. On the
other hand, though, the inevitable anarchy of autonomy is based
on the erroneous assumption that individuals are totally transparent
to themselves; and the inevitable tyranny of heteronomy is based
on the equally erroneous assumption that individual persons are
totally transparent to society—at least to the ideal society run by
savants. It can be argued that the schizoid social contract qua social
compromise described by Socrates in the *Crito* and advocated by
Glaucon in the *Republic*, and then followed more or less by modern
social contract theorists, is preferable to both of these extreme
political options.

    However, the reason that this balance in a society constituted by revelation does not lead to the schizoid state of human life that we have just seen is that both the individual person and the society itself are totally transparent to God. "For humans only see appearances, but the Lord sees the heart" (I Samuel 16:7). "Above all, the heart is deceitful; it is wounded (*v'anush hu*). Who knows it? I the Lord get to the bottom of the heart" (Jeremiah 17:9–10).[40] It is revelation that makes this fundamental truth known to the people—both collectively and individually—to whom God has chosen to reveal God's self and God's law. Revelation is from the creator God who alone has perfect vision of the whole and everything in it—we humans included—because "He made us and not we ourselves" (Psalms 100:3). God's commandments are addressed to all created entities: human and nonhuman, individual and collective. The only way of life, then, that is truly sufficient to our nature must come from the Unique One (*ehad*) who transcends the limits of created nature itself. As the *Mishnah* puts it, "Beloved are Israel having been given a desirable vessel [the Torah], and it is an additional act of love that it is made known to them [by God] that this desirable vessel is that through which the world is created."[41] Israel's revelation thus privileges her to be aware of what is the true fulfillment of human nature, a nature that reflects the nature of the whole created universe.

God's authority is the total authority unique to the creator of the universe. Obviously, it is not "autonomous" in the modern anthropocentric (and ultimately atheistic, in my opinion) sense of that word that we have seen above. It is not "heteronomous" either because it does not come from an "other" (*heteros*). It does not come from a stranger, whose authority, as we have also seen above, is only valid when limited and distributed, but invalid when unlimited and ubiquitous. God is closer to our nature than any of us are to ourselves (*autos*). With all "other gods," however, we are esentially alienated from our nature.[42] As the Talmud puts it, "God does not deal with his creatures as a tyrant."[43] That is why the Mishnah teaches, "God wanted to benefit (*le-zakkot*) his people, so he multiplied commandments for them."[44] God can benefit the people much more than they can ever benefit themselves.

For theologians who have been open to the influence of philosophy, the natural law that humans can discern from the dim mirror of nature is part of the larger divine law that is revealed more directly by God. We see this in theologians as otherwise disparate as Maimonides, Aquinas, and Calvin.[45] However, unlike later rationalists, they do not think natural law and divine law are identical.[46] Unlike later fideists, they did not think that natural law and divine law are antithetical.[47]

For philosophers who have been open to the influence of theology, natural law is seen as coming to nature from the divine lawgiver, even though these philosophers can be agnostic about any particular historical revelation. Indeed, as Strauss's oldest disciple Harry V. Jaffa has shown, the very term "natural law" is itself an oxymoron in ancient pagan philosophy, for *natura* or *physis* is the opposite of *lex* or *nomos*.[48] Hence that term could only enter philosophical discourse that is open to the influence of theology. When the word *law* is used nonfiguratively, it presupposes that there is a lawgiver.[49] Therefore, natural law presupposes, in the words of the Declaration of Independence, "Nature's God," who being the *creator* is not the same as "the God *of* Nature." Nevertheless, natural law is the province of philosophy and not theology precisely because it is not directly derived from the words of revelation but, rather, from reflection on the limits or ends of the human condition itself. To confuse theology and philosophy at this key juncture is to commit a most disastrous category error.

Philosophy's Challenge to Theology

Strauss was quite astute to see that the philosopher's problem with revelation derives from the question he raised in his article "The Mutual Influence of Theology and Philosophy," namely, "is the tradition reliable?"—that is, the tradition through which revelation is transmitted to all of us who are not prophets.[50] (The assumption of the Bible and the rabbis is that all the people of Israel, at least when the first two commandments of the Decalogue were uttered, were themselves prophets for that moment.[51]) Moreover, he raises the question of "one particular divine code [being] accepted as truly divine" and "all other allegedly divine codes [being] simply denied."[52] In other words, there are competing revelations, and even if there were only one, how do we know that it is accurate?

Philosophy, of course, cannot answer either of these questions. A philosophical answer would have to judge which revelation, if any, presented the best law inasmuch as revelation for the three religions of revelation—Judaism, Christianity, and Islam—is explicitly normative. But, as Strauss rightly points out in this essay (speaking as a Jew about Judaism), "if this is the case, is then the allegedly revealed law not in fact the product of reason, of human reason, the work of Moses and not of God?"[53] It is one thing for philosophy to admit the possibility of revelation; it is quite another thing for philosophy to claim that it can validate revelation. No true theologian could ever accept such external validation. As the Bible puts it, "There is no wisdom, there is no understanding, there is no counsel, over above (*le-neged*) the Lord" (Proverbs 21:30).[54] Revelation is only validated by the experience of responsively hearing the voice of God, or by the trust one has for those who have transmitted the story of revelation and its normative content.

However, what philosophy can do for theology is to elucidate its *conditio sine qua non*, its minimal condition, without judging its *conditio per quam*, its ultimate ground.[55] Philosophy and theology can agree on what the moral prerequisites of a society worthy of human loyalty are to be. Strauss speaks of "a broad agreement between the Bible and Greek philosophy regarding both morality and the insufficiency of morality; the disagreement concerns that 'x' which completes morality."[56] The rabbis speak of the area of interhuman relations (*bein adam le-havero*) with which part of the Torah is concerned as being most akin to the workings of human reason, as being that "which even if it were not written, it should have been written."[57] Aristotle saw custom (*ethos*) as being capable of rational explanation (*ēthikē*).[58] And both the rabbis and Aristotle, *mutatis mutandis*, saw the realm of the interhuman as ultimately subordinate to the realm of the divine-human. Here philosophy as practical reason, the practical reason that discerns natural law, is of most help to theology because it prevents theology from sinking from the level of the superrational to the level of the subrational, that is, to the level of superstition and fanaticism. So also does practical reason prevent metaphysics—theoretical philosophy—from sinking to the level of irresponsible flight into fantasy. In our day, practical reason prevents both *Torah* and *theōria* from sinking to the level of ideology, which argues neither from revelation nor nature, both of which are public (as Maimonides emphasized), but only from the private vision of the ideologue. In other words, the enemy of both *Torah* and *theōria*, in both ancient and modern times, is gnosticism, of which ideology is only its modern manifestation.[59]

Let me give one example of how this philosophical influence on theology works from the writings of Strauss's favorite Jewish theologian, Maimonides. The Torah commands the people of Israel to exterminate the Amalekites. "Blot out the memory of the Amalekites from under the heavens" (Deuteronomy 25:19). Two grounds for this command seem to be found. One is that of revenge for the unprovoked attack of the Israelites by the Amalekites when they left Egypt (25:17–18a), an attack upon noncombatants as well as on combatants. The second is that the Amalekites "did not fear God" (25:18b), fear of God being a biblical term for elementary human decency and restraint.[60]

If the ground of revenge is emphasized, then the present moral condition of the Amalekites is irrelevant: an old score is to be settled. Israel is to do to Amalek as Amalek did to Israel. To use a rabbinic term, it is "measure for measure" (middah ke-neged middah).[61] However, if the ground of fear of God is emphasized, then what if the present moral condition of the Amalekites has changed? What if they have repented of their evil, either all of them or even only some of them?[62] To interpret the commandment as being categorical rather than hypothetical would be blatantly unjust. Therefore, Maimonides, basing himself on earlier rabbinic speculation—not legislation per se—writes in his code of Jewish law, the Mishneh Torah: "Even though Scripture says about Amalek 'Blot out the memory of Amalek' (Deuteronomy 25:19) that only pertains to those who did not accept peace terms (she-lo hishleemu)."[63] Thus he changed what appeared to have been a categorical imperative into a hypothetical imperative. As the commentator on Maimonides, Joseph Karo, pointed out, basing himself on Maimonides' whole ethical approach, "this means they accepted the seven Noahide laws . . . thus removing themselves from the moral category of 'Amalek' and becoming proper (ha-kesherim) Noahides."[64] "Noahides" is the rabbinic name for humankind; and "the seven Noahide laws" is the rabbinic term for natural law, as I have argued elsewhere.[65]

In other words, criteria of rational morality are invoked to interpret revelation. But, unlike modern Jewish thinkers such as Hermann Cohen, against whose approach to Judaism Strauss argued more than once, the criteria of rational morality do not constitute revelation.[66] There is much more to revelation than morality, but not anything less. As Maimonides emphasized elsewhere, all philosophers are not prophets, but all prophets are first philosophers.[67] In the end, the theologians can account for philosophy, but the philosophers cannot account for revelation.

Thus Deutero-Isaiah, in his messianic vision states:

All the nations are gathered together, the peoples are assembled. Who among them can tell this and let us understand the first things? Can they put forth their witnesses and be justified so that they will be heard and say 'it is truth' (*emet*). You are my witnesses, says the Lord, my servant whom I have chosen, so that you may know and be certain of Me and understand that I am He, before Me no god has been and after me none will be. (Isaiah 43:9–10)

In the earliest translation of the Bible, that of the Septuagint into Greek, we see that "first things"—*ri'shonot*—of the Hebrew text is translated *ex archēs*. Since it is not unreasonable to assume that the Greek translators were aware of the earlier philosophical use of *archē*, for example by Aristotle, we can see a text like this laying the groundwork for philosophical theology from Philo on. That is, this theology insists that it can recognize the authentic insights of the philosophers about the "first things" and then witness the revelation that shows what the philosophers alone could not see.[68] To do this, these theologians themselves have to already be philosophers. Being in this tradition myself, I must therefore respectfully disagree with Strauss who insists that philosophers cannot be theologians and vice versa. In this tradition, theology presupposes philosophy, and philosophy intends theology. Furthermore, theology itself admits of philosophical analysis every bit as rigorous as that which is applied to the study of any other area of significant human experience. Revelation itself is a prime datum.[69] Being itself a creation of God, like nature, revelation cannot be inconsistent with what we know about nature, and there must be significant commonality between the methods used to study both data, therefore.[70]

Conclusion

Since I have learned much from Leo Strauss, learning that directly pertains to Torah itself, I am duty-bound to pay him honor—a duty that is also a pleasure.[71] Let me close with a rabbinic word about what our relationship to a deceased teacher might be. "Levi bar Nazira said that whoever quotes a teaching in the name of the one from whom he heard it, the lips of that teacher move along with his, even in the grave."[72] In order to explain this cryptic dictum, the interpretation of a later scholar is brought by the editor of the same text. He says, "it is like drinking good old wine: even after the wine has been drunk, its taste remains in one's mouth." With such a taste in one's mouth, one not only continues to enjoy the wine, one will also be much better prepared to distinguish good wine from bad, the true from the false. After drinking this good old wine, he or she will never again be the same. So it was, so it is, and so it will be when we are privileged to learn from Leo Strauss.

Notes

1. Based on Strauss's own criteria, it seems paradoxical for anyone to claim to be his disciple, that is, to be a "Straussian." Let it be remembered that the only two valid forms of ultimate knowledge, for Strauss, are either philosophy or theology. If Strauss was a philosopher, then philosophers only know what is true by their own "unassisted efforts" (*Natural Right and History* [Chicago: University of Chicago Press, 1953], 85). They cannot be the disciples of anyone else in the strict sense of the term nor can their students qua philosophers be their disciples. So, in order to be his disciples, Straussians must see Strauss as a theologian, that is, someone who transmitted a tradition based on revelation, which is the necessary aid to anyone who desires to know that revealed truth. Whether Strauss saw himself as a philosopher or not is subject to speculation; however, I do not see how anyone can see him as a theologian, whatever his respect for theology, especially Jewish theology, happened to be. Hence, could one not see "Straussianism" as a misplaced desire for revelation and, accordingly, inconsistent with everything we do know about Strauss's own position?

2. The main point of these intramural disputes among Straussians seems to be how important Judaism was in Strauss's thinking. For the view that Judaism is peripheral in Strauss's thought, see Thomas L. Pangle's introduction to Strauss's *Studies in Platonic Political Philosophy* (Chicago: University of Chicago Press, 1983), 19–24. For the view that Judaism is more central in Strauss's thought, see Harry V. Jaffa, "Crisis of the Strauss Divided: The Legacy Reconsidered," *Social Research* 54 (1987): 583; and K. H. Green, *Jew and Philosopher: The Return to Maimonides in the Jewish Thought of Leo Strauss* (Albany, N.Y.: SUNY Press, 1993), esp. preface. Here again, I do not know enough about Strauss to decide who is right as regards his thought. However, it is only the latter reading of his thought that could possibly make it a matter of serious interest to contemporary Jewish thinkers.

3. See D. Novak, "Jewish Theology," *Modern Judaism* 10 (1990): 322–3.

4. Published posthumously in the *Independent Journal of Philosophy* 3 (1979): 111–8.

5. A Hebrew translation of the original English lecture appeared long after it was given in *Iyyun: Hebrew Philosophical Quarterly* 5 (1954): 110–26. For all of Strauss's love of Jerusalem, note: "In this city and in this land, the theme of political philosophy—'the city of righteousness, the faithful city'—has been taken more seriously than anywhere else on earth. Nowhere else has the longing for justice and the just city filled the purest hearts and the loftiest souls with such zeal as on this sacred soil" (*What Is Political Philosophy?* [Westport, Conn.: Greenwood Press, 1959], 9).

6. "Mutual Influence," 111.

7. Ibid., 118.

8. Ibid., 113.

9. Ibid., 114.

10. See *Hegel's Logic*, trans. W. Wallace (Oxford: Clarendon, 1975), sec. 14: 19–20; sec. 24: 41–2.

11. See Hegel, *Phenomenology of Spirit*, trans. A. V. Miller (Oxford: Oxford University Press, 1977), 453ff.; and Spinoza, *Tractatus Theologico-Politicus*, trans. S. Shirley (Leiden: E. J. Brill, 1991), chaps. 13–15.

12. See D. Novak, *Jewish Social Ethics* (New York: Oxford University Press, 1992), 27ff.

13. See ibid., 45ff.

14. See Maine, *Ancient Law* (Oxford: Oxford University Press, 1931); Tönnies, *Community and Society*, trans. C. P. Loomis (East Lansing, Mich.: Michigan State University Press, 1957).

15. *Republic*, 431A. See Aristotle, *Magna Moralia*, 1213a7.

16. See *Republic*, 433A–B, 441A, 494A.

17. *Politics*, 1254a20.

18. Hence *autarkeia*, "self-rule," for Aristotle, means the reasoned self-control of the rational person. Even when he speaks of such a person being "like a law unto himself" (*hoion nomos ōn heauton*—*Nicomachean Ethics*, 1128a10—my translation), he does not mean that this person's will is the ultimate criterion of his or her action. Rather, he means that this person's *nomos* is modeled after the greater *physis* in which it participates by its aspirations. (See *ibid.*, 1141a20; 1177a25–30; 1177b25–30.) *Nomos* originates in humans, but *physis* is prior to it and is its ultimate standard. (See below, n. 47.)

19. *Groundwork of the Metaphysic of Morals*, trans. H. J. Paton (New York: Barnes and Noble, 1964), 103.

20. See *Critique of Practical Reason*, trans. L. W. Beck (Indianapolis: Indiana University Press, 1956), pt. 2: 157.

21. See Thomas Aquinas, *Summa Theologiae*, 2–1, q. 90, a. 1

22. See D. Novak, *Suicide and Morality* (New York: Scholars Studies Press, 1975), 83ff.

23. See *Groundwork*, 102ff.

24. See *The Open Society and Its Enemies*, 1, 5th rev. ed. (Princeton: Princeton University Press, 1966), 86ff.

25. See *Politics*, 1262a5ff.

26. See *Nicomachean Ethics*, 1177a25–30, 1177b30–1178a1.

27. See Hegel, *Philosophy of Right*, trans. T. M. Knox (Oxford: Oxford University Press, 1952), sec. 324.

28. See Glendon, *Rights Talk: The Impoverishment of Political Discourse* (New York, 1991); Sandel, *Liberalism and the Limits of Justice* (Cambridge: Cambridge University Press, 1982). For Rawls's debt to Kant on the question of autonomy, see his *A Theory of Justice* (Cambridge, Mass.: Harvard University Press, 1971), 251ff., 563ff.

29. See, e.g., Ronald Dworkin, *Taking Rights Seriously* (Cambridge, Mass.: Harvard University Press, 1978), 171–172, 205; John Finnis, *Natural Law and Natural Rights* (Oxford: Oxford University Press, 1980), 223ff.

30. See his *Sources of the Self: The Making of the Modern Identity* (Cambridge, Mass.: Harvard University Press, 1989), 511ff.

31. See Hermann Cohen, "Einheit oder Einzigkeit Gottes," *Jüdische Schriften*, ed. B. Strauss (Berlin: C. A. Schwetschke, 1924), 1:87ff.

32. *Republic*, 358Aff; *Crito*, 51D. See Strauss, *Natural Right and History*, 119.

33. See *Apology*, 29D.

34. See *Civilization and Its Discontents*, trans. J. Riviere (Garden City, N.Y.: W. W. Norton, 1958), 25.

35. See Augustine, *Confessions*, 1.1.

36. See *Proslogion*, chap. 2.

37. Eruvin 7.11.

38. See, for example, *Babylonian Talmud*: Baba Metsia 19a; Berakhot 27b; Maimonides, *Mishneh Torah*: Mamrim, 2.9.

39. See Maimonides, *Mishneh Torah*: Gerushin, 2.20.

40. See Hannah Arendt, *The Human Condition* (Garden City, N.Y.: Doubleday, 1959), 302, n. 2 regarding Augustine, *Confessions*, bk. 10.

41. Avot 3.14. See *Bereshit Rabbah* 1.1.

42. See *Mekhilta*: Yitro regarding Exod. 20:3 and Isa. 46:7, ed. Horovitz-Rabin, 223.

43. *Babylonian Talmud*: Avodah Zarah 3a. See Shabbat 88a.

44. Makkot 3.16 regarding Isa. 42:21.

45. See Maimonides, *Mishneh Torah*: Melakhim, 8.11–9.1; Thomas Aquinas, *Summa Theologiae*, 2–1, q. 94, a. 4 ad 1; John Calvin, *Institutes of the Christian Religion*, 2.7.10; 4.20.16.

46. Thus Kant replaces *Gebote Gottes* with *göttliche Gebote* (*Critique of Pure Reason*, B847), which means that whatever is divine is ipso facto rational and, conversely, whatever is not rational is ipso facto not divine.

Along these lines, he is followed by his greatest Jewish disciple Hermann Cohen. See his *Religion of Reason Out of the Sources of Judaism*, trans. S. Kaplan (New York: F. Ungar, 1972), chap. 16: 338ff.

47. One of the most influential expressions of this kind of fideistic antinatural law position in Judaism today is that of Marvin Fox in his widely discussed 1972 essay, "Maimonides and Aquinas on Natural Law," *Dinē Israel* 3 (Eng. sec.); now reprinted and slightly revised in his *Interpreting Maimonides: Studies in Methodology, Metaphysics, and Moral Philosophy* (Chicago: University of Chicago Press, 1990). The following quote (p. 126) epitomizes his views: "In ancient Hebrew thought there is only one source of the knowledge of good and evil—the commandments of God as they are revealed to man." For a critique of both Fox, who errs on this point for theological reasons, and Strauss, who errs on this point for philosophical reasons, see Novak, *Jewish Social Ethics*, 25–33.

48. See his article on "Natural Law" in *The International Encyclopedia of the Social Sciences*, 11:80; also Helmut Koestler, "The Concept of Natural Law in Greek Thought," in *Religions in Antiquity: Essays in Memory of Erwin Ramsdell Goodenough*, ed. J. Neusner (Leiden: E.J. Brill, 1968), 521ff.

49. Thus, Spinoza, who wanted to sever philosophy from any connection to theology, distinguished between *lex*, when used for nature, from *ius*, when used for human society. *Ius* presupposes a temporal will; *lex* expresses the eternal natural order. See *Tractatus Theologico-Politicus*, chap. 4.

50. "Mutual Influence," 115.

51. See *Babylonian Talmud*: Makkot 23b-24a; also, Maimonides, *Guide of the Perplexed*, 2.33.

52. "Mutual Influence," 112.

53. Ibid., 115.

54. See *Babylonian Talmud*: Berakhot 19b.

55. One can see this distinction in the way Aristotle relates justice and friendship. As he writes, "Friends do not need justice, but the just need friends" *Nicomachean Ethics*, 1155a26—my translation. What he seems to mean here is that justice is presupposed by friendship, hence it is already in place before persons can be friends to each other. It is tacitly assumed. However, justice per se is insufficient for a fulfilling human life. It is form not content. *Philia* is the ground and content (for Aristotle, the *telos*) of *dikaiosynē*; and *dikaiosynē* is its necessary condition. For my own more Kantian treatment of the logical relation of ground and condition in the ontological relation of revelation and reason, see D. Novak, *Jewish-Christian Dialogue: A Jewish Justification* (New York: Oxford University Press, 1989), 129ff.

56. "Mutual Influence," 111.

57. See *Mishnah*: Yoma 8.9; *Babylonian Talmud*: Yoma 67b; *Mishnah*: Baba Batra 10.8 and R. Israel Lipschütz, *Tif'eret Yisra'el*, n. 84 thereon.

58. *Nicomachean Ethics*, 1103a17.

59. See Hans Jonas, *The Gnostic Religion*, 2d ed. (Boston: Beacon Press, 1963), 320ff.

60. See Gen. 20:11; Exod. 1:17.

61. *Babylonian Talmud*: Sanhedrin 90a.

62. See Gen. 18:23–25; Jonah 3:8–10.

63. *Mishneh Torah*: Melakhim, 6.4. Rabbinic sources for this ruling are *Sifre*: Devarim, no. 204 and *Palestinian Talmud*: Shevi'it 6.1/36c.

64. *Kesef Mishneh* on Maimonides, *Mishneh Torah*: Melakhim, 6.4.

65. See D. Novak, *The Image of the Non-Jew in Judaism: An Historical and Constructive Study of the Noahide Laws* (New York and Toronto: E. Mellen Press, 1983), esp., 275ff.

66. See *Spinoza's Critique of Religion*, trans. E. M. Sinclair (New York: Schocken Books, 1965), intro. 15ff.

67. See *Mishneh Torah*: Yesodei Ha-Torah, 7.5; *Guide of the Perplexed*, 3.29.

68. See H. A. Wolfson, *Philo* 2 (Cambridge, Mass.: Harvard University Press, 1947), 439ff.

69. As such, my difference with Strauss can be specifically connected to the debate among scholars about whether Maimonides' reference to his major legal work *Mishneh Torah* as "our great compilation" (*Guide*, 3.29—Arabic: *ta'alifana al-khbir*; Hebrew: *hiburenu ha-gadol*) is a statement about its quantity or its importance in relation to the *Guide*. The latter is Strauss's view; see *Persecution and the Art of Writing* (Glencoe, Ill.: Free Press, 1952), 39–40. For the former view, see Isadore Twersky, *Introduction to the Code of Maimonides (Mishneh Torah)* (New Haven: Yale University Press, 1980), 18–19. Over and above what Maimonides' true opinion was, *Mishneh Torah* is in many ways—including theological ways that include philosophy—the more perennially interesting work. For its reflections are more beholden to the most perennially interesting Jewish data: the commandments. The *Guide*'s reflections, on the other hand, are far more beholden to an ontology that presupposes a by now irretrievable natural science and an ethics that presupposes a by now irretrievable political order. See D. Novak, *The Election of Israel: The Idea of the Chosen People* (Cambridge: Cambridge University Press, 1995), 237ff., esp. 239–40, n. 151; also, *Law and Theology in Judaism* 1 (New York: Ktav Publishing House, 1974), 142–3. This specific question was the subject of my very first conversation with Leo Strauss, sometime in the spring of 1960 in Hillel House at the University of Chicago.

70. See Maimonides, *Guide*, 1.65 and 55.

71. See *Mishnah*: Avot 4.1 regarding Ps. 119:99 and 6.3 regarding Ps. 55:14.

72. *Palestinian Talmud*: Berakhot 2.1/4b regarding Cant. 7:10.

Afterword

Jenny Strauss Clay

I have never spoken or written publicly of my father, perhaps because others can and have done such a good job of it, speaking with eloquence and understanding of his work. And, then, there is the fact that I have thrown my lot with Athens, and not even the Athens of philosophy, but the Greece of the poets, thus doubly disqualifying me from a serious say in the central issues to which Leo Strauss devoted his life's work.

Over twenty years after my father's death, it is for me deeply moving to participate in a project dedicated to a reconsideration of what was perhaps the core of his thought: the problem of Jerusalem and Athens, the tension between the imperatives of philosophy and of revelation.

Although not prone to vanity, he would, I think, be pleased by this volume and the conference that it follows. I also think he would have been amused by his posthumous fame, or perhaps, notoriety. Much of it has been disseminated by his students and their students in turn. His name appears in the popular press, and his influence is detectable in the work of fashionable intellectuals, who discreetly choose not to mention his name. Indeed, discussion of such questions as that of nature and human nature by political theorists today would not have been possible or, at least, taken seriously, without the influence of Leo Strauss.

I cannot help but note that the conference "Jerusalem and Athens" took place at the University of Virginia, where ten years before his death my father gave the Page-Barbour Lectures. These

193

were subsequently published as *The City and Man*, perhaps the most Athenian of his books. It seems to me, then, altogether appropriate and in some sense fitting to restore—in this place—the necessary balance, or rather, tension, insofar as this volume focuses on the other pole of his thought, Jerusalem.

Let me close with a question that is not merely meant as a provocation. If I understand him correctly, Strauss would consider a conference and then a volume devoted to Jerusalem and Athens paradoxical, if not impossible. For if such an enterprise were to go beyond a presentation and exposition of respective claims and foundations to a genuine confrontation of those claims and those foundations, by which I mean a reasoned dialogue represented by this book, then wouldn't Athens have already won?

Index

About the Contributors

Hadley Arkes is the Edward Ney Professor of Jurisprudence and American Institutions at Amherst College.

Allan Arkush is associate professor of Judaic Studies at Binghamton University.

Jenny Strauss Clay is professor of classics at the University of Virginia.

Werner Dannhauser is professor emeritus of government at Cornell University and visiting professor of political science at Michigan State University.

Hillel Fradkin is vice president for programs at the Lynde and Harry Bradley Foundation in Milwaukee, Wisconsin.

Frederick Lawrence is associate professor of theology at Boston College.

David Novak is the Edgar M. Bronfman Professor of Modern Judaic Studies at the University of Virginia.

Susan Orr is a program specialist at the National Center on Child Abuse and Neglect, U.S. Department of Health and Human Services.

Kenneth Seeskin is professor of philosophy and chair of the Department of Philosophy at Northwestern University.